MW00579529

BARBED WIRE

Barbed Wire

An Ecology of Modernity

REVIEL NETZ

Wesleyan University Press MIDDLETOWN, CONNECTICUT

Published by
Wesleyan University Press,
Middletown, CT 06459

ISBN 0-8195-6719-1 cloth
Printed in the United States of America

Set in Ehrhardt type by
BW&A Books, Inc., Durham, NC

5 4 3 2 1

Cataloging-in-Publication Data
appear on the last printed page of the book.

To Maya and Darya

CONTENTS

MAPS AND FIGURES

MAPS

FIGURES

ACKNOWLEDGMENTS

Research for this book was begun when I was at MIT as a fellow at the Dibner Institute for the History of Science and Technology. Then, and since, I was fortunate to have access to important collections: at Harvard, the Widener Library and the Baker Business Library (housing the U.S. Steel and Wire Company archive); at Stanford—where I teach—the Green Library and the Hoover Institute Library. During my stay in Moscow (teaching for the Stanford Overseas Program), I studied at the archive of the Memorial Society, with its unique collection of unpublished memoirs from the Stalinist era. I am filled with gratitude to the staffs of all those libraries—a gratitude multiplied by wonder and admiration at the selfless generosity of the members of the Memorial Society in Moscow.

Myles Burnyeat, Paul Laity, Richard Milner, Tom Radko, and Suzanna Tamminen have all, in turn, read my original manuscript and convinced me to proceed with it, first in abbreviated form as an article published by the *London Review of Books* (July 2000), then as this book. Further comments were made by many friends and colleagues, of whom I mention just a few: Maya Arad, Moritz Epple, Lori Gruen, Arne Hessenbruch, Marie Huong Nguyen, Andrea Nightingale, Leonard S. Reich, Aron Rodrigue, Relli Shechter, Walter Scheidel, Amanda Vinson, James R. Voelkel, Kelly DeVries, and Nicolas Wey-Gomez, as well as two anonymous readers for Wesleyan University Press. Maya Arad, in particular, has commented on the manuscript several times over, guiding it as it achieved its style. Responsibility, of course, remains with the author.

Ariel Tsovel's research and activism inspire my own work in animal history. He wanted me to produce work with both intellectual and political dimensions; I hope I did.

INTRODUCTION

Define, on the two-dimensional surface of the earth, lines across which motion is to be prevented, and you have one of the key themes of history. With a closed line (i.e., a curve enclosing a figure), and the prevention of motion from outside the line to its inside, you derive the idea of property. With the same line, and the prevention of motion from inside to outside, you derive the idea of prison. With an open line (i.e., a curve that does not enclose a figure), and the prevention of motion in either direction, you derive the idea of border. Properties, prisons, borders: it is through the prevention of motion that space enters history.

Abstract topological structures—closed, open lines—need to be implemented. Their physical (and social) implementation may vary. We may have absolute material barriers, whose function is to make motion impossible: such are walls, in aspiration. Or there may be more subtle obstacles, whose function is to make motion inconvenient and therefore undesirable: these, in general, are fences. Finally, there might be purely symbolic definitions of limits—a yellow line painted on the pavement—respected solely by virtue of the habits of social practice. Yet as with all other forms of coercion, even the symbolic definition of space relies ultimately on the potential presence of force (where there is a yellow line, there are usually also police nearby).

The ubiquitous presence of potential force is indeed a universal of history. Force, brute or refined, is what societies and histories are built of. Note, however, that with the prevention of motion, force—in the most literal sense, of applying physical pressure to bodies—assumes a special kind of necessity. Quite simply, being in a place is something you do with your *body*—nothing else—and therefore, to prevent your motion from one place to another, your body must be affected. The history of the prevention of motion is therefore a history of force upon bodies: a history of violence and pain.

Facilitation of motion is another important theme of history. In this book, I will often have occasion to mention not only dividing lines but also connecting lines: sea-lanes, trails, railroads. It should be seen, however, that the prevention of motion is in a sense more fundamental than the facilitation of motion. A train is worthless unless you can prevent some people—those who did not buy your tickets—from boarding it. Like all property, the train becomes valuable only when access to it can be controlled, and so the system of the railroad—lines that connect points—is anchored by the system of *stations,* buildings whose walled lines enclose space and control motion. A world where the railroad exists without the station is unthinkable, because without control over motion, value cannot be formed. Value arises from lines of division—even when they happen to enclose lines of connection. To understand history and its motions, then, we must first understand the history of the prevention of motion.

This book follows one of the major threads of this history. I show the conditions for the invention and spread of a simple but highly significant technology: barbed wire. Starting with a description of its origins in the colonization of the American West, I move on to describe its eventual role in modern warfare, and then in the modern forms of human repression, offering finally some remarks concerning the general lessons that may be derived from the growth of barbed wire. Throughout the book, I glance beyond barbed wire to the space it has enclosed. Around the strand of history made of barbed wire, I weave a chapter of modernity. Barbed wire allows us to see a more fundamental ecological equation, whose main protagonists are flesh and iron. Here is how modernity unfolded: as iron (and, most important, steel) became increasingly inexpensive and widespread, it was used to control motion and space, on a massive scale, exploiting its capacity for mass production and its power of violence over flesh. This massive control over space was the defining characteristic of a certain period of history: the eighty years from 1874 to 1954—from the invention of barbed wire to the downgrading of the Gulag. Throughout this period, barbed wire constructions were at the forefront of the major events of world history. This was not an accident; barbed wire was what this period required. This book tries to explain why. Thus the book is about what may be considered the age of barbed wire: the period of the coming of modernity.

This history took place precisely at the level of *flesh,* cutting across geographic as well as biological boundaries. It was not humanity alone that experienced barbed wire. The tool was created to control animals by inflicting pain on them. The enormous sweep of barbed wire through history—ranging from agriculture to warfare and human repression, encompassing the globe—is due to the simple and unchanging equation of flesh and iron. The first must yield to the second, followed by the inevitability of pain. The history of violence and pain crosses species, and so, as a consequence, did the history of modernity.

It is only by considering reality at this level, going beyond humans alone, that history can make sense. Indeed, although much has been written about some technical aspects of the invention of barbed wire, the particular thread followed in this book seems hardly to have been noticed at all. Some authors have written about barbed wire in agriculture, many more about concentration camps, but few have even mentioned both in the same breath.[1] This is precisely what needs to be done if we wish to understand either concentration camps or agriculture. Both belong to the same world and follow the same history. This book is largely about the environment—literally—that gave rise to concentration camps: as it were, an environmental history of Auschwitz. It thus has to start where environmental history does, in the encounters between humans and other animals. For animals are always part of the social picture; their flesh, suffering and consumed, motivates human history itself. When we set out to offer a history that mentions animals, we should understand that the history of animals is not merely an appendix, a note we should add because it is missing in our present traditional, human-focused history. Rather, the history of animals is part and parcel of history—that reality where all is inextricably tied together, humans, animals, and their shared material world.

1 EXPANSION

The American West and the Invention of Barbed Wire

Your first question is simple: when and where was barbed wire invented? Let us start with the simple answer: barbed wire was invented in 1874, for use on the American Great Plains. Let me be more precise so that we may begin looking for the essence of the tool. Its goal was to prevent the motion of cows; its function relied on violence; its success depended on deployment on a vast scale.

The question may be restated: why would America need, in 1874, to prevent the motion of cows on the Great Plains,[1] and why would it do so through violence deployed on a vast scale? Now we reach some difficult questions whose answers might reveal the nature of barbed wire.

Barbed wire was created as a result of a special kind of colonization taking place in the American West. This colonization had two features that, combined, set it apart from earlier colonizing episodes. First, it was new in terms of space: an entire landmass was to be exploited (and not merely some selected points on it). Second, it was new in terms of time: the colonization was to take place very rapidly. Earlier human expansions on similar scales had taken generations, but this one was to take no more than a few years. There were precedents for massive colonizations, and there were precedents for rapid colonizations, but there was no precedent for a colonization that was simultaneously massive *and* rapid. Thus a new way of control over space was called for: one based on violence deployed on a vast scale.

In this chapter's first section, "Unpacking the Louisiana Purchase," I consider the rise of the cow on the plains, leading to the immediate background to the invention of barbed wire. Section 2, "How to Fence a Cow," describes how cows were controlled by barbed wire. We see how space and its animals were suddenly brought under control following the introduction of barbed wire. In section 3, "How to Fence the World," I consider the shape of the industry following its globalization. The problem of control over animals was universal, and it resulted quickly in a system, based on the one used in the American Northeast, reaching around the globe. The following two chapters will trace out the consequences of this globalization.

1. UNPACKING THE LOUISIANA PURCHASE

No one quite knew what to do with Louisiana—nor, indeed, where precisely it was. The French colonial claim of that name, dating from 1699, more or less coincided with the borders of the Great Plains (though the term was not used), and the borders were left intentionally vague so as to leave room for hypothetical future expansion. In truth, control over space was a mere act of cartography, and to name this particular space after Louis XIV was about as practical as Galileo naming Jupiter's moons after the Medici. The territory was so little known that one could not define it with any prominent features of the topography. Thus authors were reduced to the indefinites of symbolic space. Take, for instance, Du Pratz in 1763: Louisiana was "that part of North America which is bounded on the south by the Gulf of Mexico, on the East by Carolina . . . and by a part of Canada; on the west by New Mexico, and on the north by parts of Canada, in part it extends without assignable bounds to the terra incognita adjoining Hudson Bay."[2] Exactly the same ambiguity applied to all the other parameters—Carolina, New Mexico, Canada. The equation was not meant to be solved. Anyway, by 1763 the question was moot; France was defeated, and her possessions were divided, east of the Mississippi (i.e., Quebec) to Britain, west of the Mississippi (i.e., Louisiana) to Spain. This defined the eastern border and made the western border unimportant. (Louisiana was now merely the name of another Spanish colony, just like Texas to its West.) Not that any of this really mattered to the Indians or the bison—the true inhabitants of the plains—whose life was dominated by another, more real geography of the spread of horses, guns, and smallpox. In Europe, however, the spaces of the American continent took on dramatic dimensions. Returning in 1800 from his failed Egyptian expedition—where he tried to derail the British Empire through the East—Napoleon decided to attack from the West. Napoleonic pressure returned Louisiana to the French, a base from which to disrupt British power in Canada and in the Caribbean. No more luck for Bonaparte here than in Egypt, though; a slave revolt in Haiti made the French position in the Caribbean tenuous. Meanwhile American diplomats, worried about the presence of the bellicose French at the mouth of the Mississippi, inquired whether New Orleans could be leased. Napoleon, quickly reconsidering his position, retroactively made the entire operation into a real estate investment. He offered the territory to the Americans, all for $15 million. The Americans, by no means naive themselves, then obtained excellent conditions of payment, the entire sum paid in American public debt. In 1803, when the transaction was made, almost nothing changed hands. Napoleon sold the Americans the promise of space and was paid with the promise of money.[3]

Absurd as they might seem, early-day colonial claims were not irrational. Inside the phantom territories staked by such claims, real interests were protected. This was the trader's colonialism that made its big profits not by covering areas but by connecting points: a plantation, a mine, a market, a port. The spatial commodity exploited is distance. Sumatra is very distant from Italy, Peru is very distant from China, Jamaica is very distant from France. Pepper, silver, and sugar, crossing such distances, multiply enormously in value. By gaining control over this network of shipping from procurement to consumption, one obtains a tremendous source of profit and power.[4] In this type of colonialism, then, perimeters of influence were meant to enclose not a space but a series of points, and details of border and control over space were irrelevant.

Distance would always remain valuable, and it still is: the value of the sweatshop is a function of its distance from its clientele. The geographic distance allows a vast separation between the extremes of poverty and affluence. Connecting these two extremes is crucial to the contemporary world, as it has always been to colonialism. However, in the nineteenth century, a new kind of colonialism emerged: not the trader's but the *investor's* colonialism. The investor does more than connect: he invests and develops, turning as much as possible of a land into usable resources. This new colonialism, then, would be the investor's colonialism—based on the profits to be made out of intensive production on a vast scale. The spatial commodity for this colonialism is not distance alone but also area itself. Thus borders would now be defined, and their interiors thoroughly controlled. And this was to happen now, following America's acquisition of the West. In the nineteenth century, America led the way to the world in making the transition from the trader's to the investor's colonialism. In taking up the Louisiana claim, America entered, without knowing it, not only a new space but, more important, a new way of handling space. This would ensue in ever-widening cycles of violence.

It started with Texas. A Spanish territory in 1803, Texas came to be part of the newly independent Mexican state in 1822. Its many colonists from the United States took a dim view of the antislavery position of the Mexican government. They fought for their freedom to own slaves—gradually drawing the United States itself into their protection, which, in the brief war of 1847, finally led to the United States being in possession of the West.

At this point, the countdown began for the American Civil War. The issue is this: Land, alone, does nothing for humans. It has to be used in some definite way: cultivated; grazed by animals; mined; built. Each land use determines a different ecology and thus a different society. To reach for land is to try to extend a certain social order into it to the exclusion of others. Decisions are painful, especially when different social orders coexist already. To open new lands is therefore to open old wounds; America's wound, of course, was slavery. This land use was based on extensive agriculture in large fields, poor in technology, rich in the unskilled, coerced labor of draft animals and enslaved humans. It was most profitable in the global products of classical trader's colonialism: sugar, tobacco, cotton. It assumed little investment and much transportation. Contrast this to the land use of the farmstead, where a paterfamilias would govern a large family and its livestock to make a living from a land intensively cultivated, partly for internal consumption, partly for the sale, to nearby urban centers, of high-quality produce. This is based on cheaper transportation, but more intensive investment. From the census of 1860, we can take the following two questions: (A) the numbers of acres of improved land (irrigated, fenced, etc.) on the farms; and (B) the number of acres of unimproved land on the farms. A vote for Lincoln was directly correlated to the ratio of A to B. Connecticut had nearly three improved acres of land for each unimproved acre; South Carolina had nearly three unimproved acres of land for each improved acre. This was the divide defining the Civil War.

We can mark the big divide as follows: between a northern country, where fields were controlled by the intensive use of the fence, and a southern country, where fields were controlled by the intensive use of the whip. At issue, in other words, was not just the moral sentiment of abolitionism—which, it is only fair to say, did greatly move many Americans—but the realities of control. The North wanted to see an America with acre after acre of improved land supporting both families and urban centers, all inspired by the intensive economy of the northern American town. The plantation owners of the South wanted to prevent just this outcome of an America governed by the cities of the North. The South needed to grow, demographically, just as the North was growing, and the South needed new slave states, if only to have new slave state senators.

Now the settling of the plains themselves gained a new urgency. It was progressing apace; the bison were retreating, and the railroad was beginning to send its branches west of Chicago. The continental rail project—to connect California with the East, gathering all the West along the way—exacerbated the sectional strife and got stymied by it. The decision about a route for this train would be, symbolically as well as practically, a decision about which part of the nation had first claim to the West. Hence no decision could be made. Nor could any explicit political decision be made for the settlement of the plains. Yet throughout this all, American agricultural practices were brought into Kansas and the entire Plains, changing the land and driving away the bison and the Indians. In Kansas, Southern and Northern farmers faced one another in what became throughout the 1850s a bloody skirmish, a prelude to the Civil War. Simultaneously, the West was being integrated into the East, and the South was breaking away from the North—and the two processes were one.

To repeat: there was a fundamental asymmetry between North and South. Northern farms were outposts of agricultural production sent out by an urban, industrial economy; this is ultimately why intensive farming made sense for them. Southern farms were all the South really had. Like the entire Caribbean area, the South was all, essentially, no more than an outpost of Europe. The sectional divide was thus a relic of the trader's colonialism, of a time when America was made up of discrete entities serving separate European functions. With its railroads, with the explosion of its urban life, the North was now ready to become its own center, and the center for the entire continent. More than this, the North was ready to become the center of the continent *as a continent,* the entirety of its land being developed for the support of Northern cities. This was why Southerners felt threatened, and why they lost. When Lincoln came to office in 1861—a president whom Southerners perceived, somewhat falsely, to be a Free-Soiler—and when the South finally seceded, the war was fought not merely to resume an American system. The war, instead, *created* such a system. Now it was to be, for the first time, a single structure, with a single center based in America itself, on the northern Atlantic seaboard—all intensively developed. The war started because there was a West to incorporate, and it ended with the West—as well as the South—both incorporated into capitalist America.

In Lincoln's Congress—the Southern filibusterers now having seceded—all the gridlocked issues of the 1850s were pushed into motion. The main goal was to develop land in the West; the main tool the government had at its disposal was land in the West. Thus the curious nature of the legislation, offering uncharted lands to those who would chart them. The Pacific Railroad Act established a northern route for the railroad, offering its developers, as incentive, 6,400 acres of western land (more would be decreed in the future) for each mile constructed. Meanwhile, toward the foundation of state colleges, the Morrill Act gave western land at the rate of 30,000 acres for every senator and congressman each state had. These colleges, let us remember, were primarily supposed to produce agricultural experts—which, in the early years, is what they largely did. Funded by the intensive cultivation of land, their intellectual production served to intensify agriculture further. Finally, the Homestead Act was the crucial legislation that set out the basic form of settlement for the West. The act promised each individual settler, following five years of residence and improvement, 160 acres of land. This envisaged small-scale, intensive family farming. The railroad, agricultural science, Northern farming families—all were expected to replicate soon, on the Great Plains, the economic achievement of the North.

This was all enacted in 1862 in Washington, D.C., while not far off, Americans were dying in numbers—and ways—unimagined. The Civil War was the fourth cycle of violence unleashed by Louisiana, following Texas, Mexico, and Kansas, but nothing had prepared for what happened now. It was as shattering to contemporary Americans as World War I would later be to Europe. It was strange and frightening; while warring, war itself was changing. No one knew iron could wreak such havoc. Ironclads, introduced in 1861 by the South and soon mass-produced by the North, made wooden military ships obsolete overnight. Railroads allowed the concentration, never seen before, of hundreds of thousands of soldiers. Rifles—an invention assembled together during the 1850s—changed the space of battle itself. If you impart spin to a bullet by shooting it through a rifled, or spiral-grooved, barrel, it gains in precision and thus in effective range. The smoothbore musket had a range of not much more than a hundred yards; the rifle had one of about six hundred, covering a space thirty-six times greater. From 1862 onward, the hundreds of thousands of soldiers amassed by the railroad carried with them rifles instead of muskets. Iron made battles larger: the rifle made the field of killing greater, and the railroad enlarged its reach in terms of human population. A soldier could be drafted in Boston, within a few weeks arrive in Pennsylvania, and there become tangled in an area of tens of square miles of unremitting violence—the worst of them all, the field of Gettysburg, where more than 50,000 were killed over three days' fighting in July 1863. Death was agonizing; rifles were at an interim stage of technology, forceful enough to get the bullet inside the body even at long range, but not quite forceful enough (as twentieth-century guns would be) for the bullet to exit the body following impact. Civil War bullets typically rested inside the flesh, ensuring inflammation and, in most cases, painful death.[5] All in all, more than 600,000 Americans died in the four years of the war. The brutality of the frontier skirmish—the Indian wars, Texas, Mexico City, Kansas—returned, magnified many times over, to the centers of American civilization. I will return to this dialectic of frontier and center—the brutality of the first returning to haunt the latter—in the next chapter.

Not that the American frontier skirmishes ever stopped. The Civil War had its Indian War built into it. Indeed, some tribes made the wrong tactical decision, siding with the South—particularly in the Indian Territory. This was very convenient for the North, as ultimately it would allow the federal government to discontinue the grant of *any* territory to the Native Americans. But the same was true everywhere. The skills, the brutal attitudes, and the technologies developed in the Civil War were seen in the West as well. Even as the Civil War was still raging, rifles shot more bison than humans.

These were the cycles of violence: from the Texans' war against Mexicans, through the Mexican-American War, and then through the North-South skirmish, particularly at Kansas, came the Civil War itself; and this led immediately to further cycles of violence, aimed now at the Indian and the bison. In November 1864, General Sherman was marching from Atlanta to the sea, everywhere proclaiming the cause of liberty. Just then, far to the West, the Cheyenne Indians were invited by the American settlers to come to Sand Creek, Colorado. The Cheyenne were promised that they could hunt there, but on November 29 they were hunted themselves. Local Colorado militia forces surprised the Cheyenne in their tents, and all were killed—hundreds of men, women, and children. Skin cut off a dead body had an enormous fascination for the killers of the West, and the scalps of Cheyennes were now displayed, to applause, in Denver's public theater.[6]

Such excesses were indeed less common, and an outcry took place when news reached further east. But America did not really have an alternative Indian policy. To start with, the main piece of official policy were forts garrisoned across the West to protect the growing railroad and the concomitant agricultural settlements. In topological terms, then, the Great Plains were a plane surface, across which points (garrisons and settlements) were connected by lines (railways and trails), the surface as such still belonging, in a sense, to the Indian and the bison. Precisely this topology was to be changed. The bison—the basis for the Indians' way of life—were being finished, and the Indians were urged to settle down, to get out of the way. Instead of Euro-Americans being confined to points on the surface, the Indians were to be reduced to their points—the reservations—the entire surface now becoming European. This was the enlightened alternative to Sand Creek. Indians, on the whole, realized they had no other option, but many resisted. They had moved to the plains from the East, generations ago, because their agriculture was failing under European pressure; they had taken to hunting because, with their resources, successful agriculture on the plains was impossible. They suspected they were being condemned to a life of destitution, and they were right. But all their courage and equestrian skills notwithstanding, the Indians had no chance. With the typical advantages of guerrilla fighters—better mobility, knowledge of the land—surprise and individual successes were always possible, most spectacularly at Little Bighorn, when on June 25, 1876, Colonel Custer was caught and killed with his force of 220 soldiers. But in fact, these were already the last moments of Indian resistance. They had nothing to roam the plains for. The bison were now dead, replaced by railroads and farmers. As the Indians retreated to their pitiful reservations, the cow began its trek north of Texas, eventually to introduce there an economy based in Chicago. And this, finally, was the culmination of American history in the nineteenth century. Texas led to Mexico, which led to Kansas, which led to the Civil War, upon whose conclusion America could move on to destroy the Indian and the bison. The final act in the subjugation of the West was under way: the transition from bison to cow.[7] This was the immediate consequence of the Civil War: the West was opened for America—and America had filled it with cows.

We are getting near the invention of barbed wire, then. So let us focus our attention on western cows, at the moment when they replace the bison. Was this, in reality, a deep transformation at all? The answer is complicated. At first glance, the new order could be said to be no more than a shift of species and of race: bison replaced by cows, Indians replaced by Euro-Americans. Neither shift, in itself, involved, at first glance, a dramatic change.

Take first the animals. The Texas longhorn cow, instead of the herds of wild bison, now roamed the plains. We should not be misled. When one thinks of a cow, what comes to mind are, perhaps, dairy cows seen in European fields—heavily bred and disciplined so as to produce a breed as docile as a spaniel. But the longhorn was different—in fact, could not survive otherwise on the open plains. The ancestors of these cows had gone wild after being brought to America by Spanish colonizers. The same happened to many domesticated species brought to the New World. Animals, let loose on a new continent, outgrew their European past, indeed, their European masters. The local ecology had little to resist the new species, and a few escapees would be enough to establish a huge population, gradually shedding its domesticated habits.[8] Beyond the limited domain of European settlement and domestication, a penumbra of feralized animals could be seen on the American continent. Here were wild horses—as many as two million of them—famously contributing to the last stage of Indian life.[9] So, to a lesser extent, were wild cows. In the 1870s, they were just being brought back to the fold, and the Texan breed was still remarkable in its ferocity. Nearly self-sufficient, they were thus not totally unlike the bison that they had replaced.

As for the Indians—for the last century subsisting almost exclusively by hunting the bison—they too were replaced by a breed not quite unlike them. Euro-American men, mounted on horses, gathered and herded the cows, roaming the same plains as the Indians did, following the same constants of grass and water, living in similarly small bands with little attachment to settled community. Life on the plains, then, did not change much.

The essential ecological structure was in a sense preserved as well. The sun's energy was stored up by grass. The grass was consumed by vast numbers of large bovines. These in turn were herded and killed by small bands of humans. At first, perhaps, not quite as many as the bison; the bison population is now estimated to have peaked at about 30 million near the beginning of the nineteenth century, while cattle numbered perhaps over 11 million by 1880. But then again, the rise of the cow came after a long period of degradation, as overroaming, human impact, and ecological catastrophes gradually reduced the capacity of the plains to carry bovines. Taking a longer view, we can say that the bovine population (i.e., either bison or cows) started from around 30 million at the beginning of the nineteenth century, collapsed to perhaps 15 million in the 1860s before the final onslaught on the bison herd, then bottomed out in 1880 at 11 million before climbing back to nearly 24 million by 1900. The death of the bison was in a sense merely a crisis of transition from one bovine ecology to another.[10]

Bovines, far more numerous than any other mammals, continued to dominate life on the plains. They were dominant also in the sense that they governed space, at least locally. Just as the bison did, cows roamed freely most of the time—and just as the bison did, cows did it all under the surveillance of small bands of humans. Finally (and here is the essence of the continuity) the cows, like the bison before them, accounted for the presence of the humans. Everything about human life on the plains was built around the protection of bovines for the sake of their future killing, just as it had been since the start of the Indian hunting experience on the plains. In a sense, the American West had to start from somewhere, so it started from where the Indians left off. There was nothing better to be done with the land.

Below the ecological continuities, however, ran deep differences, most obvious in the nature of the killing. The basic structure of the history of the Great Plains was the evolution of methods for killing bovines. In fact, killing a bovine is not an easy thing to do. A bison, in particular, is a swift, agile animal. Of course, the bison did not evolve to be protected from humans, but it had enough experience with wolves and other mammal predators to teach it caution. Prehistoric Indians could hardly face a bison and try to kill it; it would, quite sensibly, run away. This was the bison's mistake: it should, of course, have turned around and tried to ram the Indian, but the bison never realized how much weaker humans are than wolves. Thus the Indians could elaborate their method of killing. It worked like this. First, the hunt was at the level of bands—a band of Indians gathered together against a band of bison (single bison or small groups would not be affected by the method I describe). The bison would be frightened, literally, out of their wits. The humans egging the bison on would gradually herd them along a predetermined route. There they reached a precipice (the plains, in fact, do have their hills). The bison, being closely packed, could not change direction at the last moment. Most if not all would fall over the brink, which, even if not very high, would suffice to shock them so that they could be done away by the band. Notice that all tribe members participated in the exercise, which was almost pastoral, rather than hunting, in nature.[11] Then, in early historical times, dramatic changes took place, and the Indian hunting method changed completely. With the horse—rapidly made available on the plains during the eighteenth century—equestrian hunters could now outrun the bison and kill it from horseback. Note the advantage: killing was possible all year long, not only during the rutting season (when bison would form their great bands). Note also that, now being more capital intensive, so to speak, killing a bison became more specialized and involved a division of labor. The Indian women, with a lesser contribution to food procurement, developed the specialty of making robes from bison hides into something of a manufacture business. Soon Euro-American merchants, reaching up the river on the Mississippi, would prompt the Indians to kill bison specifically for the purpose of robe making.[12] Finally there came better guns, and in particular the much more precise rifles, invented in the 1850s and used, as we have seen, to great effect in killing humans, too. Armed with these, Euro-Americans overwhelmed the bison—already decimated by Indian overkill. Now the killing of the bison was more capital intensive (you needed to own a rifle), but almost labor free. There was no problem whatsoever in getting the bison into rifle range, so that the plains practically became bison-killing factories, with rifles for machines. The hunt peaked in 1872, and the plains were practically clean of bison by 1883; according to one estimate, more than 5.5 million bison were killed in the peak years of the early 1870s alone.[13] At this point, division of labor as well as capital investment went one step further. The Euro-Americans were killing bison not to eat their meat but to transport the unprocessed hides east. The bison, killed by the products of American machinery, were further processed by this machinery—and then became part of it. The bison hide was processed by the American tanning industry to produce, in particular, the strong belts required for running factory machines.[14]

The cow brought this process to its logical end. We have seen how the bison, in the final stage of its existence, stopped being consumed or processed on the plains; the cow was not even *killed* on the plains. The plains merely transported the cows now and gave them whatever meager nourishment would sustain them through the process. A cow would typically begin its life in Texas; herded north, it would roam under the guidance of humans somewhere in the plains, then be herded again eastward (sometimes by rail), often to be better fed and cared for there, briefly, nearer a major center of slaughter (Chicago itself, or some urban center further east). This last stage of care was necessary because of the immense hardship the cows had just been through. Walking the entire American Midwest, often under inclement weather and in inhospitable terrain, was an experience reflected by the animals' physical state—and so in their commercial value. To make them more profitable, therefore, they were allotted a brief period of comfort before death, as if to compensate for the months and years of deprivation. Finally, however, the animal would be brought into a city to be killed there, its carcass processed and then finally consumed. During this process, many humans would be involved: usually more than one group of cowmen and farmers, freight train personnel and retailers, farmers again, and then a butcher, leading finally to the consumer.

Horse, steamboat, gun, railroad—as each tool of control over space reached the plains, a further step was made toward capitalism. Now, finally, capitalism was reached. The prehistoric bison hunt represented a precapitalist economy, with the killing limited by humans' precarious hold over their environment. The historic bison hunt by Indians represented the unstable interface of capitalist and precapitalist economies. With relatively little division of labor and thus a huge profit margin for the merchants, greed overcame reality. Extremely vulnerable in this exchange, becoming ever more dependent on American merchants, the Indians were driven to overkill and to ruin the basis for their way of life. At this point, with hardly a life left in the bison herd, Euro-American hunters, representatives of a more sophisticated capitalist system, came in to exploit what was for them merely a valuable, if dwindling, natural resource. The handling of cows, finally, represented a fully capitalist economy, with sharp division of labor. Killing was now made fully calculated and economical. There was more revenue in a cow than in a bison, but less of a profit margin: more thought, therefore, would go into the cow's killing. The cow economy—as well as the cow ecology—would not have the simplicity of structure that the plains had at the times of the bison.

This new complexity had two aspects. First, the biological dominance of cows in respect to other nonhuman species would soon be challenged: land would be used not only for the feeding of cows but directly for agriculture. Second, and related, the relationship of cows with humans was much more one-sided than bison-Indian relations had ever been. Of course, the Indians were dominant enough relative to the bison; they could kill hundreds and hundreds of them with great ease. But, after all, the bison was also the great imponderable of Indian life on the plains, the beast whose numbers and appearances were to be determined by forces beyond human control. For capitalist America, nothing was supposed to be beyond human control.

What is control over animals? This has two senses, a human *gain*, and an animal *deprivation*. First, animals are under control as humans gain power over them—most importantly, as humans gain control over animals' biological cycle (procreation, growth, and death). Such control transforms biological patterns into marketable commodities: this is the essence of domestication. Second, animals are under control when they are deprived of their powers of activity. To survive, an animal must develop a certain control over its environment: it can move, trace food, graze or kill. To complete the control over the animal—to reduce it to a mere passive member in a fundamentally human society—is the other side of control over animals. Where they cannot be domesticated, then—that is, when they cannot be reduced to mere passive members in an otherwise human society—animals have to be kept away or destroyed. When all animals have been either subdued or destroyed, a share of land has been cleared from animal power and brought fully under human control. The fact is, control over animals is rather like control over humans: you can either make them do what you like them to do or else get them out of the way. This is how societies are made: human societies as well as the larger, multispecies societies that humans have created.

Now, large animals living in large social groups—the kind, that is, of most direct value to domestication—combine the considerable force of each member to create, in their herds, a powerful social organism. Thus they pose an especially difficult task in trying to bring them into human society. Facing the bison, the human problem was stark, and the solution adopted by Europeans was very simple, that of extermination.

But even with fully domesticated animals, it takes a considerable amount of effort to set up a constant counterforce so as to keep the animals at bay. Even domesticated animals, after all, are still alive. And so they would, unless specifically controlled, go where they want, eat what they want. Hence the problem of subduing the cows on the plains. It was to solve this problem that barbed wire was invented.

2. HOW TO FENCE A COW

All those land grants—to the homestead, to the state colleges, to the railroad—were so many Louisiana Purchases. When you got there, there was not much to it. America evolved through the experience of the Atlantic, the Gulf, the Great Lakes, the Mississippi. Farmers built their life based on the expectations of copious rainfall and its attendant vegetation. Now they got to plains that evolved through the experience of aridity—mostly less than sixteen inches of rain per year. (Boston has over forty inches; New Orleans has over sixty.) Who would live there? Grass, bovines, wolves and other predators, humans foremost among those other predators. Grass could survive on little, unpredictable precipitation; bovines could survive on grass. Wolves and humans could then survive on bovines.[15]

From the point of view of the individual cattle ranger, that was just fine. The West may have been won by the North, but the immediate gain was made, once again, by Texas Southerners. As we have seen, the immediate aftermath of the killing of the bison was the herding north, from Texas, of the longhorn cow. In one respect already, this was part of capitalist America—the cow was to be killed in Chicago or further east. But in other ways, the practices of the range were simply transmitted north.

This explains the continuity with the bison-hunting practices described in this chapter's first section. In other words, the West now had a range, not ranch, business. Do not be confused. In contemporary agriculture—which tends to be, strictly speaking, a ranch business—the terms "range" or "open range" came to have the more narrow meaning of any animal raising that does not involve strict imprisonment inside a building. In the original sense, the distinction between "range" and "ranch" was different. A ranch is an enclosed piece of land; the range is space, unlimited. Originally, Texas cows were fed off the land and moved through it, all throughout the plains—just as the bison did. Control over parceled units of land—the essence of the land grants—was at first out of tune with the actual economy. The economic value of cows resided in their self-reliant properties—they found their own nourishment, and this meant, especially in the difficult conditions of the Great Plains, that they had to operate in open space. The profitability of animals was, at this stage, partly a result of animals acting independently, exercising their powers. A ranger has the animal not merely to be killed eventually but also to do the work for him: the ranger does not look for food and water for the cow; instead, it is the cow herself who seeks those resources. The range industry makes its profits by combining the killing of animals with their forced labor. (This, we should note, was hard labor, under very harsh conditions.) To reduce the motion of cows, then, is to reduce their labor and thus to take away from the owner's sources of profit. The truth was, there were so few resources on the plains that settling anywhere in particular, at first, made little sense. Better to move on with your cows, finding grass and water along the way. As the Indians were being consigned to their reservations, Texans were taking up a quasi-nomadic form of existence. Life was endless motion, and human survival was impossible without the horse.

Nor, indeed, would there be any compelling reason for an owner of cows to fence them so as to gain control over them. Not only did cows manage to survive on their own; they could also be relatively easily collected for marketing by small numbers of humans on horseback. Within the arid plains, river valleys—7 percent of the land—were the only space that mattered. The promise of an open plain actually reduced to the reality of branching rivers, on which, historically, life depended. Of course, cows might wander off, but one did not need constantly to inspect each of them individually. Control could be maintained in other ways: the river would determine the areas where cows could roam. They were boxed by the climate and geography of the plains. This way, herds would be assigned separate spaces along the banks of rivers. For practical purposes, a river's bank does not have its space open in all directions. Inland, away from the river, thirst blocks the motion of cows; the river itself blocks motion on the other direction. The rectangle along the riverbank has therefore only its two short edges open. All you need is to patrol these two edges.

Most important, you rely on the practices of the cow itself. This is the principle of domestication: study the habits of an animal and use them against it. The cows could become free from humans, but they were the captives of their habits. They were conditioned to protect themselves against predators by forming into close herds. Their gregarious habits are precisely what humans exploit. Cows just will not disperse. Had some herd realized in 1866 what it was up against, it could have made the rational choice and dispersed in all directions. No amount of cowboy skill would have been able to collect all the cows, and those that were left on the range would have had, at least, a sporting chance against the occasional wolf. But the cows never realized this; they kept going together, assuming that this was—as it had been thousands of years earlier—in their best interest.

Hence moving cows over long distances is a fairly simple task. The mounted humans who controlled the herds—frightening them all the way up to Chicago—kept an eye on them not so much to prevent them from running away but rather to prevent other predators from taking away the prize. Control over the cow itself was easy; this, after all, is why the animal was domesticated in the first place. No need for fencing, then, as far as the cow itself was concerned.

The threat of other humans was a special problem, of course, but once again, the division of land was not necessary for this purpose either. The goal for this type of economy was to establish control not over land directly but over the cows on it. Instead of marking the land, it was more rational to mark the cows. Thus, to guard against theft, owners branded their cows—an ancient practice applied systematically in the West.

For humans, of course, symbols are more than just practical tools; they embody culture. Branding was, and still is, a major component of the culture of the West. Ranches, for the last century, have often been named after their brands; pride is taken in mastering this symbolic system that defines human control over space and over animals. Ranchers will show off their ability to recognize the many symbols invented. The ritual is still central to ranching life: tying the animals' legs tightly together; setting a fire; carefully heating the branding iron (large, so as to make an articulate, clearly visible mark); then applying the iron until—and well after—the flesh of the animal literally burns. As put by Arnold and Hale (western authors writing in 1940), "There is an acrid odor, strong, repulsive . . . [the animal] will go BAWR-R-R-R, its eyes will bulge alarmingly, its mouth will slaver, and its nose will snort." (At this stage, typically, a bull will be castrated, and in many cases, a cut will be made in the ear as a further symbolic mark.)

A complicated ritual: as the same authors note, "[the inventor of branding] could hardly have suspected how much fun and interest would eventually center around cattle-branding."[16] The entire practice is usefully compared with the Indian correlate. Indians marked bison by tail tying; that is, the tails of killed bison were tied to make a claim to their carcass. Crucially, we see that for the Indians, the bison became property only *after* its killing. It was only then that the bison made the passage from nature to human society. The cow, on the other hand, was a property—indeed, a commodity—even while alive. It would be branded early in its life.

In the special case of calves born free, branding was the moment when a cow passed from nature to culture. A feral calf caught on the Texas plains, unbranded and technically called a "maverick," would be branded and thus made a commodity. Once again, a comparison is called for: we are reminded of the practice of branding runaway slaves, as punishment and as a practical measure of making sure that slaves—that particular kind of commodity—would not revert into their natural, free state. In short, in the late 1860s, as Texans finally desisted from the branding of slaves, they applied themselves with ever greater enthusiasm to the branding of cows. Sometimes whole herds would be collected through "mavericking" (the technical term for hunting and branding wild calves). Such herds would gain their marketable value by being herded north, as far as Chicago. This was a fortune that required, as investment, nothing more than motion and violence.

Violence, of course, was everywhere in the West. Central control did not yet extend across the land as a whole but was still limited to the network of military garrisons. Beyond that, power was wielded by small, mounted bands, ready to kill: the same kind of people who had fought for Texan slavery against Mexico, and then against Indians, or against each other in the Civil War. The habits of violence were endemic to the land. The combination of violence and motion, after all, is what made the West so cinematic.

But the West was even more interesting than that. Its myth was based not merely on violence and motion in the raw but on another, more subtle encounter: that between violence and motion, on the one hand, and civilization, on the other. This myth is fully based on reality: the North had won a war designed to make the West into an extension of its prosperity based on the prudence of farmers. It had also won this war through the experience of violence and lawlessness. Hence the liminal character of the West.

Consider, for example, James Butler Hickok, at one of the mythmaking moments of the West. The year was 1871, and Wild Bill, as Hickok was popularly called, was employed by the city of Abilene, Kansas, to act as its marshal. Abilene had been made practically overnight by the Illinois cattle trade when, in 1867, the rail terminus to Chicago opened there. The economy was booming: the cattle needed pens, attracting settled farmers; the cattle drivers looked for gambling and sex, attracting an altogether different kind of population. This led to the division of the city, neatly marked by the railroad tracks, between law and lawlessness. On one side was a midwestern small town transplanted further west; on the other side was the demimonde of a border town. Wild Bill was hired to prevent any spillover across the tracks. He was considered successful, but he was also deeply resented by the Texan herdsmen, particularly because of his past (born in Illinois, his adult life was divided between fighting Indians and fighting Southerners). Toward the end of the cow season, on October 5, he was passing the Alamo Saloon when a shot was fired, narrowly missing him. The Texan Philip Coe, pistol in hand, explained that "he shot a stray dog," and then fired again at Wild Bill, who immediately shot Coe twice in the stomach—as well as fatally shooting a bystander who came to help. This turned out to be Wild Bill's friend Michael Williams. Grief-stricken, Wild Bill set out to chase the Texans from town; a marked man, he lived now in constant fear for his life. This is the stuff western myth is made of; but consider the denouement of the combat. Abilene decided that it had had enough, and it could from now on live on marketing the growing agricultural produce of the county. The Texan trade was asked to move to other rail termini, and Wild Bill's contract ended.[17]

Here, then, is the historical development. The economic value of the plains was, to start with, marginal. At first they attracted primarily cow owners. However, the very act of pushing the cows into the plains raised their value, even if only a little. This rise in value justified a certain amount of Northern investment, such as the extension of the railroad or the settlement of new towns. This investment, in turn, raised the value of the land even further, so that an economy based purely on cows on the open range was no longer justified. The cow ecology would have to adjust to a much more competitive use of the land. And Texas, after all, did lose the war. The extermination of the bison made the Great Plains into a vacuum that Texas got sucked into—to get entangled in the web centered in Chicago.

Competitive use of the land was marked not only in the North-South confrontation of the saloon cities but also among the Texan herd itself. There were more and more cows now in an area devastated by the transition from the bison, and further reduced by the encroaching agriculture on its most fertile lands. To remain competitive, you had to secure the grass for yourself, and the cattle industry moved into buying and claiming land—fraudulently claiming homesteads or (especially in Texas itself, whose landholding system was not influenced by the Homestead Act) directly leasing vast estates from the state.[18] As the 1860s turned into the 1870s, control over cows had to be supplemented by control over the land itself. Where the cows would go was now something to be fixed. Farmers, as well as the railroad, needed to make sure cows would keep off their lands; cow owners needed to secure land to which their cows, and no others, could get access. All those cows, all this motion: it now somehow had to be delimited.

That, in itself, was nothing new. Ever since domestication, the control of animals on agricultural land had always been a complicated operation—especially considering that animals were in fact always forced to provide the main source of muscle power on the farm and as a result were part of agricultural production itself. Modern capitalism insisted on this discovery: that private ownership of the land could lead to intensive investment and thus to much-higher profits. The enclosed field, kept for the use of a single owner, was one of the hallmarks of capitalism in Britain and therefore also later in the United States.[19] Such fields could have been defined symbolically but more often were fenced by some combination of various materials easily available in northern Europe and in northeast America: stone, hedges, and—especially in rain-rich Atlantic America—wood.[20] With the expansion of agricultural land in America, the capital represented by fencing grew immensely; an often-quoted report by the Department of Agriculture in 1871 put the total value of fences at over $1.7 billion, and the annual cost at about $200 million, so that "for every dollar invested in live stock, another dollar is required for the construction of defenses to resist their attacks on farm production."[21] The purpose of such reports was to suggest a transformation in the use of fences: instead of keeping animals out of fields, they should be used to keep animals inside given boundaries, so that agricultural fields could make do with more symbolic fencing. Here was the trouble, then: such symbols would not do with animals, and no police force would buttress such a symbolic definition of space to make it effective to prevent animals' motion. They must be stopped by force; but where would the money come from to stop those herds of animals in this vast new land of the West?

The West had all those animals, and it did not have the means to stop them. The traditional materials of fencing were scarce, the most traditional of them—wood—nearly absent. Even the earth, a dusty, crumbling land—ideal for the grass—did not produce the right sort of stones. And while hedges could and were grown, they had their own limitations. As George Basalla, a historian of technology, notes for Osage oranges (the most prominent hedges of the American West in the 1860s and 1870s), "They were slow to develop, could not be moved easily, cast shadows on adjoining crops, usurped valuable growing space, and provided a shelter for weeds, vermin and insects."[22] In other words, hedges were inappropriate for the special colonization process going on in the American West, in which vast stretches of land were brought under control during a brief span of time, and the entire process was to be achieved with maximum flexibility and profit. This was colonization driven not by the life cycles of growing populations but by the expectations of capitalist investment. The three to four years it took an Osage orange to grow (as well as its element of waste) now became a major drawback. Four years, in the life of the plains, could be an eternity—the time it took, for instance, for Abilene to become a center for the cow industry and then to get out of that industry altogether. Geography was shifting daily. Something had to be found, quickly, to control the cows.

Fencing materials had to be imported, and the growing rail network—the essential infrastructure for the entire growth of agriculture in the West—transported those materials. Wood was shipped to the West in vast quantities; after all, American houses were built of wood in the West, just as they were in the East, and the railroad itself consumed timber.[23] But the vastness of the spaces involved made such shipping doubly unprofitable for wooden fences—both because of the vastness of spaces to be enclosed by such fences and because of the vastness of the space to be traversed by railroads put in place to carry such loads.

Thus a new technology for fencing was made a necessity—as stressed by the literature on the invention of barbed wire. But notice that the necessity was made by people, not given by nature. It did not derive from sheer geography—the presence of this space, the absence of those woods. It derived from the way in which America sprang upon the West, to enmesh it, almost in an instant, into its economy.

But let us return to the problem as it was perceived by individual Americans. They confronted animals; they were trying to control them. Such a task could be conceived as a kind of education: how to get an animal to do as you wish? This is essentially how the task was perceived in 1873 by Henry Rose, a farmer in the village of Waterman Station, Illinois. Trying to control a "breachy" cow, as he referred to her, he conceived of the following plan. He attached a wooden board, studded with sharp pieces of wire, right next to her head. Thus the cow, he reasoned, would be cured of her mischievous tendency to pass through loose fences. Now whenever she tried to squeeze herself through a limited space, pushing against barriers, she would cause herself considerable pain.[24] Of course, the idea of education through pain was familiar. Children at the time, after all, would regularly have their bare feet lashed with hickory sticks for failing to remember the multiplication table.[25] Children needed to learn arithmetic, and animals needed to learn fences. There are even specific precedents for Rose's experiment: for instance, we may compare it to the triangular yokes with which hogs were collared in seventeenth-century Massachusetts.[26] These yokes were intended to prevent hogs physically from crossing through fences, rather than to make pain ensue from such attempts; but essentially Rose's idea was an extension of the idea of the collar and similar attachments to the bodies of animals. The wooden board served as a tool for constant surveillance and punishment, even in the absence of the human. After a while, it occurred to Rose that the fence itself could teach its own respect, serve as its own surveyor; instead of the sharp wire being attached to the cow's head, it could be attached to boards of wood on the fence itself. The experiment made, Rose was satisfied: the cow learned not to approach the fence. Other Americans made similar trials during the same period. Adrian Latta, for instance, attached sharp spikes to the bottom of his family's fences (he himself was only ten years old at the time, 1861) to prevent hogs from crossing underneath. He noted that "the hogs got through a few times after the barbs were put in. However, the barbs had the desired effect as the owner saw his hogs were getting terribly marked and kept them at home."[27] So instead of education, Latta's aim was sheer violence—aimed directly at hogs, indirectly at humans. If Latta's inspiration was perhaps nothing more than juvenile sadism, William D. Hunt took as an inspiration the venerable idea of the spur. This ancient invention consists of a roughly cut piece of metal that, thrust against the flesh of the animal, goads it to abrupt reaction. Hunt's patent, issued in 1867, positioned spur wheels on wire. The animal, pushing against the wire, would be wounded, though real injury would be prevented as the spur wheel turned under the animal's thrust. This, in retrospect, was a mistake: Hunt's spur wheels were, so to speak, too lenient, so that animals were not ultimately deterred by them. The same went for Michael Kelly's patent in 1868: cut nails thrust into wire. Once again, the nails would simply rotate on their wire when pushed against by the animals. Still,

Kelly was sufficiently concerned about the injury this might cause to animals that he called for tarred rope to be strung along the fence so that animals could see it in the dark and not get accidentally injured.[28] The peculiar experience of Henry Rose was meaningful: by starting from a corrective collar, he was prepared to the fundamental idea that, by causing pain, the fence could create the habit of its own avoidance. The genius of the new technology was that—once again—the cow's habits and skills were enlisted against her. Rose's fence acted not on the cow's skin alone but also on her memory and judgment, and these were ultimately used for her control. No need for the farmer to constrain his violence, then; make the cow feel the pain, and she will do the rest. Ultimately this was how hedges functioned—and the Osage orange, in particular, was protected by sharp, strong, long barbs, in retrospect highly suggestive of barbed wire.[29] Rose patented his idea and took it to be displayed in a farm exhibition in De Kalb, Illinois, near his hometown.

Notice that, with Rose's invention, iron barbs supplemented wood and did not replace it. However—as we have seen with some alternative inventions—others were already experimenting with materials. In the mid-nineteenth century, organic components gave way rapidly to their metallic counterparts. Iron production was exploding, and the material was searching for applications. In 1852, Samuel Fox invented the use of wire ribs for the frames of umbrellas—a huge British industry—replacing whalebone; the same was happening in the (generally similar) industry of corsets. Staying in the same domestic setting, we may take the production of strings for musical instruments; here, once again, wire became cheap enough around midcentury to begin to replace the guts of sheep. With the mass production of steel wire at midcentury, the piano began to be mass-produced as well—a major development in European culture. Umbrellas, corsets, and pianos were all important industries. Closer to home, though, for the interests of American farmers, was the production of rope, revolutionized in the 1840s as hemp began to be substituted by iron. Iron strings had tremendous strength, and most important, machines could be produced to automatically strand such strings into a braided rope.[30] This immediately suggests an idea: if the linear strings can be twisted together to construct stronger ropes, attached linearly, they can also be netted together, on a planar pattern—a fence made of wire. These, of course, are a familiar feature of our own contemporary landscape: fences made of woven lattices of wire, once again an invention of the 1840s and the 1850s. Butts and Johnson from Boston, for instance, advertised their "patent wire fencing" in 1856 "for enclosing railroads, canals, fields, cattle pastures, cemeteries, gardens, heneries, and for ornamental garden work, grape and rose trellises, etc."[31] Whatever were the real hopes of Butts and Johnson, such lattices did not fence in cattle: these structures are rather delicate and are made even more vulnerable by the contraction and expansion of iron under changes in temperature. Even determined humans can, with patience, run down such fences; they are no obstacle at all for herds of cows.[32]

It is here, finally, that barbed wire comes in. One of the visitors to the De Kalb fair, Joseph F. Glidden, formed the following idea: instead of attaching Rose's barbs to wood, they could be coiled around one of the strands in a double-stranded wire. The double-stranded structure, as well as the coil of the barb itself, would keep the barb in place. In short, unlike previous inventors, and emboldened by Rose's idea, Glidden decided to make the barb fixed so as to resist the cow in its approach and to inflict real pain. Further, Glidden's main technical idea—stranding two wires and a series of barbs between them—came from the experience of stranding wires together to form ropes, where the crucial fact was that machines already existed for the operation. No special new ingenuity was required: standard practices could be extended to achieve the mass production of barbed wire. And this is how barbed wire was born. In a sense, it was a natural idea, the confluence of all that went into the West: violence and the need to control space, iron, mass production. At any rate, a number of visitors to Rose's exhibition at De Kalb went away with the idea of attaching barbs to iron fences instead of wooden boards.

Glidden's original patent was quickly joined, apparently independently, by five other barbed wire patents, and most began production almost immediately.[33] Already in 1876, half the rights in one of the main patents were bought by Washburn and Moen, a Massachusetts-based iron and steel company, and in this way barbed wire reached the mainstream of manufacturing industry.[34] It was an extension of existing technologies, and so, although it had been invented on the prairie, it was soon taken up by the mass producers of steel and iron.

Washburn and Moen knew what they were doing. Barbed wire was an instant success. In the spring of 1875, the first commercial leaflet produced by the fledgling Glidden company claimed that the fence had been tested already by more than a thousand farmers—hardly a hyperbole, as the statistics available from later in the decade would indicate. Some of the selling points Glidden made were especially interesting:

> It is the cheapest and most durable fence made.
> It takes less posts than any other fence.
> It can be put for _ the labor of any other fence.
> Cattle, mule and horses will not rub against and break it down.
> The wind has no effect upon it and prairie fires will not burn it up.
> Stock will not jump over or crawl through it.

Two major claims emerge. First, the technology had the advantage of violence, so that it more effectively protected the space it enclosed. Indeed, not only was it a kind of fence that protected the inside it surrounded—but the fence protected itself as well. Second, the technology had the advantage of iron. The material was more resistant to natural forces. Combining the two, the power of violence and the power of iron, led to the major advantage of the technology at that stage. Lighter materials were required now to construct a fence, hence less labor, hence ultimately the fence's competitive pricing.[35]

Here is how Washburn and Moen were to state the case in 1880, in one of their early pamphlets. Taking forty rods of three-row fences as the unit of comparison (about one hundred meters of fenced length), we have the following:

WOODEN BOARD FENCE		BARBED WIRE FENCE	
1,000 feet pine fencing	$15.00	136 lbs barbed wire	$14.96
80 posts	$16.00	40 posts	$ 8.00
15 lbs nails	$ .60	2 lbs staples	$ .20
Labor	$ 2.50	Labor	$ .50
Total	$34.10	Total	$23.66[36]

The beauty of this pricing scheme is obvious: the main component, the one on which Washburn and Moen make a profit—barbed wire itself—is priced artificially high, just below the price of the main alternative piece of hardware, pine. The entire barbed wire fence is made competitive only because barbed wire, especially owing to its lightness, is cheaper to erect: fewer posts and nails are required, and much less labor. Notice, however, that posts *are* required—and were usually made of wood. This is an important aspect concerning the growth of barbed wire: it did *not* replace wood. That is, barbed wire did not at all result in a *reduction* of the importation of wood to the West. It did not, after all, replace existing wooden fences: instead, barbed wire fences were erected where no fences had been erected before (and none, probably, would have been erected otherwise). Thus barbed wire actually led to a *growth* in demand for timber. As the West was becoming capital intensive, the North was being deforested.[37] Barbed wire represents therefore not the replacement of wood by iron but rather a more effective combination of the two. It uses wood for its capability to sustain weight, and iron for its capability to take on precise, strong forms. In this, barbed wire resembles the two other typical technologies of the period, the railroad and the telegraph line, all consisting of repeated bases of wood, set perpendicularly to support long lines of custom-made metals. (The telegraph, another huge wire-based industry, used copper rather than iron.) Short posts of wood, repeated at regular intervals, supply these objects with a solid hold on the surface of the Earth; metal lines, attached continuously, make them stretch without a hitch to an indefinite length. In combination, such objects can accomplish a task, defined along immensely long lines, and in this way they reshape space—railroads and telegraph lines by connecting distant points, and barbed wire by defining lines of limit. This is the material context in which the growth of barbed wire should be placed.

The spread of such lines determines the transformation of space. From 9,000 miles to 30,000 miles of tracks: this was the growth of the American railroad during the 1850s, the period during which northeastern America was forever reshaped by train.[38] By 1880—a mere six years after its first patents—something like 50,000 miles of length were fenced by barbed wire.[39] We are therefore justified in comparing the revolution of barbed wire with the revolution of railroads; both transformed space almost instantaneously. The difference lies in the intended species—and is also the difference between lines as connectors and lines as dividers. While the purpose of trains was to make motion *possible,* for *humans* (as well as for their commodities), the purpose of barbed wire was to *prevent* motion, for *animals.*

The key to the entire success of this technology was, of course, its ability to stop cows. We have looked at how manufacturers priced (or at least attempted to price) their barbed wire, but whereas prices could be fixed on paper, animals had to be stopped in the real world, and humans had to be shown that. This was indeed the marketing strategy employed by the distributors of barbed wire. Let us look at an event that acquired an emblematic significance in the literature on barbed wire: the exhibition in San Antonio in 1876. Three years earlier, the farmer Henry Rose had displayed the fruit of his farm experiment on his cow. Now the salesman John Gates offered a far more striking spectacle. (Gates, at this point, was a mere agent for barbed wire manufacturers, but he was destined—as we will see in the next section—to become an international iron magnate.) Part of the central plaza next to San Fernando Cathedral was surrounded by barbed wire fences, and dozens of fierce-looking longhorn bulls were packed into this space. Here is the view to have greeted you, stepping out of the cathedral: the animals deliberately frightened and provoked; they charge against the fence and are repulsed by the sheer pain of sharp metal tearing flesh; they are wounded, and their wounds exacerbate their rage; further charges, further pain, and instinctive withdrawal; finally, resignation. The spectacle was indeed symbolic: it showed how, without the slightest touch by humans, the fiercest, and at that point least domesticated, bovine animals could be made to respect a definition of boundary: the bulls learned to avoid the fence. Barbed wire could succeed as a tool of surveillance and education.

It became clear that cheap, flexible, and effective means were available to control the movement of cows, even without the need for human intervention. Sales skyrocketed—from 5 tons in 1874, the first year of production, to 300 tons in the following year, surpassing 10,000 tons by 1878 and 100,000 tons by 1883.[40] Of course, the artificial prices that the manufacturers tried to keep did not hold. Even in 1880, actual prices paid were about half those mentioned in Washburn and Moen's advertisement quoted earlier.[41] By 1885 the price was halved again, and by 1897 it was more than halved again. At that time, the original patents began to expire, driving prices down even further. This made the invention of new patents an attractive business, and new technological advances made the technology more economic and effective. Most important, it was realized that steel, while more expensive to produce per ton, could resist animal power with much lighter strands, so that overall the price per mile would be lower with steel than with iron.[42] Steel barbed wire became more and more common during the late years of the century. (Its greater power would be significant during the next century, when barbed wire was to meet humans rather than cows.)

Instead of being a prohibitive element of cost, fences now became a cheap, labor-efficient resource, and so fencing could be extended not only in space but also in its intended uses. It is probably true that barbed wire was invented in Illinois with the farmer in mind, to protect his fields from animals; but almost immediately, barbed wire was used by owners of cows. Just as they were struggling with the diminishing resources of grass and water, they were now saved by the growing resources of iron and capital. The central fact was that as the economy gradually made its upturn from the financial panic of 1873, capital began to pour into the West, driving more and more cattle there, attempting to acquire more and more land. From 1876 onward, more than 200,000 cattle were moved annually north from Texas to form the basis of new ranches.[43] Hundreds of companies formed, mainly on the Atlantic seaboard and in Great Britain, attracted to what was perceived as a bonanza.[44] The usual logic of concentration of capital applied: as pointed out in a government report at the peak of this process, "generally it is found that the average cost per head of the management of large herds is much less than that of small herds. The tendency in the range cattle business of late years has therefore been toward a reduction in the number of herds, and generally toward the consolidation of the business in the hands of individuals, corporations, and associations."[45] Larger herds require larger space, and the larger a space is, the smaller the ratio of unit of perimeter to unit of area. This, then, was a further crucial element of economy: fencing became cheaper, paradoxically, on the immense units of space used by large herds. It also became more necessary as the same spiral of overuse continued to force fiercer competition for resources. The result was that lines of fences were set to define territories on which companies grazed their cows—whether those companies had legal title to that land or not. In 1885 it was reported that almost 4.5 million acres had been illegally fenced in this way.[46] Illegal as well as legal fencing led to wire cutting, typically as owners of smaller herds entered spaces controlled by owners of larger herds, to use their grass and water and, frequently, to steal their cows. Warfare surrounding wire began here: from Texas to Montana, big firms owned by Atlantic capitalists fought against adventurers who thought they could still make big money on violence alone. But this was not the Texas of the 1830s or even of the 1860s. Gangs of hired guns were employed by the big firms and provided with lists of small-time rangers to be killed.[47] The big-ranch business was busy, in short, driving out the range business (and the small-ranch business), much as the cow business had earlier driven out the bison business. The comparison is meaningful: in a sense, cows were driven off the land just as surely as the bison had been. The only difference was that whereas the bison were killed, the cows were imprisoned, in an Archipelago Ranch, so to speak, strewn across the plains.

To illegally fenced land, one should add several million acres of legally fenced grazing lands (especially in Texas, where the legislation was more favorable to large landholding). A notable example was the XIT Ranch in the Texas Panhandle, named after the ten (X) counties through which the ranch extended; by 1885, it had 50,000 cattle fenced inside 476,000 acres. This may be compared with the size of the territory owned in the West through the Homestead Act by 1884—just over 16 million acres.[48] In short, then, about a decade after the introduction of barbed wire, it was already used to surround cows as much as, and even more than, it was used to surround farmlands. All of this, it should be stressed, had never been envisioned by Rose, who had thought in terms of the age-old confrontation between a single farmer and a single animal. The mass scale of it all came out of the West itself and, in this way, re-created the tool beyond the imagination of its inventors. It could now be used to redefine space itself.

A striking example of the new manipulation of space made possible by this new technology was drift fences. Faced with a bad turn in the climate, what cows remained on the range would instinctively turn south—to compete there for diminishing resources. Texans (and Oklahomans) therefore looked for ways to prevent the motion of cows from north to south, in particular since the same kinds of climatic conditions that made such prevention desirable also made it difficult for humans to stay on the open range and to stop the animals in person. Beginning in 1881 or 1882, therefore, a new type of fence was gradually built: a long line of fortification against the North, as it were—built by many individual landowners, with little coordination, but effectively constructing, ultimately, a barrier across the entire Texan Panhandle. Those fences worked; cows, even those that were not yet fenced in, could be relied upon to stay in the North and not to compete for southern grazing land. No cow was now free from having its motion limited by barbed wire, and the basic geography of the land was now redefined. The climax of this development came in the severe winters of 1885–1886 and 1886–1887. Heavy blizzards drove cows in many tens of thousands southward, but just like the bulls of San Antonio, they could not pass through the barbed wire; weakened by the storm, they now were wounded and frustrated. Even in their concentrations of hundreds upon hundreds, they could neither break through the barrier or generate enough warmth between them to survive. Trapped like that, they died, perhaps as many as two-thirds of the cows in the open field, dying of starvation and of cold. Not all victims, of course, reached as far south as the drift fences, but those that did—the ones who had the most chance to survive—were perhaps those that suffered the most.[49] Such images—piles of the dead, huddled together, desperately crushed against barbed fences—are eerily reminiscent of twentieth-century images (I will return to such historical continuities later in the book).

In short, barbed wire was a success. It could stop animals, no matter how many, no matter how desperate. At first it was not clear that the static violence of barbs alone could make wires sufficiently effective, so manufacturers erred on the side of caution, supplying sharp and large barbs. These barbs met semiferal animals, accustomed to free roaming. Crashing against the wire—as they did at Gates's display at San Antonio—cattle would inevitably get seriously gouged. Open wounds ensued, which in the warm, humid summers easily lead to screwworm infestation. The screwworm fly was an endemic part of the southern plains cow economy. Its life depended on the wounds of large, warm-blooded animals. In those wounds the female would lay its eggs. When they emerged, the worms could literally eat the animal alive. All of this was extremely disagreeable to the cow owners: "A particularly disgusting and sickening job was when cows or calves got screwworms in their mouth or gums. . . . [This sometimes happened when] [t]he cow or calf—if they could reach the wound—would try to lick the worms out of the lesion. . . . You couldn't use any medicine—just remove the worms and hope you got them all. It sure wasn't a job for anyone with a 'queasy' stomach."[50] The owner's concern was not just aesthetic. Besides the loss of value owing to the death or severe illness of cows, screwworms were a severe drag on the cow economy in two ways: they demanded skilled labor, and (since birth invariably led to wounds) they made it undesirable to allow birth during the summer, thus curtailing the natural growth in the number of marketable cows.[51] The plains were rapidly moving away from the simple nature-turned-into-profit of the mavericking days. Barbed wire created the conditions for a new type of cattle industry; simultaneously, it was a constant source of loss to it. Thus we should not be surprised that, among some farmers, barbed wire was unpopular. Farmers in the late 1870 were surrounded by barbs they had not asked for, causing damages they could not control. Now, an interesting feature of barbed wire is its symmetry. While it is possible in principle to have barbs arranged so that they point in just one direction, it is far simpler to have them double pointed, so that the wire can be made "blindly," without figuring how the barbs precisely fit. In other words, the topology does not distinguish "inside" from "outside"—violence is projected in both ways. In a very real way, barbed wire is contagious: by enclosing a space, it is thereby automatically present in all areas bordering on that space. Imagine that you are a farmer, used to controlling your animals without barbed wire, now finding yourself adjacent to it. This could happen anywhere, especially since almost from the beginning, the railroad had used barbed wire to prevent animals from straying onto the tracks and causing damage to the trains.[52] Take, for instance, Mr. Palmer, a representative of Jericho to Vermont's General Assembly, who in 1880 drafted a bill to limit the use of barbed wire. He focused on the injuries caused to horse and cattle by railroad barbed fences and concluded that "the public sentiment of the community was against its use in these three cases: along highways; between adjoining landowners without mutual consent; and between railroads and pastures without the consent of the farmer."[53] Bills to prohibit the use of barbed wire were put forth in several states, always defeated in the West but, for brief periods, made law in some eastern states. Mr. Palmer actually succeeded (as did some of his colleagues in Connecticut and Maine), but by the end of 1880s, no state made barbed wire illegal any longer; the plains had reached the North.

Some compromise had to be made between the conflicting interests. In fact, following the first years of violent encounters between animal and iron, a new relationship was gradually established. To some extent, barbs became less sharp (less "vicious," to use the technical term). It is instructive to compare the declared objectives of barbed wire patents between their introduction and their later accommodation to farmers' needs. In 1876, Parker Wineman of Illinois boasted of his barbs that they "will be sure to penetrate the skin and give pain";[54] five years later (i.e., immediately after barbed wire began to be politically contested), Joseph H. Connelly of Pennsylvania stated that his particular invention "will resist force and turn stock without entangling or otherwise injuring them."[55] One such invention is typically praised in a Washburn and Moen leaflet: "the barbs are short and lance shaped, so that there is NO DANGER OF INJURY TO STOCK. . . . They will prick and scratch but NEVER TEAR THE SKIN. . . . It is well known that the sensation of pain is at the surface of the skin, hence the smart or prick . . . is all that is required. NO WOUNDS ARE MADE, consequently NO LOSS OF CATTLE in the southwest from putrefying sores, in which flies deposit their eggs."[56]

As humans learned more about animal pain, animals learned more about human violence. Animals learned to avoid barbed wire, and sometimes they were deliberately taught. A commercial leaflet encouraging the use of barbed wire advises the farmer "to lead [young horses] to the fence and let them prick their noses by contact with it . . . they will let it thoroughly alone thereafter."[57] This expresses the special interest humans always had in the physical fitness of horse, whereas cows were generally expected to pick up such knowledge through sheer experience. Their knowledge was apparently transmitted between generations, by the experience, for example, of calves following their mothers (one should remember that the cow economy of the nineteenth century still did allow calves to grow up following their mothers). To close this circle of mutual knowledge, finally, the stage was reached where manufacturers, exploiting the knowledge gained by animals, produced more conspicuous barbs, now functioning not only as instruments of direct violence but also as a more indirect instrument of intimidation (in the technical language, barbs became more "obvious"). This transition was essentially complete by the end of the 1880s, when the success of barbed wire as a tool for the education of cows can be considered complete. Simultaneously, more and more cows were fenced in, rather than fenced out, partly because of the general trend to establish landholding, and partly to "protect" the cows. The topology was now inverted, just as it had previously been for the Indians. Instead of fences preventing the motion of cows from outside a closed line to its inside (protecting the property of farmers), fences now prevented the motion of cows from inside a closed line to its outside (imprisoning cows inside ranches). Fenced inside, cows could be taken care of in the case of screwworm infestation, and winter catastrophes could not return in such harshness—so that, to a certain extent, cows were fenced in to protect them from fences.[58] Cows and plains were transformed, so that barbed wire became both natural and necessary.

With the gained perspective of nearly a decade of barbed wire use, Washburn and Moen adopted an almost historiographical tone in their commercial leaflet of 1883, already quoted briefly. The analysis offered is especially sharp and acute, and it is worthy of lengthy quotation as a summary of the early development of barbed wire:

> The fence of plain wire was far from satisfactory. . . . It had no terrors for trespassing animals. . . . [S]omething else seemed to be needed to realize the perfect fence, and this came in its own time, in Barb Fence.

> Barb wire was invented by a farmer, to meet farmer needs [it should be understood that Washburn and Moen, having won the ranch business, were now busy introducing barbed wire into cultivated areas, hence the stress on the "farmer needs"], in 1873, at first a crude working out of the parent idea; the making of fence wire repellent by borrowing from nature the principle of the sharp pricking thorn, thus appealing to the sense of pain and danger that resides in the skin of the farm animal.
>
> The principle which was first sharply challenged as cruel, has, on the contrary, been found to be humane, for these accidents of the old style were common [a litany of non-barbed-wire fence complaints follows]. . . . [T]he accidents from barb wire have been mainly of a trivial character [in a brilliant rhetorical move, following the description of accidents involving traditional fences, the author is now able to refer to wounds caused by barbed wire as "accidents"—even though, of course, the causing of wounds is the essential function of barbed wire], which, in such cases, have been warnings, salutary in their effect, and have educated the beasts in the new law of respecting fences.

This, then, was the basic function of barbed wire: a form of education—of manipulating animals—through violence. From a broader perspective, we may conceive the manipulation, or transformation, as follows. As mentioned earlier, cows brought to America by the Spanish multiplied immensely on the loose, so that a new breed of semiferal cows was created on the margins of Spanish settlement, especially in Texas. This breed was gradually redomesticated by Anglo-Americans, until faced with the need to use those animals in the conquest of the West, the process of redomestication had to proceed much more quickly. Barbed wire served to retame, by a shock, an entire breed, partly through its immediate impact, and partly through its indirect biological effects. Fenced cows could be bred in a more controlled way. Ranches, defined in space, became also defined in stock (and gradually, as a rule, limited in numbers).[59] Breeding generally took the form of the introduction of bulls from eastern states—a docile and fat breed.[60] Backed by eastern investors, eastern owners came to hold more and more of the ranches, so that eastern cow-handling practices gradually became dominant.[61] Eastern capital, eastern iron, eastern semen: all were pouring into the West to turn it into a new, artificial land for the use of the East.

All of this, let us remember, was based on a simple fact about Texan cows—indeed, about most animals. Therein lies our misfortune: our skins, just a little beneath the surface, are endowed with special nerves activated by pressure rising above rather low thresholds. You can use those nerves against us. By cutting through the boundary of our skins, you can act to protect the boundaries of your property, your prison, your border. Iron, for instance, is a useful tool. It is harder than flesh; pressed against it, iron will first push the flesh inward and then (particularly if the iron's surface, like that of a barb, is sharp) cut through the skin to impact on the nerves. The nerves send a report to the brain, and there the report undergoes some process—we do not know quite what—that leads to something else—we cannot explain quite what. This is what we call pain, and apparently it is something truly universal, cutting across species, places, and times. A useful tool of globalization, then.

3. HOW TO FENCE THE WORLD

Joseph Glidden was not so sanguine. A cautious capitalist, worried that his invention might fail through bad marketing, he kept sending anxious letters to his agents. On September 15, 1875, he was admonishing Sanborn (who had shown signs of straying from the plains marketing strategy): "we do not expect the wire to be much in demand where farmers can build brush and pole fences out of the growth on their own land and think the time spent in canvassing such territory very nearly lost even if some sales are made."[62] Sanborn should stick to his domain, the plains of Texas. Glidden's perspective, writing from De Kalb, Illinois, was defined by the plains, but as soon as production moved to Massachusetts, the perspective widened dramatically. New England had an experience of world commerce; barbed wire now was to join this global trade. Already in 1877, Ferdinand Louis Sarmiento was working in the South American continent as an agent for Washburn and Moen, busily seeking outlets for barbed wire.[63] In December of that year, for instance, he managed a public relations coup: Carl Glash, director of the Imperial Botanical Gardens in Rio de Janeiro, issued an endorsement of a barb fence erected there that he found "exceedingly complete and useful." This fence, probably one of the first to be erected anywhere outside the United States, "was erected to enclose a collection of rare water and wild fowls and animals brought home by H.I. Majesty Dom Pedro II from his late North American and European trips." It did not take long for barbed wire to reach beyond the botanical gardens. Essentially, barbed wire was used, at first, wherever conditions approached those of western America. The most obvious parallel was Argentina, where the huge plains of the Pampas were held by semiferal and feral animals, as well as by Indians. The Argentinean Indians were totally destroyed by 1879, and throughout the 1880s, fenced cattle—and wheat fields—covered the Pampas.[64] Parallel historical circumstances made the Pampas similar to the Great Plains. This similarity could now be exploited by American producers, who moved in to supply the Pampas with the technologies of the Great Plains. Soon barbed wire defined the Pampas just as it did the plains. It was estimated that by 1907, barbed wire in Argentina was already sufficient to surround the perimeter of the republic 140 times.[65] Everywhere, Washburn and Moen were aggressively seeking the prairie lands of the world, sending out powers of attorney in 1880 to diverse places such as Tasmania and the other Australian provinces, New Zealand, Cuba, Ceylon, and Russia.[66] In their correspondence, they repeatedly stressed how much further growth could be expected as a function of the global area covered by plains throughout the territories to which they had extended their patents. In 1884, when Washburn and Moen were working on a global arrangement with Felten and Guilleaume, from Mulheim, Germany, they claimed that they had already obtained patents "covering [Australia], New Zealand, India, Italy, Sweden, Austria and Denmark, representing a territory in the prairie countries only of those named . . . of 5,470,952 square miles in which no barbed wire can be sold without direct infringement . . . a territory compared with the territory of the United states as two is to one, or ensuring as soon as barbed wire is properly introduced in said countries at least 300,000 tons of sales per annum." (It would seem that Washburn and Moen had, somewhat disingenuously, measured Siberia as an equivalent of more fertile prairie land, ultimately revealing an almost prophetic vision for the future of barbed wire.)[67] In the end, Felten and Guilleaume obtained the following arrangement, which I will spell out so as to give a sense of the massive amounts involved—and how these were to be calculated across the globe. Felten and Guilleaume were to produce in the United States up to 1,000 tons per year, to be sold outside North America. They were also to produce, without limits, anywhere in Europe (or in other countries where they owned rights), paying Washburn and Moen two dollars for every ton sold in Britain and one dollar for every ton sold elsewhere, except for the amounts of 250,000 tons in both Germany and France, which could be produced and sold for domestic consumption free of charge to Washburn and Moen. Try to concentrate on that figure—a quarter million tons, almost as many miles—sold in Germany and France alone! This arrangement was continued in 1889, with the Germany/France clause changed to allow the sale of up to 1,000 tons anywhere in Europe, for domestic consumption, free of charge.[68] Yet at this stage Felten and Guilleaume were already Washburn and Moen's minor global partners. In 1891, Felten and Guilleaume's royalties paid to Washburn and Moen came to a little less than half those paid from Johnson and Nephew in Britain.[69] Johnson and Nephew's factories at Manchester and Ambergate, with about a thousand workers,[70] were among the largest producers of barbed wire at the time—American production, as we will soon see, was rather more dispersed during that period. British producers were, however, rightly concerned: German products were now dominant in Europe, while America had become a net exporter of iron products rather than a market for them. The huge production of Johnson and Nephew was thus based on export to the British Empire, with important consequences for colonial war—as we will see in the next chapter.

An important area for the introduction of barbed wire was Australia and New Zealand.[71] These continental areas were now opened for settlement, calling for some of the most radical ecological transformations Europeans effected anywhere in the world. Barbed wire reached Australia at a stage comparable not to the American cow but to the American bison: where human domination over other animals calls for extermination. Barbed wire's violence could easily be extended to extermination as well—simply by fencing water sources.[72] As for control over domesticated animals, the Australian tendency, at first, was to rely on plain wire. This was a sheep economy, based (as is usually the case with geographically marginal animal economies) not on the export of flesh but on that of other, less perishable animal parts—in this case, wool. Already in the 1860s farmers realized that wire fencing could be cheap and effective against such animals, and sheep and a radical transformation of the Australian ecology resulted with wire alone, barbs being introduced only gradually, later in the century, when the price of barbed wire was no longer higher than that of plain wire (in the twentieth century, of course, it was all barbed wire). Now that sheep could be perfectly controlled without an investment in the unreliable labor of shepherds, their numbers skyrocketed. From 6 million sheep in 1861, New South Wales had 57 million by 1894, now clearly the dominant animal on the land, with wire fencing the dominant land feature.[73]

South Africa—as usual—was even a more special case. Unlike other major areas of European colonization, it already had established agricultural practices, all based on animals. Black agriculture used the ox as the major source of muscle power and the cow as the major source of food. The Boers—descendants of seventeenth-century Dutch settlers—had already adapted European agriculture to South Africa. They gradually reverted to a form of low-capital agriculture with strong dependence on pastoralism and hunting. All of this was now coming more and more under the power of the British Empire; Boer resistance to it would lead to important consequences for the history of barbed wire (to be seen in the next chapter). But even before formal British domination, Johnson and Nephew were taking over the land with their barbed wire. The land was ready for the change. In 1886, mines were discovered in the Witwatersrand—legendary treasures of gold. Almost instantly came the railroads, new immigrants, new cities. In the countryside, it was now more profitable to produce wheat for the urban market. The many governments of South Africa supported the new intensive agriculture; in 1890, for instance, the Orange Free State—a Boer government—made fencing a legal obligation. Relations of humans and animals were quickly changing. In 1892 the *Friend of the Free State*, an Orange journal, painted a vivid picture of the new methods of hunting game: "The modus operandi is to drive all the game against a farmer's fence and then shoot them down, regardless of course of the cost of the fence." These hunters were very inconsiderate, the journal suggested, but there was some hope in the future: "When fencing is more general, however . . . [they will have] to give up their favourite pastimes."[74] Soon an animal apartheid took shape: on the one side Boer and British cows, fenced in, on the other side wild animals as well as cows belonging to blacks, fenced out of the best lands. Barbed wire was a tool in the white landgrab, with the blacks removed to marginal, unfenced land. This could still feed all animals in good years, but when the rains failed, disaster would strike. No one can tell the exact impact on wild animals, but the impact on the black economy was obvious. By the century's end, more and more blacks were forced to become farmhands on white farms, a major step toward white ascendance. A new way of controlling the land, designed to make more efficient use of it, transformed the relations not only between humans and animals but also between different human groups—distinguished by their different access to the new technologies of control over space.[75]

Everywhere, the world system was building up its stocks of

barbed wire. The center was casting its net wider. Even American producers came to rely more and more on export. The dominant American producer from 1899 onward, American Steel and Wire Company, produced 34 percent for export in the first eight years of its activity (1899–1906), but 44 percent in the following eight years (1907–1914). Taking into account foreign production, it is likely that at the end of the nineteenth century, the point had already been reached where more barbed wire was installed outside the United States than within its borders. But still, the absolute importance of the American market should not be lost from sight: with more than 100,000 tons consumed annually, the United States was, throughout, the mainstay of demand for barbed wire.[76] It remained a leading net exporter well into the twentieth century. As late as 1932, barbed wire imports into the United States did not exceed more than 20,000 tons. About half of these came from Germany.[77] The very existence of barbed wire export from Germany into America was in fact significant: the Old World would not allow the New World to monopolize barbed wire.[78]

Even Europe, a growing barbed wire producer, was itself grudgingly becoming a consumer for its own domestic consumption (and not just that of the colonies). In the decades following Glidden's original cautious estimate, barbed wire returned to reshape old, established agriculture. J. Bucknall Smith, an engineer, sounded a note of alarm in 1891, writing from the perspective of British wire production. "Our American friends may run locomotives and trains through their public highways [but should we?]. . . . Similarly, although barb-wire fencing is admirably adapted to the protection of landed property, and for enclosing live stock, in a large portion of the States or our colonies, &c., nevertheless we should scarcely be pleased to see it applied to our parks or promiscuously along our public roads." Smith had a deep insight into the historical process around him. The world was diverging—centers of polite society, where violence was now viewed with unprecedented disgust,[79] and, away from them, areas of economic expansion where unprecedented violence and power provided the profits to sustain polite society itself.

There is a paradox about the modern reshaping of space. Capitalism is based on spatial division of labor, assigning entire domains to a specific kind of production that cannot survive without interacting with the world economy as a whole. Thus it leads simultaneously to two opposing processes: as parts of the world become mutually dependent, they also diverge from each other. Barbed wire, contributing to the integration of the animal industries of the world with the world's urban centers, also formed part of the growing divergence between urban and rural. This had two aspects. First, the rural world was being unified; across the globe, different rural economies became part of the same system (as, of course, was happening at the same time to the cities themselves). Second, the rural world was, as a whole, pushed out of sight of the urban world, creating a major cultural divide.

The globalization of the rural world was keenly felt on the Great Plains themselves: they were now part of a world system, based on the urban centers of the northern Atlantic. This world system was not merely financial but also biological. I have mentioned the growing domination of the cow industry in the West by eastern breeds. This gave rise to concerns. It should be understood that historically, Texas was very different from the truly intensive cow districts of the world. In places such as, say, England, cows lived next to urban centers so that their milk could be transported and consumed by city dwellers. Thus a much more dense population of cows could be profitable. With its growing density—as well as its greater motion, a commodity in a world connected by rail and steamboat—this Old World of cows was also susceptible to new outbreaks of disease. A major epidemic of rinderpest in 1865 shook everyone in the cow economy. Shivering, frothing at the mouth, refusing all food, cows died in the millions—sometimes as many as half the herd.[80] The epidemic began to be monitored in Britain, quickly traveled on to the Continent, then to New England.[81] Texas, however—its cows herded much less intensively, and, in this period, almost a cow world unto itself—was spared. As Swabe has shown, the 1865 rinderpest epidemic was a major event leading to the new veterinary regime of the 1870s. In Europe, an attempt was made to control the motions of cows on the basis of science, the old practice of the quarantine applied with great force.[82] This, then, was the background for the alarm of the United States Treasury Cattle Commission, expressed in Chicago on August 23, 1881: "That a very large proportion of our country has, up to this time, remained exempt from [rinderpest] is owing chiefly to the fact that the current of our cattle traffic has heretofore been mainly from the west toward the seaboard; but the business of purchasing calves from the eastern dairy districts and scattering them throughout the western states and territories, which has, within a year or two past, assumed such mammoth proportions, has augmented the danger . . . tenfold."[83] It should be noted that the commission had no regulatory power, and anyway, the commissioners had missed the point. What had saved the Texas cows was the isolation of the plains, but their very economic value now ended that isolation. Soon they would have (on top of the screwworm) all that cow flesh is heir to: rinderpest, anthrax, tuberculosis, foot-and-mouth disease—and many other diseases, filling the journals of veterinary science, for decades to come, with useless medications.

All of this was being segregated from the urban sight. A crucial development was the invention, in the 1870s, of refrigerated train cars. Refrigeration along a distance, for the first time, made it possible to build a spatial separation between the killing of animals and the life of humans. It should be understood how Sisyphean a task it is to kill an animal. You stop its heart beating, and still, billions of organisms go on thriving inside. You think you have gained full mastery over the animal by slitting her throat, but all you have done is to start a new battle, now for domination over the dead body. So now the dead animal has to be boiled, frozen, inundated with minerals—everything to kill the microorganisms. (More recently, radioactive exposure has been added to the arsenal in this fight.)[84] Ultimately this is a losing battle, and the longer you take between killing the animal and consuming it, the more likely it is there will be nothing left for human consumption at all. This is very unfortunate for the manufacturers, for, as I have mentioned already, profits are always proportionate to distance. Historically, the animal industry could produce such distance-based profits only by severely limiting itself. Hides and other tissues of the body (such as horn), already semidead, can be used as something more akin to mineral resources. Hence the original killing of the bison. But this leaves out most of the animal's body. Heavily salting the animal is another solution, but this gives up the most lucrative business of the more upscale, raw flesh. That is the sadness of it, you see: people *like* the taste of blood. So sausage is not the best source of profit. As an alternative, you can let the cow grow in a faraway place (to profit from cheap land, resources, and labor) and then transport it, still alive, somewhere near a center of consumption, to be killed there. But this implies investment in slaughterhouses on prime real estate (in the American context of the 1870s, this meant property in New York). There is also the wasteful need, already mentioned, to revive animals somewhat after transportation with expensive feeding near urban centers. No: a way had to be found to make the dead flesh of animals a raw commodity and to make it participate in the new network of transportation.

This network itself provided the solution, and once again, the American West led the way. Chicago became the meeting point for two commodities: cows from the plains, and ice from northern lakes and rivers. Cows would now be killed in Chicago and transported to the East. This invention, evolving simultaneously with barbed wire and reaching perfection in the late 1870s, ensued in a new, macabre railroad car architecture. The passengers were dead carcasses, closely packed together as they dangled from the center of the car like tuxedos on a huge coatrack. From both ends of the car, they were guarded by boxes of ice and brine; a ventilation apparatus blew frozen air into the compartment. These new cars created a buffer zone between a polite urban world, where animals were seen more and more as nothing more than meat, and a violent rural world, where the killing of animals became more and more profitable.[85] Now that the American killing of cows was nearly all concentrated in Chicago, killing and processing could benefit from the concentration of capital. Huge factories were built, based on what came to be known as the "disassembly line." Living animals were transformed into so many products, for although iron replaced so many organic resources, such resources were never discarded. The animal that was not eaten had to be used. Some of it went into products used by humans—buttons, for instance, made of bone. These would ultimately be replaced by synthetic products such as plastic; more significant in the long run was, so to speak, the recycling of the animal, that is, using its carcass for such purposes as fertilizer and animal feed.[86]

At the two ends of the carcass trains, worlds were disengaging. Agriculture was intensifying, and the lives of plants and animals were now spent in worlds created by the agronomists' manuals, far from the imagination of the city. This, in turn, drew away from the animal. Muscle power was reduced in value, especially as the millennia-long tying of the horse to the wagon was giving way, by century's end, to the forces of steam and electricity. The streets saw fewer horses. They also saw fewer animals brought to be killed (once a typical urban sight). The town butcher became a dealer of packed meat, and killing was relegated to faraway meatpacking factories.

Which is all to say that control over space was ever more perfected. Raise in Texas; kill in Chicago; eat in New York. Or raise on the Pampas; kill in Montevideo; eat in London. The northern Atlantic had now truly dominated the spaces of the plains. Let us not forget the true order of causes. To begin with, the inhabitants of the northern Atlantic shared a dietary heritage that prized the flesh of bovines.[87] (In the next chapter, I will explain why this was the case.) In the early nineteenth century, Americans liked to eat beef à la mode, which was ground cow flesh, incised and stuffed with bread crumbs, spices, and butter (of course also a product of the milk of cows). Most common was the fried steak, often served—in affluent northern cities—for every meal, breakfast included.[88] This breakfast steak was the ultimate cause of all we have seen so far. In America, it was not the West that shaped the eastern diet; it was the eastern diet that shaped the West. The same elsewhere: that so much of the globe was now given over to growing cows was an expression of how much the world was governed from Boston, New York, London, and Berlin. No rice eaters, there.

No sentimentalists, either. Americans embraced the violence of barbed wire, just as they embraced the violence of competition to which it gave rise. In the dynamic years of the American steel and iron industry, barbed wire was crucial—the spur that pushed the industry in its most significant development. We have seen how half the rights in Glidden's patent were bought already in 1876 by the Massachusetts iron producers Washburn and Moen. But with the technology being so simple and lucrative, it was easily pirated. In the ten years after its invention, at least 114 companies were formed for the purpose of barbed wire production. All they needed to do was to buy a wire-stranding machine, invest in plain wire from some of the big companies in the East, and hope for good marketing in the West. Unable to drive the competitors out of the market, Washburn and Moen finally succeeded, in 1880, in making them all into licensed producers for Massachusetts itself. There were still many producers, but they had agreed to set production quotas and pay royalties to the holders of the patent. During the following decade, however, competition between the many producers did drive the price of barbed wire down—and so drive many producers out of business altogether. Price of plain wire was falling much more slowly, and margins in the industry reached critical levels. The patent expired in 1891. To stay profitable now, the few remaining barbed wire producers had an enormous incentive to reach arrangements with plain wire producers. We have met John W. Gates already, in 1876 on the plaza in San Antonio, a barbed wire salesman goading bulls into being gouged by barbed wire. He went up in the world. Now he was gouging the industry, in 1892 creating the Consolidated Steel and Wire Company, a $4 million holding company with two wire mills and three barbed wire manufacturing concerns. The years after 1893 were a period of depression. Now it was the wire mills themselves that felt the squeeze. For the wire industry to survive, it had to consolidate so as to cut its costs. Gates easily convinced more and more wire mills to consolidate with him. In 1897, finally, he approached J. P. Morgan in person. Morgan, one of the wealthiest American capitalists, was asked to underwrite a huge conglomerate encompassing most of the American wire business. Morgan nearly agreed the following year, when a war with Spain broke out over the island of Cuba (I will return to this war later). Not the time to invest in wire, Morgan considered. Gambling, Gates went ahead on his own and formed the American Steel and Wire Company of Illinois. Quick success in the Cuban War created a buzz of optimism, investment flowed into the new company, and now Gates could buy more and more steel and wire companies, incorporating, in 1899, the U.S. Steel and Wire Company.[89] The new corporation had a capitalization of $90 million, and the world had never seen its like. The company dominated the entire steel and wire industry of the United States and hence the world. Gates was now as powerful as Morgan, a leader of American industry—a giant career built on the wounded bulls of San Antonio.[90]

Everywhere industries were centralizing. When trusts along the American lines could not be formed, companies reached together to form syndicates that oversaw production and prices. Consider Provoloka (Russian for "wire"), formed in Russia in 1908, controlling the entirety of Russian wire production from Poland to the Urals.[91] Also consider the much more important Deutsche Draht-Verband GmbH, formed in Düsseldorf "as the result of a contract entered into June 6, 1914 [whose] object was to improve the manufacture of wire and to further its sales at home and abroad."[92] (German foreign policy would soon take care of *that.*) But nothing compared to U.S. Steel and Wire. The Federal Trade Commission was justifiably enthusiastic: "In 1913 this company had 268 foreign agencies, in about 60 countries. It also had 40 foreign warehouses, situated in Antwerp, Johannesburg, Sydney, Copenhagen, Barcelona, Singapore, Valparaiso, Rio de Janeiro, and other places. It ordinarily had under charter 35 to 40 steamers for the transportation of its goods, which are sold as far north as Iceland and as far south as the Straits of Magellan and the South Sea Islands."[93]

Such concentrations were a typical feature of this age of capitalism, but so was barbed wire itself. The urge of the period was to concentrate, quite literally, to bring space under control. The initial urge can be located on the prairies themselves, as entrepreneurs sought to bring land and cattle under control. This nineteenth-century capitalism was already based on the need for mass markets and mass products and therefore needed to have control on a vast scale. Hence the new kind of colonialism over an area, and the fencing of the plains. As the century ended, the fencers were fenced, and a few trusts reached everywhere—indeed, from Iceland to the South Seas. The entire structure of control over space—now global in nature—was firmly in position, and the ultimate locus of control was clearly seen to be at the center of capital, the Atlantic seaboard.

Maps 1 and 2 may be instructive in this respect. Map 1 indicates, in a rough way, the North American areas where barbed wire was chiefly distributed.[94] Map 2 indicates, with greater accuracy, the North American areas where barbed wire was chiefly produced.[95] We see, in this comparison, the phenomenon of spatial concentration. Because barbed wire is characterized by its relatively light weight, it makes economic sense to concentrate its production where the means of production are already available and then to distribute the product elsewhere. The main sites of production were the steel areas of Massachusetts, Pennsylvania, and Illinois; distribution was much wider and effectively covered the whole of the United States (and as the disproportionate role of seaports indicates, distribution was global). The light weight of barbed wire makes it into a cheap way of controlling space on the ground; it also makes it possible to produce this control over space from a few centers, so that Chicago and Pittsburgh, in this indirect way, come to control the space of America.

At this stage, two further comparisons should be made to complete this North American map. Upward, the financial and

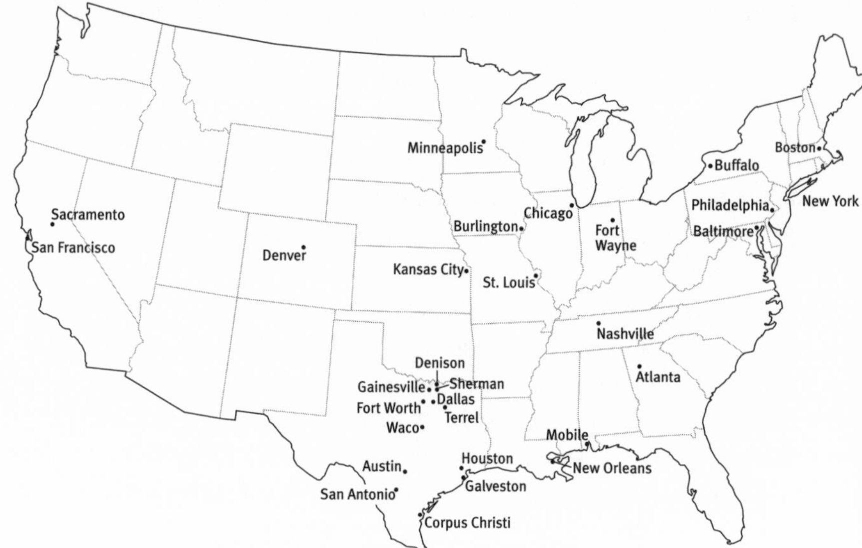

MAP 1 *Centers for delivery of barbed wire, United States, 1888. Data from Roberts Wire Company, of Pittsburgh Pennsylvania, in the American Steel and Wire Company Archives (Baker MSS: 596 DcB 1119).*

industrial control of Washburn and Moen, and then the American Steel and Wire Company, should be brought into the picture as well. Now we see the control of midwestern production by eastern capital, typical to this historical period.[96] Downward, and most important, one should add the animals themselves, all around the continent, ever more effectively surrounded and controlled by barbed wire. Now extend the picture globally, to appreciate the system just sketched, including arrangements such as those obtained with Felten and Guilleaume and with Johnson and Nephew. The resulting picture is that of the life of animals, throughout the globe, brought under human control through violence and pain, gain being extracted from this new form of control; and then control leads to control, until we reach the centers of control by capital, where violence and pain are no longer suffered or meted out, in places such as Mulheim, Germany; Manchester, England; and, above all, the American Northeast. It is unfortunate that Marx did not comment on this process, which

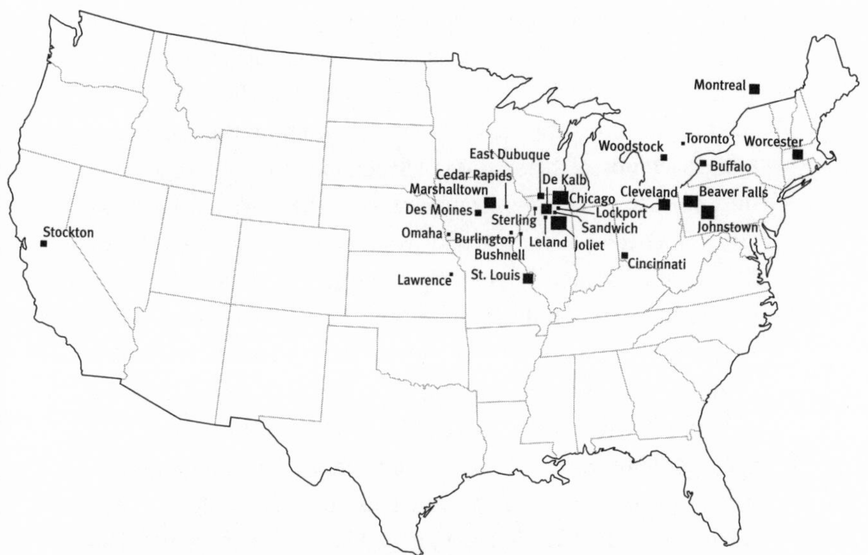

MAP 2 *Centers for production of barbed wire, United States, 1881. Data from files relating to Washburn and Moen in the American Steel and Wire Company Archives (Baker MSS 596: DcC 827).*

is perhaps a mere accident. Invented in 1874, barbed wire's economic role would become obvious only in Marx's last years. Barbed wire was destined to play a prominent role not so much in the theory of Marxism as in its practice (more on this in chapter 3).

Capitalist concentration itself, rather than the produce of the Great Plains, would be the true economic significance of barbed wire. The promise of the Great Plains gave a push to an industry of a certain tool of violence, and this industry gave a push to the concentration of capital. But the promise of the Great Plains remained deceptive. Of course, American capital did eventually develop intensive agriculture even in that arid land. Windmills brought water from beneath the surface; tractors tilled it over. In World War I and its aftermath, the production of Kansas, Oklahoma, and neighboring areas would be crucial in helping America to feed the world. But all the while, native vegetation was being destroyed, the soil overturned. Quite simply, the soil was not ready for intensive agriculture. Years of good rainfall helped the land from turning into dry dust, but when drought hit in the 1930s, the plains had already been denuded. Heavy winds always raged across the plains. Now they lifted up the soil, creating biblical clouds of black dust. Throughout the dry 1930s, these dust storms never completely ceased in the so-called Dust Bowl (an area encompassing parts of Kansas, Colorado, New Mexico, Texas, and Oklahoma). A storm could have a thick front of dust reaching up for a mile or more, weighing hundreds of tons per square mile, running across hundreds of miles on the open plains. Visibility disappeared, breathing was difficult—many people died of lung-related complaints—and everything, plants as well as animals, could be buried in the ensuing debris. The same would happen to people who had the bad luck to stray outdoors when a storm hit: "On March 15, 1935, a black blizzard struck Hays, Kansas, catching a seven-year-old boy away from home. The next morning a search party found him covered with dust and smothered. A hundred miles to the west, the same storm stranded a nine-year-old boy; a search party found him the next morning alive but tangled in barbed wire."[97] (We should recall Dorothy, another native of Kansas, having her own narrow escape.) In the traumatized ecology, rabbits suddenly proliferated, eating away the little produce that remained. Here, in the mid-southern part of the Great Plains, American colonization ensued in a terrible ecological blunder that in a sense never healed. Intensive efforts at soil conservation, as well as better luck with the rain, helped the Dust Bowl out in the 1940s, yet the area never did regain its place in the American economy.[98] Kansas, we can say, was a harbinger not of future development but of future underdevelopment. Throughout the Third World, through the twentieth century, modernism would bring the illusion of rapid development. The temptation would be to go down the path of an environmentally irresponsible monoculture, designed for the consumption of distant, rich lands. Early successes would typically lead to ecological and economic disasters. Unlike other Third World farmers, however, Kansans could vote for the U.S. Congress, and so they got their subsidies and somehow managed to extricate themselves from the legacy of the Dust Bowl.

So it is not in agriculture that the Great Plains formed a modern success story. Their significance lies in concentration, in control over space itself. This significance, however, is considerable, and it ushered in a special kind of modernity. For several decades, the plains were the prize of colonialism and an engine for historical change. At this cutting edge of history, barbed wire was created. By the end of the nineteenth century, the cutting edge of history was pulling away from the Great Plains, and barbed wire would soon make history elsewhere.

2 CONFRONTATION

Barbed Wire on the Battlefield

It was remembered as a period of peace and civilization. War was somewhere else; one could combine the thrills of warring with those of sightseeing. Let us follow, for instance, Winston Churchill, a youthful journalist-soldier. We join him in 1895 as he sails to Cuba (merely twenty-one years old, he works for the *Daily Graphic*, writing back on an insurrection against the Spanish). We catch him again in 1896, on India's mountainous Afghan border (he is a young officer, himself fighting now on the side of the colonial power). In 1898 he sails up the Nile and deep into Sudan; he is with the British army that crushes—at last—the revolt of the Mahdi. Sudan is pacified, but there is yet another revolt, yet more travels. In 1899 he is in South Africa, where the Boers try to keep their independence from the British. And here we may stop following him: Churchill's reports from South Africa, as well as his exploits there, would launch his political career, and the warlike experience of three continents would prove useful when war would—not much later—come back to Europe itself.[1]

In this global history, we need, as it were, to synchronize our historical watches. So I will start with 1873—the year Henry Rose was experimenting with wire attached to a cow's collar. In the same year, you could go to the Gold Coast in Africa to participate in Britain's Ashanti war, or you could take the silk road with the Russian armies on their way to subjugate the great Uzbek oasis Khiva (central Asia was being colonized, as part of the so-called Great Game pitting Britain and Russia against each other). Now move on to 1884. The German firm of Felten and Guillaume obtained its worldwide barbed wire distribution contract; to travel the world in that year, you should have joined the French. You could go with them either to the western Indian Ocean, where they took over the huge island of Madagascar, or to the Far East, for the Tonkin War (the French fought to carve out a sphere of French supremacy in China, to border on their colony, Vietnam). Finally, 1899—the year U.S. Steel and Wire was formed. In that year, besides going with Churchill to South Africa, you could also go with the Americans themselves—victorious over Spain—to either Cuba or the Philippines (the United States was trying its own hand in transoceanic colonialism). The year 1899 already marks a turning point: as we will see, the Boer War was about to channel barbed wire into human history itself.[2]

Is such a synchronization meaningful? That is, was there, in fact, a connection between the peaceful economic growth of the center (with inventions such as barbed wire coming out of it) and the wars overseas? Clearly there was, but not in the crude sense that European prosperity relied on the revenues of colonial expansion. Of course, it did so to a certain extent, but this can be easily exaggerated. The main source of European prosperity was in Europe itself. However, at the deeper level of space and mobility, there are important relations of the period that help to explain both the peace of the center and the war of the periphery. Both resulted from the enormous control over space enjoyed by the people of the center.

Europeans and North Americans had acquired tools of globalization: trains, steamships, and the telegraph. Hence both the internal peace and the external war. The Europeans had peace because of their interdependence; they knew that their prosperity relied on commerce crossing borders, and under such conditions, European war was seen to be so dangerous as to be impossible. Capital was invested everywhere so that the obstruction of capital flow across borders—an immediate consequence of war—would have to lead to universal financial collapse. This financial balance of terror was the main reason why everyone assumed peace in

Europe would hold indefinitely, and why indeed it had held for so long.[3] At the same time, the same tools of spatial interconnectedness that made war inside Europe so undesirable made war overseas both desirable and possible. Troops could be assembled and sent everywhere with great ease, hence expansion's possibility. And once you got your hands on distant resources and labor, you could in theory (not always in practice) produce huge profits, all based on the extension of the investor's colonialism to new territories. Hence expansion's desirability. The same territories over which Felten and Guillaume reached their agreement were the scenes of fighting itself. This fighting was designed—just as in the Louisiana territory—to clear the way for the exploitation of space.

Still, from the perspective of the history of barbed wire, colonial war was almost too simple. The asymmetry between Europeans and non-Europeans—fundamentally, the asymmetry between iron and flesh—was such that no subtle uses of violence were called for. As famously summed up by Hillaire Belloc, "Whatever happens we have got / The Maxim gun and they have not." No need for barbed wire, then. As soon, however, as both sides had similar access to iron, the simplicity evaporated. The truly bloody conflicts—as far as Europeans were concerned—involved not the fighting of "us" against "them" but the fighting of "us" against "us." At the turn of the century, colonial powers overreached and met each other, especially in the meeting of old colonialists and new ones. In 1898, Spain, the founder of American colonialism, met its heir—America itself—in Cuba; from 1899 to 1902, Boers, descendants of Dutch settlers, clashed against British interests; in 1904 and 1905, finally, Russia—an ancient empire—met the rising empire of Japan. These three wars made colonial war, finally, into a serious challenge, calling forth new solutions. We will see the significance of the Spanish-American War in the next chapter. In this chapter, we will see how, in the Boer War and the Russo-Japanese War, barbed wire was brought into warfare, leading the way to World War I itself.

Why was barbed wire important for military applications? For an obvious reason: in war no less than in peace, barbed wire could enhance human control over space. My argument in this chapter is twofold. One part of it is that the ecological background we saw in the previous chapter explained, as cause and effect, the military developments we will see in this chapter. Because barbed wire became widely available as a tool for controlling agricultural space, it also came to be used by armies. The second part of the argument is more subtle: that the ecological and military changes are related not only as cause and effect but also as two aspects of a single phenomenon. Land was being brought under more control, and this would be seen *simultaneously* in agriculture and in war—both can be considered, at a certain level of abstraction, as expressions of the same relations: space being brought under control; flesh being brought under the violence of iron. I have argued this already for Louisiana: agriculture and war are two species belonging to the same genus. In this chapter, we will see more examples of this family relationship.

The military growth of barbed wire was brought about by three main avenues, which I will consider in sections 1 through 3. Section 4 brings them all together.

Section 1, "Conquest by Iron," describes how barbed wire opened the way for a new kind of control over colonial space, total and massive in scale—comparable to that of America over the Great Plains. This was first achieved by the use of barbed wire in the Boer War. We may consider this as the *strategic application of barbed wire*.

Section 2, "Crisis of the Horse," examines how in their battles —just as in their daily, urban lives—Europeans marginalized their animals. In the new ecology of the battlefield, characterized by land broken by cultivation and fortification, horses had no place. As it were, European warfare was traditionally an open-range business, based on the free motion of large animals. With the end of the European range, the horse was removed from the battlefield just as the cow was removed from the fields. This has a deep historical significance, as more than any other animal, the horse defined European ecologies, European ways of life. The crisis of the horse as a tool of war was a decisive moment, defining the coming of modernity to the continent. We may consider this as the *ecological consequence of barbed wire*.

Section 3, "Perfection of the Obstacle," shows how military space was reshaped, not only on the vast scale of whole lands but also in the immediate scale of human encounters. Barbed wire transformed military tactics by making it possible to produce, cheaply and rapidly, highly effective obstacles; the consequences of this transformation were first made clear in the Russo-Japanese War. We may consider this as the *tactical application of barbed wire*.

Put all of these together—the strategic and tactical applications of barbed wire as well as its ecological consequence—and you have World War I. With it came the breakdown of the European center together with its peace and prosperity. This we will see in section 4, "The Obstacle Triumphant." The collapse of Europe would finally lead to the new inventions of human repression for which the twentieth century is famous, and for which we mostly remember barbed wire. I will consider these consequences of European collapse in chapter 3, but let us first look at Europe at its moment of global conquest.

1. CONQUEST BY IRON

The Boer War was not fought just for abstract space; it was fought for gold. Colonialism, we remember, was the expression of free capital flows. This, in turn, rested on the unique achievement of the age: for the first and only time in history, nearly the entire world had adopted a single financial system—the British one. It was based on the vow made by central banks to convert their currencies, on demand, into gold, all following Britain's lead. Thus financial risk was immensely reduced. All this was based on the banks of the city of London, and in fact, this financial role was now the main basis for the centrality of Britain in the world system. The United States had already overtaken Britain in industry, and so, soon, would some parts of western Europe. But they all looked to London and to its gold. If iron was the metal that produced colonial power for Europe, gold was the metal that fixed this power for London.

Little wonder, then, that the goldfields of South Africa gave rise to such British concern. There were plenty of them: they sprang forth from the earth from 1886 onward, to constitute, eventually, more than half the world's gold reserves.[4] London, then, could not allow South Africa to slip from its hands. Hence Britain's most painful war since Napoleon.

In the previous chapter, I noted the transformation of South African agriculture: it all came out of the gold. The basic configuration was this. The Boers—descendants of seventeenth-century Dutch settlers—had moved in the nineteenth century to build their own free republics deep in the South African plain (the veld). There they pursued their frontier agricultural life, relying heavily on stock raising and hunting. The coastal areas—the Cape and Natal—were British possessions, crucial (even after the opening of the Suez Canal) to British control over the Indian Ocean. Then the mines were discovered. Intensive agriculture changed, as we have seen, the relationship between humans and animals and, as a consequence, the relationship of two groups of humans: whites (who owned the new agriculture and excluded the blacks from it) and blacks (who were marginalized from the land and therefore had to become, more and more, merely a workforce for the whites). Now we should note the friction caused between the whites themselves. The gold was not distributed in an equal pattern; as if to mock London, it was all in Boer territory. This was hardly to the Boers' advantage. A theme of nineteenth-century history was the rapid population drifts due to discoveries of gold: California, Australia, Alaska, and the Boer republics. In all such cases, the absolute numbers involved were small, but as they were imposed suddenly on a sparsely populated landscape, they radically transformed it. Now there was suddenly a large non-Boer population in the Boer republics, the foreigners, or *Uitlander*. By 1896, their number reached 44,000 in the Transvaal—the chief Boer republic—alone, and it is likely that the Boer republics already had more male *Uitlander* than male Boers (this is what counted in those male suffrage republics). Most of the *Uitlander* were British, which provided London with its excuse. Arguing with a certain degree of plausibility, British diplomats claimed to worry about the treatment of the *Uitlander*, demanding that they should not be discriminated against, that they should be given access to citizenship, and so forth. Worries turned to ultimatums, and finally the Boers refused to give the *Uitlander* outright citizenship—which would have amounted to giving up on the Boer republics. When war came in October 1899, both sides went to it with a warm glow: they were fighting for the cause of European liberty.[5]

At first, all went according to plan: the Boers, as could be expected, had the initial initiative; the British, as could be expected, then mustered their forces and rolled the Boers back. By June 1900, the Boer capitals were taken, and the war seemed to be over.[6] It also seemed to have been an ordinary war: fortresses besieged, troops deployed for engagement; victories in battle, followed by daring marches, carrying the day. In fact, the war was not over, and it was not ordinary.

For the Boers refused to see the fall of their capitals, or their defeat in battles, as the end of their struggle. Regrouping and rethinking their strategy, they moved into guerrilla war. Small units of mounted soldiers—commandos—harassed the British invading force, cutting train routes and taking small units by surprise. They did not concentrate, and they did not stay put. The Boers were well prepared for such a struggle: they knew the land, they had plenty of horses, and, with their hunting experience, they were good sharpshooters. Their goal was to make invasion less profitable for Britain and, most of all, to try to raise the substantial Boer communities of the Cape and Natal into rebellion so that, with the entirety of South Africa in arms, occupation would become a task to daunt even the British Empire. The goal of the British army was now defined as a mirror image of that of the Boers: to contain and subdue the last fighting forces of the Boers, and to prevent the importation of guerrillas into firmly British controlled areas.[7] In guerrilla and counterguerrilla warfare, winning a war was not about identifying the stronger party, capable of controlling the centers (as the preceding, traditional war of battles and sieges had been), but about the ability of an occupying force to exert total power.

Part of the problem had to do with the civilian infrastructure. To prevent commandos from receiving shelter and produce from their own people, the British broke Boer civilian life. Farms were systematically burned, their noncombatant inhabitants brought into what the British called "refugee camps" or simply "concentration camps." I will return to consider this in more detail in the next chapter; in this respect, as well as the strictly military one, the Boer War was a watershed of history. But let us now concentrate on the military problem. This was essentially a problem of motion, its facilitation and its prevention. Which side would have the ability to concentrate its power at the place and time to suit its purposes? The British relied largely on trains, the Boers on horses. The train is much more vulnerable (it involves much more infrastructure than horse mobility does), and a basic Boer strategy was to blow up the tracks. The British had to find a way to protect the railroad, and, somehow, to cut the motion of horses.

This, then, is the basic problem of imperial control over land, and the British were heirs to a long tradition—which they were about to revolutionize. It should be understood how difficult control over land is. How far does naked force go? Historically, it went as far as your soldiers went; so how would you keep control when the soldiers were away? This was always a complicated task, and successful empires usually relied on local leaders, with their own network of local authority. The topology was always based on power being present at isolated points. The standard European war brought troops so as to concentrate them on a single battlefield or to march them into major cities. The guerrilla topology was different, involving an open plane; in the Boer War, this was the South African veld. The Boers controlled the plane, and the British controlled the points. This had to be brought under total British control, the topology inverted so that the British would control the plane and reduce the Boers to unconnected points. But how to achieve such a task?

The solution found by the British was revolutionary, but they were driven to it almost by accident. The tools themselves, as it were, suggested the solution. Start with the railroad. All over the world—even where there were no Boers around to try to blow it up—the railroad was being protected by barbed wire (to prevent stray animals from interfering with the passage of trains). Obviously, then, the British now set out to protect their railroads with barbed wire. However, humans could (as they so often did in the American West) simply cut the wire and then blow up the tracks or cross with their horses. Barbed wire alone was not enough; for barbed wire to protect the railroad, the wire had to be protected itself. Thus another idea followed naturally: set up garrisons along the railroads. This, however, seemed impractical for what the British still hoped would be a short war. It simply took too long to build fortresses for garrisons—"blockhouses," to use the technical term. Not so, it was soon discovered: mass production and iron could set up a system of barbed wire and blockhouses in a surprisingly short time.

In February 1901, the Twenty-third Company of Field Engineers, led by Major S. R. Rice, came up with the perfect solution.[8] Take sheets of iron and fix them upright with wooden posts. Use two layers of iron, spaced six inches apart, and fill the space with fine gravel (each blockhouse needed five cubic yards of these; such quantities were easily available in South Africa). Fashion in this way a regular octagon of about two yards on each side (about fifteen feet in diameter). Put anything on top, and the result is a small iron hut and a very effective protection against rifle fire. Gradually, the engineers found that iron was not a limiting factor, and several layers of skin were used, supported by earthwork, eliminating the use of wood. As time went by, more and more sides were added to the octagon. The polygon came to approximate a circle—the most efficient space-enclosing figure. (In this back-to-basics construction, the British were learning some geometry.) But such modifications aside, Rice's invention was essentially the final form. Soon the Twenty-third Company became itinerant housing contractors.

The blockhouse was not comfortable. Usually, six people—one noncommissioned officer and five regulars—were envisaged to live in some 150 square feet. But the blockhouse was extremely quickly built—eight thousand of them were erected during the war (mainly, it should be mentioned, by local African labor), which represents about fifteen blockhouses per day on average. They were also very cheap. A blockhouse cost a mere sixteen pounds to build. Add in fifty pounds for the cost of one mile of barbed wire entanglement, and you have a very reasonably priced system. (Of course, for very little additional money, each blockhouse was itself further surrounded by many layers of barbed wire.) Production went ahead rapidly; by the end of March 1901, nearly all railroads were protected by lines of the new system. Finally, the blockhouses were connected by telegraph. Now we have all the three typical technologies of the time arranged along a system of lines: railroad, surrounded by barbed wire, which in turn encompassed a telegraph line. The blockhouse system was thoroughly modern.

The distance between blockhouses was set, at first, at about one and one-half miles. The entire system rested on an equation involving space and time. The spatial parameter was provided by the effective range of a rifle—at that point, over three-quarters of a mile. The temporal parameter was set by barbed wire. Cutting it—especially the thick, deep entanglements laid down by British military engineers—was a slow business. Thus an attempt to cut the line in daylight would make the attackers into static targets for bullets. The night posed more of a problem, but with iron so cheap, this could be solved as well: blockhouses were built more closely together (now separated usually by not much more than half a mile), and rifles were put on "fixed sights," to cover the barbed wire line. Adding in a pastoral note, the engineers attached bells to the wire; the advancing Boers and their mounts—like Alpine cows—would fill the veld with the melody of tinkling bells, immediately followed by rifle shots, of reasonable effectiveness. (Wild animals would often get entangled in the wire, triggering false British alarms.)[9]

At this point, the British realized they had obtained something unexpected. The goal of the blockhouse system was originally to protect the railroad network. Thus the topology was understood in terms of connecting points. However, lines on a plane do not merely connect points; they also divide areas. This is what the British suddenly had—a net spread across the veld. This was a spatial application of "divide and rule." The land was parceled into separate cells surrounded by barbed wire, and in June 1901, when the British understood this effect, the blockhouse system spread its wings and began to be established apart from the railroad itself. It now became much more than a railroad defense tactic: it was a pure space-controlling mechanism.

Consider first the arithmetic. Eight thousand blockhouses, and 3,700 miles of length, were thrown over the space of the veld.[10] This comes to about £300,000, that is—to make the useful comparison—the value of some ten tons of gold, or the gold mines' prewar output for a mere month.[11] Iron was cheap. Even more startling, however, is the following comparison: the total British expenditure on the war was about £200 *million*. The entire wire system cost a little over one-thousandth of the war cost. Barbed wire and blockhouses formed an extraordinarily cost-effective method of waging war.

Now consider the geometry. South Africa is a big country: it has today about 500,000 square miles. Most of these are covered by desert land or are in the British coastal areas (although some of the system did penetrate there, as blocking Boer penetration into the old British colonies was a major concern). Say, for the sake of discussion, that the area to be brought under control was about 250,000 square miles. In other words, it was like a square with 500 miles in each direction. This might seem a forbidding magnitude, but less so with the ability to deploy barbed wire quickly on a mass scale. We have at our disposal 3,700 miles length of wire. This—still thinking in the simple terms of the square, equally divided—allows us to throw three lines horizontally, and three

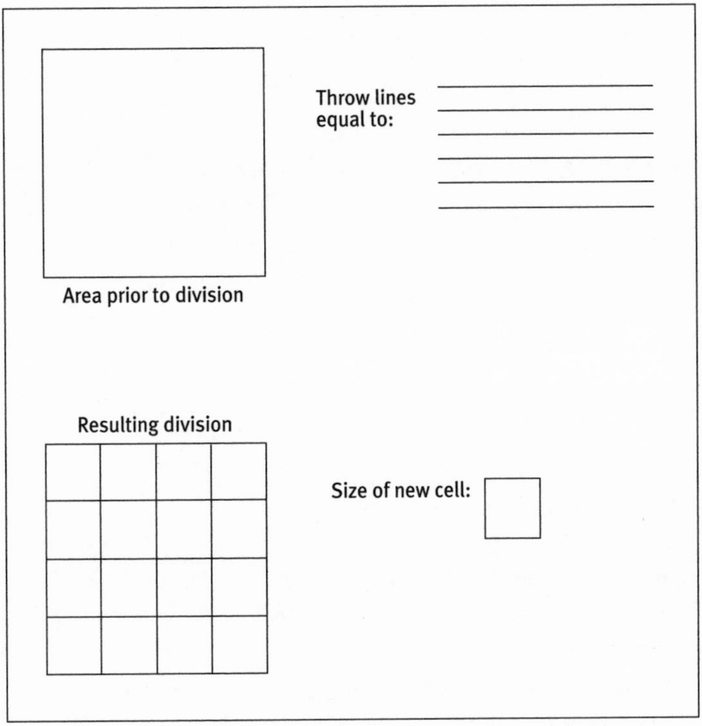

Throw lines equal to:

Area prior to division

Resulting division

Size of new cell:

vertically, with 700 miles to spare. Thus the big square is divided into sixteen smaller squares (see figure 1). Each cell is now not much more than 100 miles by 100 miles and is much easier to bring under control separately. Now compare this to the actual map of the South African barbed wire lines (map 3). By fitting the pattern of the lines to the real geography, effective cells became much smaller. Thus began the hunt for the Boers.

This was known as "the drive." In the previous chapter, we saw how, with the coming of barbed wire to South African agriculture, some Boers devised the hunting method of driving animals onto fences and killing them there. Now the hunters were hunted themselves. Large columns of British soldiers would push through the veld. They had thousands of soldiers concentrated and, significantly, had artillery, which the Boers could not match. The Boers would try to follow their basic guerrilla strategy—

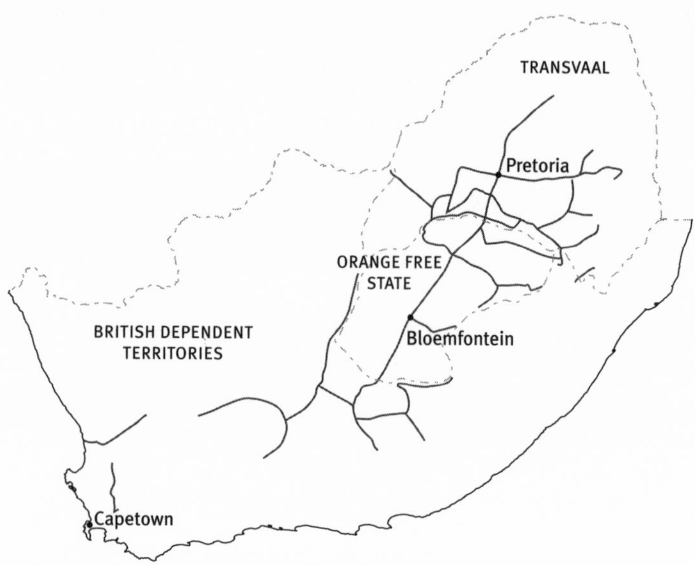

MAP 3 *Lines of barbed wire, South Africa, 1902. Based on maps in War Office 1906, <page no. TK>.*

harassing the British but avoiding pitched battle. Here was the Boers' dilemma. On the one hand, if they tried to escape in small bands, they would be effectively blocked at the barbed wire lines. On the other hand, if they tried to move as large groups—those that had a chance to overwhelm the line—then they would be unable to slip away quickly, and so they risked dangerous battles against the columns themselves. Most typically, the Boers went for small bands, which were frequently caught at the lines. The British counted their "bags": 321 Boers killed or taken prisoner in the first week of December, 435 in the second week, 453 in the third week, and so on.[12] Of course, the Boers kept inflicting casualties, and till the end, they always managed to surprise the British. On occasion, the Boers could even beat a badly organized column. Overall in the war, about twenty-two thousand British soldiers died, many more than Britain intended to lose on colonial expansion. But the Boers did not lose many fewer—seven thousand warriors died (so did many Boer civilians in the concentration camps, as we will see in the next chapter), and many more

Boers became prisoners of war.[13] Their numbers dwindled, and their strategy was lost: now that space itself was subdued, they could not be much more than a nuisance. In April 1902 the Boers sued for peace, and soon the war was over.

It would be a mistake to think of the blockhouse system as a magic wand that won the war for Britain. It was an important tactic, effective because of special conditions. In some ways, the war was unique. The typical asymmetry between colonizer and colonized was disrupted. The Boers had superiority in their use of individual horse and rifle. A single Boer was a more effective source of violence than a single British soldier—hardly ever the case in colonial war. Hence the need for such massive techniques for control over space. On the other hand, there was still considerable asymmetry. The Boers did not have much artillery to speak of, which allowed for the iron-encased but otherwise exposed blockhouses. Most important, the Boers had very limited manpower, which was the main reason for their final defeat: this would not be reduplicated in future wars between industrial nations. Thus the Boer War did not offer immediate guidance for either colonial or metropolitan war. But it did show something of great historical significance: the way was now open for imperial powers to extend their control over space across the entire land governed. The modern form of control over space, first tried on the Great Plains over the bodies of cows, now entered human history itself.

Modernity, for the first time, made control from the center a real possibility, based on the ease of deploying iron. There are many examples of such attempts at centralized colonization based on the blockhouse system, but let us take, for instance, northern Morocco—a harsh, mountainous, and rebellious land. No one had ever really controlled it, but that is what the Spanish were now determined to do. Spain—humiliated by its defeat by the United States in Cuba in 1898—was eager to seek some colonial adventure, and so it joined France in 1904 in the division of Morocco: the majority was French, but a considerable chunk of territory to the north became Spanish. To start with, this was purely nominal. Spain merely kept the city of Ceuta on the African shore—an ancient Spanish possession—making no more than a gesture toward the interior. Soon, however, mines would be found (iron, in this case, not gold), railroads would be built to the mines—we already know the sequence—and then would come the local attacks on the railroad, and in reaction would come the beginning of genuine modern colonialism. By 1921—this was now the natural thing to do—*blocaos* were built across the land: sandbag, iron, and wood structures, typically rectangular (twelve by eighteen feet—different geometry from the British circular blockhouse, but of similar size). Obviously, they were surrounded by several entanglements of barbed wire. About 150 such *blocaos* were constructed, and they were meant to be positioned across the entire land, in good sight of each other. Things did not work so well in practice, however, as plans were not fulfilled, and the *blocaos* were left without connection. When organized rebellion broke out in 1921, many of the *blocaos* were overrun at first, but those that remained were the basis for pinning down the rebels to a limited domain. With French help from the other side of the border, the Moroccan rebels were hunted down, much as the Boers were.[14] When this was completed, by 1927, Spain could claim to have total control over *something*. The hero of this success—General Franco—would eventually extend modern forms of control to Spain itself.

Let us take one more example, that of Palestine. It is especially interesting: here we can see military and agricultural history naturally come together. The basic facts are familiar: Zionist ideology aimed not only at reclaiming land for the Jews but, as it were, at reclaiming Jews for the land. Jews were to redeem the insult of being shut off from agricultural labor (and then being stigmatized for their merchant professions) by taking to the land—with a vengeance. They were to create perfect agricultural communities. Thus it was crucial to gain physical control over the land. In the Balfour Declaration of 1917, the British seemed to ally themselves to Zionism; the area came under British control in 1918, and many colonies were set up in the following years. The vast majority of the population was still Palestinian, but the plains of Palestine began to have a pattern of alternating Palestinian and

Jewish villages. The land use, however, differed radically between the two kinds of villages. Palestinians had low-intensity agriculture, with the large open field of the traditional village; the Jews —constrained, at any case, by their small numbers—had compact settlements surrounded by clearly demarcated fields of intensive agriculture. Hence the divergence in reactions when war started to intermingle with agriculture.

Palestinians never accepted the Balfour Declaration. They could hope, at first, that their clear majority in the land would force Britain to consider them as the only real partner in Palestine. Yet now Jewish immigration was multiplying: between 1931 and 1935 alone, Jewish numbers in Palestine doubled. They now had about 30 percent of the population. Like the Boers, Palestinians faced the possibility of eventually being swamped by their *Uitlander* (with the difference that the immigrant wave was caused not by gold but by Hitler). However, it became clear that—with all the concessions it was willing to make—Britain did stand by its commitment to Zionism. In 1936 the Arab Revolt broke out. It was fundamentally guerrilla warfare; small bands of warriors either harassed Jewish settlements or attacked the tools of central British power: bridges, railroads, and electricity lines. The British had a textbook response. They built a network of police forts across the land; the capstone of the system was a barbed wire fence surrounded by heavy entanglements, laid across the entire northern border of Palestine with Lebanon—over one hundred miles in length. (It served to stop the main source of ammunition and replacements for the rebels.)[15] Significantly, the British subcontracted this operation to Solel Bone, the building firm created by Zionist organizations; the British recognized that the Jews were their allies in adopting the tools of modernity.

Meanwhile Zionist settlers were scrambling to define possible future borders. A new system evolved of colonization under military threat: wall and watchtower. Trucks would arrive at the designated settlement position, with the prepared tools: wooden boards, gravel, and barbed wire. A 35-by-45-yard rectangle was surrounded by two skins of wooden boards filled with gravel. (Because the structures were relatively large, and driven by trucks, wood was preferred over iron.) Inside this small court, a watchtower was built with similar wooden boards. Surrounding it all were several layers of barbed wire. Leave inside a few tents, and you have a small settlement, built in a day. Tomorrow you can start tilling the surrounding land, and when attack comes, you have a base to fight from.[16] In other words, the blockhouse was transformed into the nucleus of agricultural settlement. It is significant that the Arab rebels hardly made an attempt to do more than harass such settlements; ultimately, they did not have the modern tools necessary to fight a fortified position. Their guerrilla war petered out, largely because of its perceived futility.

In 1948 the British left, and the Israelis (as they were now called) and the Palestinians were fighting for their national lives. We can now understand the Israeli advantage in the war. The fundamental fact of this struggle—the defining moment of the Israeli-Arab conflict—was that the Jews lived in fortified settlements, and the Palestinians did not. Thus the Israelis had a ready-made basis from which to control the land. Palestinian villages were easily penetrated, their inhabitants removed, and the houses eventually destroyed. A familiar pattern: centers of control were connected, and the previous topology of Jewish settlements scattered across the land was transformed into total Israeli control over the land as a whole.

It is often pointed out that Israel—a very late and unlikely colonialism—was in fact a remarkably successful one. Just as the entire world was being decolonized, Israel was founded as a viable state, almost completely replacing a previous settlement of long standing, all at the heart of the Muslim world. The basic reason for this is quite simple. It was not that colonialism in general was a technical military failure but that colonizing nations decided to cut their losses. But unlike other would-be colonialists, Zionists were anxious to throw into Palestine whatever manpower they had. This, then, is the major consideration, but we can add another, more subtle explanation, based on the historical perspective we have gained so far. Israel succeeded precisely because it was so late—because it was so deeply imbued with modernism. The irony is that Zionists really did come to the land with peaceful intentions—which was precisely what prepared them for war. Because they strove to become modern farmers, Jewish settlers in Palestine prepared themselves all along to become modern fighters. They aimed to control the land, and in the early twentieth century, this meant using the modern means of control over space. And since they had those means, and the Palestinians did not, the outcome of the conflict was predetermined.

The Boers, the Moroccans, the Palestinians—examples of dispossessed people can be multiplied. Everywhere were people whose presence on their land became precarious with the rise of new means of control. The next section considers another precarious presence of great ecological significance: the horse.

2. CRISIS OF THE HORSE

Assume, for the sake of argument, that you are a horse. Then you would just wish to eat grass in peace. But this will not do; there are always those who wish to eat *you*. What to be done, then? Just stay alert and, at the first sign of trouble, run for your life, relinquishing your green corner. There will always be others.

This, we can say in retrospect, is a mistake. Compare the bison's error: it reacted to the threat of predators by fleeing en masse, a huge stampede of bison flesh—which the Indians exploited to hurl the bison over the cliffs. Or consider the cow: it reacted to the threat of predators by herding together, a huge error, as humans could easily control cows by manipulating them as a herd. All failed to foresee humanity and so became its victims; the horse, finally, can claim to be the animal most cunningly exploited by men. A human reaches a horse; he restrains it somehow; he settles on its back; he fights for position there and keeps it. All of this is difficult but possible for humans. At this point, finally, the horse makes its mistake. It should have stood still, should have waited patiently for the human to get tired of the game, but no: the moment the horse is frightened—and nothing is as simple as frightening a horse—it will bolt, running away as quickly as it can. Thus humans gain an enormously powerful tool of motion—reaching speeds as high as thirty-five miles per hour.

From this point onward, the horse will always be surrounded by tools of violence, designed to cause it the pain and fear that translate into its motion. Violence was the spark to light this engine. A whip in the rider's hand, ready to strike the horse's back. A spur at the heel of his boot, to thrust its sharp point into the horse's side. Finally the bit, inside the horse's mouth, to hit against its most sensitive flesh and startle it so as to get the most rapid reaction. The details are complicated, of course: the horse needs to be broken (an apt metaphor), conditioned to an individual rider's violence so as to react to a particular kind of pain with a particular kind of motion. Still, the main principle is simple and relates directly to the evolution of barbed wire (itself inspired by ideas such as the spur and the collar). We can look at it like this: violence often controls motion not by making the recipient static but by moving the recipient in the desired direction. The barbed wire fence works, fundamentally, not by stopping animals but by *moving* them—away from the fence. Negative motion—motion in the direction opposite to that desired by the animal—equals the prevention of motion.

The spur, the bit, the whip: more than any other animal, the horse was surrounded by human tools, indeed, was transformed into an artificial, composite organism. Iron-made horseshoes came to enhance the equine hoof (especially in wet northern Europe, where hooves otherwise tend to crack). Further tools, such as reins, neck collar, and blinkers, also served to channel the horse's reactions. Finally, since a horse is really an inconvenient place for a human to sit, saddle and then the stirrup were added to give the rider some measure of comfort and stability.[17]

The horse is a capital-intensive animal, but the investment is quickly repaid. The Indians learned to hunt the bison from horseback, beginning the demise of the bison herd. Similar scenarios were replayed wherever the horse was adapted for human hunting. We can look at it like this: some animals have developed speed as an evolutionary strategy of avoiding predators. Humans exploit this skill, extracting the reaction of a certain prey animal—the horse—in order to hunt other prey animals. When the man on horseback rides to pursue, say, a fox, there are two hunted animals: not only the fox itself but also the horse. One animal is hunted to be killed once and for all; the other has the dubious advantage that, instead of being killed, it has to live through a lifetime of being pseudo-chased, whipped and spurred into constant flight.

The horse enhanced human hunting; it enhanced human violence in general. This has two aspects. With the mobility of the horse, humans could choose the time and place for violent action, and they could exploit the thrust of speed.[18] Either way, mobility would necessarily prevail over static enemies, either by running them down through gradual harassment or by crushing them through what is known as shock combat.

Where only one side had the horse, it could be remarkably effective. In the sixteenth century, a few hundred horses brought over to America by the Spanish were sufficient to destroy whole empires.[19] More than three hundred years later, Colonel Callwell could still suggest as the recipe for British colonial wars that they should primarily rely on the horse: "Savages, Asiatics and adversaries of that character have a great dread of the mounted man."[20] Indeed, this was the very trouble with the Boer War: the Boers had no such dread, and they used horses themselves, more effectively than the British did.

Everywhere, European conquest owed much to the horse, and it can be argued, in general terms, that the unique success of Europe was based on its special combination of the horse with civilization. This, in fact, is a difficult combination to achieve.

To combine the horse with civilization is to combine it with agriculture. This, however, was the historical exception. The point is this: to create a truly effective fighting instrument out of a horse, much preparation is required, and horse and rider must be thoroughly conditioned to each other. Yet the most natural setting for developing this conditioning is hunting, and in an agricultural community, hunting cannot be more than an occasional pastime. Hence a basic bipolar structure of Eurasian history. On the one side were agricultural empires whose surplus and organization supported powerful armies. These extended through the best agricultural lands, from the Mediterranean all the way to Japan. On the other side were pastoral people—who by necessity spent much more of their life hunting from horseback—loosely organized and relatively poor, yet extremely adapt at equestrian fighting. They lived to the north of the empires, on the steppe, the more marginal Eurasian territory extending from Ukraine to Mongolia. Time and again, the nomads beat the empires. The list is long, from the Hyksos, who overran Egypt in the middle of the second millennium BC, to the Magyars, sweeping across the Hungarian plains at the end of first millennium AD. Let us remember this lesson: the experience of hunting—of sharpening one's violence against animals—was, until very recently, the foundation for the most effective human violence against humans as well. Hunters are in constant touch with nature at its most violent: wild animals, to be found and killed. In single combat, the nomads were much more powerful than the settled farmers, whose lives involved only the low-intensity violence of control over animals in their domesticated state.

Much of Eurasian history involved farmers trying to block the motion of mounted nomads. As a single, dramatic example, consider the most remarkable premodern attempt to control motion on a massive scale. In the fifteenth and sixteenth centuries—while mounted Europeans were conquering the empires of America—the Ming built the Great Wall of China.[21] China, repeatedly overwhelmed from the north, never did solve the horse problem, nor could the Great Wall be more than a symbolic gesture. When the next tide came, in 1644, the northern Manchu found allies to open the gates for them and then quickly conquered China. Thus was instituted the last dynasty, the Qing.

The reason for the Chinese failure is quite simple. The rice ecology of East Asia created huge concentrations of population that, in turn, kept East Asia at the forefront of civilization. At the same time, these huge concentrations were precariously based on an extensive use of the land for rice growing based on enormous human labor. Thus East Asia could set aside very little land for domesticated animals, let alone for horses. Now compare this to wheat, the Mediterranean staple food. Effective wheat agriculture calls for crop rotation, where fields are kept fallow for part of the cycle, their minerals replenished in preparation for the next stage of cultivation. This immediately suggests that domesticated animals could use the fallow lands (and replenish it with their manure), and it is a natural extension of the same idea to make extensive use of the ox—a slow but very powerful animal—to carry things around. In particular, the ox pulled the Mediterranean plow, and this is the beginning of bovines as the basis of the Western way of life.

In the Middle Ages, farming moved up from the Mediterranean to reclaim the plains of northwestern Europe. This involved subtle and important changes. An endless scholarly debate concerns the relative causal significance of those changes—which change was it that determined all the rest? Scholars have tried to determine the identity of the nail in the horseshoe that lost the kingdom, but in truth, this question is misleading. In history, everything happens together: changes occur simultaneously and are mutually explanatory. The transformation of the northwestern European agriculture is a single piece: the synthesis of the medieval European ecology.[22]

We have already mentioned the horseshoe itself, a medieval development. This, together with a new collar (somewhat more effective in generating power from the horse), as well as a new plow (somewhat more effective in translating this power into agricultural work), made the horse a viable agricultural animal that competed with the ox. Further, while the ox requires less food than the horse does, the period saw an expansion in the quantity of fodder. Instead of the simple two-field rotation, a three-field rotation was instituted: autumn grains (e.g., wheat), followed by spring grains (e.g., oats), only then followed by leaving the land fallow. This meant that there was more food to go around for everyone, humans as well as animals.

Thus a new kind of society was created: an agricultural land based on the muscle of the horse. It was at this time and place, then, that the ox became less a tool of production and more an object of consumption. In other words, the Mediterranean ox was transformed into the European cow.

Western Europeans did not live on the steppe, and however avidly their knights took to hunting or, indeed, to jousting, they did not become fierce, Mongol-like centaurs. Here comes the development of the stirrup, a subject that stirs more debate than any other. White (1962) has argued that the invention of the stirrup allowed riders to balance on the horse and thus to become truly effective shock-combat fighters; critics point out that experienced steppe riders have always managed to achieve military conquest without the benefit of stirrups.[23] The stirrup, indeed, neatly sums up the European synthesis: it is a tool for adapting pedestrians for action on horseback. This agricultural land now supported an army of knights.

A final component of the European medieval synthesis should be mentioned. The European crop rotation system necessitated a division between a field where animals were grazing and two other fields used for autumn and spring sowing. Obviously, the grazing animals must be penned in so that they would not graze on the seedlings, and Europe had the wood, hedges, and stones to build such pens. Notice, however, the following complication. The amount of fencing required to divide a field into separate divisions grows enormously with the number of divisions involved. Suppose a village has sixty households. If each has three small plots, then each plot needs to be fenced separately, so that altogether 180 divisions are required, equivalent to almost thirty lines thrown over the village land as a whole. (Here I use the same calculation as the one required for the British division of the South African veld.) If, however, the land is used in cooperation, merely two lines are required to separate it into three amalgamated fields: a savings of more than 90 percent. Symbolic definitions can then distinguish the animals and strips of land belonging to each family. This was the typical solution adopted in the medieval village, so that western Europe was characterized by the large, open field. Furthermore, the growth in muscle power (available by having more animals work in the fields) allowed a large absolute growth in the size of cleared fields, so that wood largely retreated from the fertile plains of Europe. Thus a Europe of contiguous villages with open fields was created.

The social and economic significance of this development is obvious, but we should also note its military meaning. The open fields supported the horse, not only in the sense that they provided it with the oats of the three-year crop rotation but also in the sense that they were *open*. As I will explain hereafter, cavalry warfare is based on wide, open fields, so that the ecology and the military system were directly interdependent.

We may now spell out the ecological system in detail. The basic unit was the village, inward looking and tightly tied together. The world of villages was ruled by a small elite of knights, much more powerful than the peasants, as war was based on the capital-intensive use of the horse. In battle, specially bred horses were made to charge across the open fields created by villages. Horses were also the animals most often used for agricultural work, most importantly the production of wheat; cows became, instead, objects of consumption. Human diet was thus based on bread, cheese, and beef. This may be called "the European feudal diet," and surviving for centuries, it became central to Western culture. When the West came to dominate the world, its diet triumphed with it, even as the feudal ecology itself was obliterated. The same diet now came to be produced by industrialized agriculture. In dietary terms, then, the world moved into what may be called "the regime of industrialized feudalism," under which we still live. This transformation happened across the plains of the world in the late nineteenth century, and it is the basic process underlying the history of the Great Plains as described in the previous chapter. Barbed wire, we can now say, was invented as a tool for this industrialization of feudal diet.

Feudalism as a social system was long dead, and its ecology—much more slowly—was eroding as well. Cavalry now had to operate in a different world. To understand its operations, then, let us turn to the shelf—heavy with old books—of instructions for cavalry warfare. One of the best works of the genre is that of Major-General Von Schmidt (1817–1875), "the most able cavalry commander that Prussia had seen since the days of Frederic,"[24] whose posthumous notes were compiled by Captain Von Vollard-Bockelberg. "The real sphere of action for cavalry," Von Schmidt states, "its decisive influence on the enemy, in short, the very life and soul of our arm, is the charge. This is the culminating point of all instruction, and may truly be looked on as the touchstone and gauge of our work. In it the greatest calm, certainty, cohesion and order must be united with the greatest vehemence and rapidity."

The issues of calm and cohesion animate Von Schmidt's instructions throughout. They demand a certain social behavior from the riders, ultimately related to the social habits of horses themselves. Horses usually travel in small bands, organized by a defined pecking order, and they will follow other horses that they perceive to be their leaders. This is immensely useful for organizing the attack but can also serve to undo it. Suppose calm and cohesion fails: then some traffic jams are bound to occur, some horses would stop, and this would make their followers stop in their tracks, the entire attack doomed. Thus the fundamental discipline required of horsemen is that of coordinated riding, comparable to our aerial aerobatics and in a sense even more difficult. Horses, after all, do not come equipped with speedometers. Thus an intuitive understanding of absolute and relative speeds must be maintained.

This means that acceleration cannot be as rapid as that of an individual horse. An individual horse—as may be seen in horse races—can reach its full speed almost instantly (very useful to the horse, when running away from a wolf). However, a very large group of horses running at full speed—and without the demarcation of tracks available at the horse race itself—would turn into a stampede. Hence the need for passing through the stages of a horse's run, with the jargon of cavalry this gives rise to: the horse begins with the *walk*, followed by the somewhat quicker *trot*, followed by the *canter*, which, at high speed, becomes known as the *gallop*, leading finally to the extra-fast run of the *charge* itself. Here is Von Schmidt's calculation:

Against Infantry we require—

	800 paces at the trot	=	2 minutes	40 seconds
	800 paces at the gallop	=	1 minute	36 seconds
	150 paces at the charge	=	0 minutes	9 seconds
Total	1750		4 minutes	25 seconds[25]

This, however, might not be enough, as Von Schmidt was keenly aware. The horses are racing—by definition—across an open field, which is in full sight of the enemy; so they cannot be slow, unless when very far away from him, or else they provide easy-to-hit targets. In other words, the gallop has to start, in practice, even farther behind (say, at least a thousand yards away from the enemy).[26] The net result is that horses have to sustain a smooth buildup of their speed over a very long run, with perhaps two or three miles required.

This was the main goal of the training of the cavalry. The entire point was to adapt these basic principles of motion to different terrains that, after all, would necessarily come in the cavalry's way: one did not charge across an open stadium. So Von Schmidt remarks, "Of course some variation in these figures would be caused by accidents of the ground and other circumstances."[27] Consider those accidents of the ground in more detail. Once again, the biology of the horse is the vital consideration. Horses —the steeplechase notwithstanding—are poor leapers. The delicate mechanism that supports the horse's speed can easily be fractured by a bad fall, and with its superior speed, the horse could usually choose, before domestication, where it should go. Thus it formed the habit of trying to avoid obstacles rather than to attempt acrobatic leaps across them. It is in fact precisely for that reason that steeplechases exist. A fundamental requirement for the training of the cavalry was to train the horse, against its instincts, to clear obstacles. Once again, the main issue was that of order.[28] Anything short of a perfectly smooth leap would throw a jam into the calculated acceleration of the charge. In this sense, then, cavalry required the horse to be something other than what it was. How could cavalry operate at all, then? Von Schmidt's instructions in this regard are extremely revealing:

> In general at riding drill, bars, barriers, hedges and hurdles are much more used than ditches, although the latter are of much more importance, as being more frequently met with in the open than hedges or barriers. This is probably owing to the fact that artificial ditches, where much leaping is practiced, are very difficult; the edges become worn away and the leap thereby rendered unsafe; but, notwithstanding this, the leaping of ditches must be practiced more than that of barriers, and I would recommend lining the edges of the ditches with fascines, and covering them with earth; the ditches will thus be better kept, and the edges will not wear down.[29]

This extraordinary observation merits careful attention. Von Schmidt describes an *artificial* tendency to practice leaps over vertically rising barriers, because such obstacles are easier to construct and maintain in the artificial setting of the drilling grounds. These, however, he maintains, are infrequent in the field of the battle, where ditches are more common. Clearly what Von Schmidt has in mind are the rivulets and small canals that line the plains of Europe, as well as the ad hoc earthworks that could be dug, on the spot, by infantry. Von Schmidt envisions a horizontal, open plane, locally marked by horizontal lines, but with few vertical obstacles. It was on this plane that his horses could ride for four minutes and twenty-five seconds, keeping their constant rhythm of acceleration.

This was not an empty dream; indeed, this was precisely the kind of field across which European battles were waged. A battle takes place where soldiers, horses, and draft animals can be fed, so that armies could sustain no more than the briefest of sojourns through mountainous, wooded, or excessively marshy land. Thus battle had to take place in a fertile countryside. This was the one we have seen already: the countryside surrounding villages with their sown strips of open fields. Succinctly: the European battlefield was, literally, a field.

We may set out on the tour by following, for instance, Chandler's *Traveller's Guide to the Battlefield of Europe* (1966). As we drive through Europe, Chandler invites us to take detours from the main roads and visit the small villages that each, for a day, entered fame. Here are the fields near Blenheim (in today's Germany) where in 1704 John Churchill, the first Duke of Marlborough, detected that "the [French] enemy position contained serious flaws . . . ignored the need to dominate the water-meadows,"[30] and the duke's forces broke through: a decisive moment in Britain's rise to greatness. Or the fields near Austerlitz (in today's Czech Republic) where in 1805 Napoleon sent his general Soult through the open Pratzen plateau, breaking the Russian and Austrian positions. Or the fields, finally, near Waterloo (in today's Belgium) where in 1815 Wellington effectively used the dead ground behind ridges to protect his forces as Napoleon spent his army in attacks that never quite broke through the British lines. A fundamental feature of all such battles was that the few obstacles that mattered were all natural, with the possible addition of an ad hoc earthwork—all justifying Von Schmidt's insistence on the irrelevance of leaping across fences.

In 1745 the British isle saw its last significant military action, the Jacobite Rebellion. The following era, of course, saw a dramatic economic and ecological transition as modern capitalism took hold. Old landowning patterns were disrupted, and the village lands were parceled out as the property of outside investors. This was the movement of enclosure, and the misery it caused to peasants was well recognized at the time and researched since. The plight of another social class—that of cavalry colonels—still needs to be acknowledged. The intensification of agriculture would have consequences on the land, and hence on the war fought on it.[31]

The changes in the land were striking. Mingay (1977) compares two maps from Waltham, Lincolnshire, before and after enclosure, which I reproduce here (maps 4 and 5).[32] Imagine that

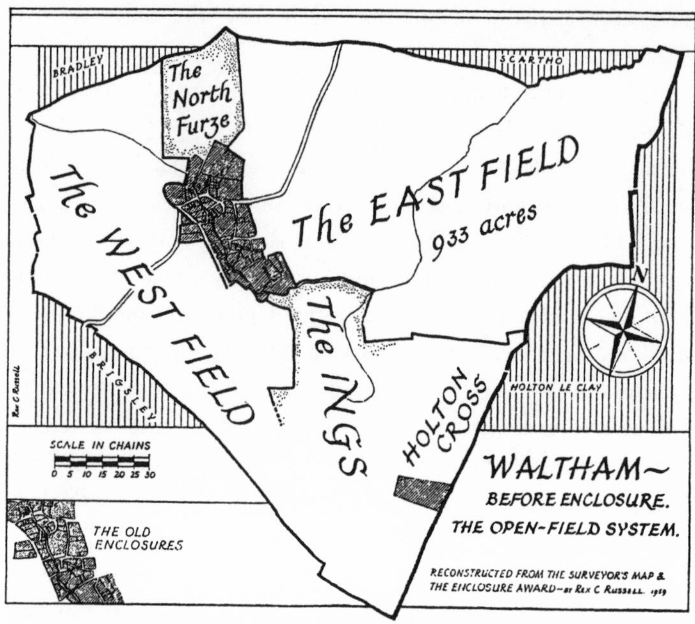

MAP 4 *Waltham, Lincolnshire, before enclosure. Reproduced from Mingay 1977, 273. Reprinted with permission, A. & C. Black.*

you cross the fields from north to south, just to the east of the village itself: about two and one-half miles distance. Before enclosure, you would cross two obstacles (map 4), whereas following enclosure, you would cross fifteen (map 5). Now try crossing those fifteen obstacles and keep your horses galloping! Which is exactly what the cavalrymen tried to do in the Franco-Prussian War of 1870 to 1871. Sometimes it still worked—there was still some room for action, and daring charges sometimes did reach some local results, greatly misleading later military thinkers. The transformation of the land was incomplete. Yet on the whole, cavalry failed.[33] See what happened where modern farmland got in the way:

> At Froeschwiller . . . General Lartigue launched Michel's brigade of cuirassiers against the Prussian infantry. . . . They set off furiously down the hill but soon ran into ground cut up

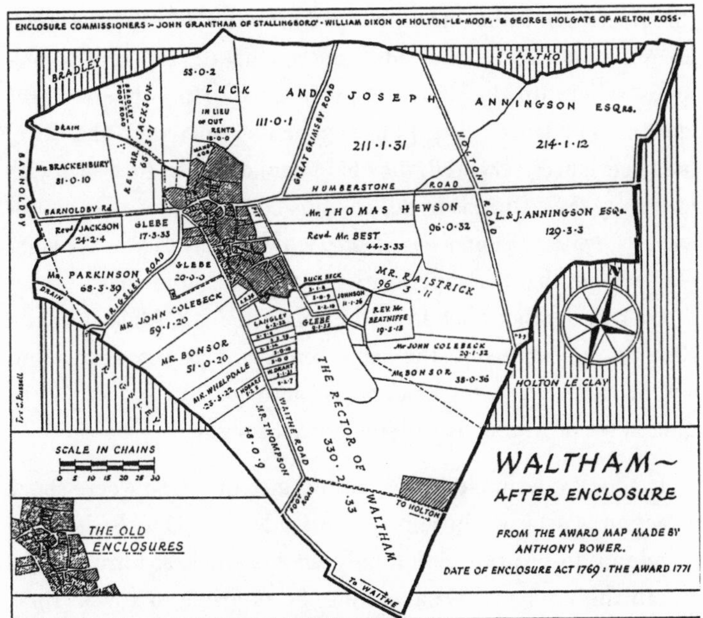

MAP 5 *Waltham, Lincolnshire, after enclosure. Reproduced from Mingay 1977, 274. Reprinted with permission, A. & C. Black.*

> by vineyards, hedges and trees. The Prussians, although tired by their earlier advance, took cover here and directed a deadly fire at the horsemen. . . . In all, some nine squadrons of cuirassiers were destroyed. It is not thought that one Prussian was killed. . . . In the afternoon another brigade of cuirassiers was thrown against the advancing Prussians. Their infantry were in extended order in just the same kind of terrain that had ensnared Michel's regiments . . . not one cavalryman got within sabre-reach of an adversary.[34]

Cavalrymen literally had the ground swept from under their feet. We begin to see many of them now entering a dreamlike world. A strange debate ran through the cavalry journals: "shock" versus "fire," that is, whether cavalry should be issued lances, or rifles only. On the bookshelf, for instance, we might find the April 1902 issue of *Revue de Cavalerie*, the journal of French cavalry (the Boers, remember, have just sued for peace, but *Revue de Cavalerie* does not yet see the wider consequences). Here is an anonymous article titled simply "Pour la lance" (In support of the lance): "The lance exists. [The regiments armed with the lance] use their lances very well; they have confidence in their arms. To take away their lance is to destroy this confidence, is to demoralize. . . . *Against Infantry and Artillery*: the superiority of the lance is so evident that this superiority requires no commentary."[35]

Or take another book from the shelf. In 1912, Major General Rimington, expressing the same sentiment as the anonymous author from *Revue de Cavalerie*, is more colorful and should be quoted for providing us with the crucial insight:

> It appears desirable to give an instance of a case where shock action is decisive. Imagine two brigades. . . . One, Red, determining to use rifle action only, adopts the best formation he can think of. . . . Dismounting, he prepares to attack. Blue, leaving a fraction of his force in guns and rifles to hold Red to his ground . . . moves round Red's flank, out of easy range and at speed, and with the remainder of his brigade attacks Red's flank, choosing the angle at which he will "go in." Red has of his own accord rendered his mobile force to a great extent immobile. [So Red is squarely defeated, and Rimington now explains Blue's success.] As regards the difficulty of hitting a galloping horseman, the following incident in South Africa may be of interest. An officer and four good shots . . . took long shots at the Boers. . . . Without any warning, suddenly about seventy Boers turned and galloped straight at [them]. "Fire steadily till I tell you to mount," was the order given by the officer, who then fired at a man in the center on a white horse and well in advance. No Boers were seen to fall. . . . When they came to compare notes, it was found that all had fired at the same man on a white horse, at whom some forty rounds had been discharged.[36]

This in fact stands to reason: the man on the white horse was moving at the speed of some ten yards per second, which is certainly very difficult to hit. Cavalry authors had their facts right on this point, at least as regards rifles (machine guns, at this stage, were a rarity: I will return to discuss these tactical details in the next section). Thus it would be wrong to ascribe the crisis of the horse to the rise of the rifle alone. Galloping horses had a chance against rifle-carrying soldiers. And Rimington, in fact, did make the right conclusion from his imaginary exercise, with the following two remarks: "Cavalry must have space to manoeuvre and fight," while conversely "Intricate ground always favours fire action."[37] Now, finally, the issue was clear: the lance and its traditional horse warfare suit open space, while fire action—that is, the horse used merely as transport to a front manned by infantry—suits "intricate ground."

But where was the ground now to be found that was not "intricate"? Lord Dundonald, arguing for "fire," spoke clearly: "the subdivision of lands into fields by wire fencing is rapidly increasing. . . . A few strands of wire, or a bit of difficult ground, will delay a mounted advance quite long enough for the rifle to do deadly work."[38] Or consider Captain Loir, a French cavalry officer writing in 1911. Like Rimington, Loir was essentially sympathetic to the lance—but much more realistic. Here is how he paints in his mind's eye an imaginary battle, where the situation is much more complex than Rimington's: "It is not a great line of battle that we are offering our enemies, but the opportunity for him to make one across difficult ground, marshes and wire fences! . . . It is of no great importance for the different units of our leading regiment to note, whether our enemy has moved with regular deploying interval at half or whole distance. All that is but a myth! In reality a great disorder results from the ignorance of the sheep and cattle enclosures, which upset the fine arrangement."[39] The cavalry officer is surprised, hitting upon those lines of enclosure. But could humans really have the right to be surprised? They set those dividing lines up, and they set them up precisely to block the motion of animals—sheep and cows, true, rather than horses. So this is what it was, really: Europeans set fences to keep cows *in*—and then, disingenuously, raised the alarm when horses were kept *out*.

We will soon see what happened in 1914, when all those officers finally did charge against each other—the disciples of Von Schmidt, Rimington, and Loir. But let us acquaint ourselves now with an even later example of the same kind of wishful thinking, from *after* World War I. I take a final quotation from those endlessly hopeful cavalrymen, this time Colonel Von Poseck. He surveyed, in retrospect, the German march into northern France in August 1914 (that is, well before the war settled into its static phase). "The advance of the cavalry was impeded by the more and more intensified cultivation of the country and the industrial works. Wire fences, drainage works, slag heaps, collieries, factory walls, railroad culverts, canals and other artificial constructions rendered harder and harder the advance itself and prevented quite often the entering into action of large mounted cavalry masses." The British cavalryman was equally disappointed, describing the Belgian countryside as "little smoky villages, coal mines, railway embankments, endless wire."[40] Von Poseck himself was still optimistic for the future of cavalry and drew from this experience the lesson that "it is very important . . . that an accurate exploration of the terrain be carried out."[41] But there was nothing to explore. Wherever one went in northwestern Europe, it was now all the same, fenced throughout. There were no battlefields in the old sense: the old troupe of cavalry players could find no theater.

Let me recapitulate the relationship found between animals and humans, ecology and history. The ecology of Europe—as of much of the world—was transformed during the late nineteenth century. Use of the land became more intensive and capital rich, and so the land itself was much interfered with. Instead of the open range of the Great Plains, or the open fields of Europe, there were now, everywhere, fenced fields enclosing intensive agricultural land. Briefly, why did that happen? Because fencing was more profitable, and because it was cheaper. Why was fencing more profitable? Because with the consumption of industrialized cities, intensified agricultural production could bring more profits. Why was fencing cheaper? Because the same industrial cities produced cheap material products such as barbed wire. In other words, a new, *modern* synthesis was created on the countryside. The medieval synthesis was based on the horse, but its modern counterpart was based on industrial produce: during this period, iron above all else.

The horse and other equids remained, for a while, as an important asset to be exploited within the new ecology, now not for speed but for endurance. Enormous fleets of horses, mules, and donkeys, powerful, surviving in the roughest conditions, continued to carry military burdens. They did so well after the invention and wide diffusion of the internal combustion engine. After all, oats were often easier to come by than oil was, roads were few, and, finally, all those animals were there, so why not exploit them? The transformation of the ecology did the horse little good. Military life was no longer that of being whipped and frightened so as to meet bullets; it was instead the sheer hard labor that the horse knew from agriculture. In World War I, a quarter million horses died with the British Expeditionary Force in France and Belgium alone—mostly from sheer exhaustion.[42] The military significance of that labor was enormous, and we can note, for instance, that fodder—not ammunition—was the main logistical item in the German army of World War I.[43] Yet even twenty years later, as Germany went into the biggest mechanized campaign of all time—the assault on the Soviet Union—it had some 600,000 vehicles, and perhaps as many as 750,000 horses.[44] Horses now came back to the steppe, a huge invading horde; now, however, they were a cart-pulling squadron, sent by a power poor in gasoline.

What was the precise contribution of barbed wire to the developments described in this section? Admittedly, it was not barbed wire alone that led to the demise of the equestrian warfare. The causes for change in the land were wider, and the transformation started before the introduction of barbed wire itself to European fields. Barbed wire was, we can say, the coup de grâce delivered to an old land arrangement that had no life left in it. But this does not make barbed wire any less significant: it was the essence of the change. The period called for efficient ways to control the land. At the end of the nineteenth century, it was wire that came to answer the call; it came, and the horse was gone. Iron replaced flesh.

Before we bid farewell to the warhorse, a final word is in order: not on the warhorse itself but on its historians. Much has been written about the demise of equestrian shock combat. Nearly all scholarly attention focuses on the development of firearms, nearly none on the development of the terrain. This, in fact, neatly reduplicates the mistake of Rimington and his contemporaries. As we can immediately note in another context, there is something extremely exciting about violent instruments such as the rifle and the machine gun. A piece of wire that a cow farmer has laid on his land does not produce the same kind of excitement. Of course, developments in firearms did change the nature of battle. However, they did not do so on their own, and firearms worked inside a certain terrain, so that it was the combination of fire and field that created the new warfare of World War I. To illustrate this in detail, I now move on to consider the history of field fortifications.

3. PERFECTION OF THE OBSTACLE

Although attack and its technologies were always the more romantic, hence noted, aspect of military life, authors had also studied, if to a lesser extent, defense and its fortifications. Once again, however, the more romantic kind of fortification was the large-scale and permanent one. The walls and castles of antiquity and of the Middle Ages were always there to be seen and to excite one's imagination. More humble means of fortification leave fewer traces and give rise to less interest. At the turn of the nineteenth century, few authors—outside the limited circle of military tacticians—even noted the rise of the obstacle, and even the tacticians usually failed to see its full significance. This would soon prove to be a serious omission.

In the world of Blenheim, Austerlitz, and Waterloo, the obstacle was perhaps of minor importance. Still, it did exist. These fields, too, all had their field fortifications: wherever you were, you reached an open field and awaited onslaught. It made sense to try to do something in advance. Mahan (1862), for instance, offered the list of what may be considered the classic obstacles of the European battlefields. The first and probably the most important were *trous-de-loup* (deep, narrow pits dug in the ground, often with sharp stakes at their bottom); it was against such obstacles that Von Schmidt had required his horses to train. Then there were many others: *abatis* (limbs of trees, entangled, their points facing the enemy), *palisades* (rows of stakes, essentially functioning as a fence), *fraises* (the same as palisades, but pointed toward the enemy), *stoccade* (the same as palisades, but constructed of small trees instead of stakes), *chevaux-de-frise* (complicated star-like structures consisting of a main body with stakes rising from it in all directions), *small pickets* (as the name suggests, short stakes—no more than three feet in length—with cords, brambles, etc., used as entanglements between them), *crow's-feet* (small pointed iron tetrahedrons, constructed so that an iron point must always project upward), and finally *inundations* and *dams*, that is, water obstacles.[45]

One immediately notes two crucial features of these obstacles: they demand much labor, and they do not assume much in terms of previously available resources. This is labor-rich but capital-poor warfare. As Mahan explains about the function of all such obstacles, none is "of much service to the assailed which is not within good striking distance of his weapons." In other words, obstacles are always intended to function in a larger system. The obstacle, essentially, slows down the attacker while weapons strike him. We have already seen the same double structure with the British lines in South Africa, consisting of barbed wire *and* garrisons, and this reveals an important distinction between the prevention of human motion and that of large domesticated animals. Given enough time, humans will always find ways around: they are more resourceful and, quite simply, more agile. The horse and cow, after all, never did climb trees. Thus obstacles, unless extremely effective, do not so much bar human motion as delay it.

Even this, however, is of great military significance. Units of time gradually became more and more important in modern warfare, for reasons well explained by Brackenbury—yet another obstacles expert—in 1888: "obstacles are of greater value now than in the past, because, however short be the time during which they detail an assailant, he will suffer much more severely during that time because of the rapidity and accuracy of modern fire."[46] Brackenbury—an intelligent and thoughtful author—went on to recite the list of obstacles, repeating Mahan's list precisely (nothing is as conservative as military manuals). Brackenbury does make the addition, however, of "wire entanglements," about which he makes the following remarkable note: "the best of all obstacles is the wire entanglement, which can be used everywhere when wire is procurable. The higher it is and the more wire the better. In woods the trees and bushes will form support for the wire, and it has the advantage of remaining in coils about the feet of an enemy, no matter how long his artillery may have played on it. The only way to defeat wire entanglement is to lie down and crawl through it or cover it over."[47] This seems to echo earlier writings, for example, those of Brialmont (1879), a Belgian author: "nets of wire constitute one of the most efficient accessory defenses. They are not seen from far off, they do not hide the fire of the defense and they resist artillery shells well. . . . In the absence of wire, one can use boards, sticks, or ropes."[48]

An interesting question arises, namely, what are they speaking of? The word "wire" is often used in the late nineteenth century to mean, where the context so demands, what we would refer to as "barbed wire" (the term had not yet become entrenched in the language). However, the wire mentioned here is probably not barbed. Brackenbury suggests crawling though it: possible with barbed wire, but extremely unpleasant and time consuming (of which fact no mention is made). A similar conclusion seems to follow from Brialmont's willingness to interchange wire with, say, ropes—as well as his failure, once again, to mention the delaying action of barbs. (Indeed, it would be extraordinary for a Belgian study from 1879 to note the existence of barbed wire, let alone its military role.) Non-barbed wire now enters the standard list of obstacles, for instance that of Wheeler from 1893: "*Entanglement*—an entanglement made by driving stout stakes into the ground from six to eight feet apart and connecting them by stout wire twisted around the stakes, forms an excellent obstacle. It is quickly made when the materials are close at hand."[49] This is accompanied by a figure that clearly shows that the wire in question was simple wire.

The major point about both Brackenbury's and Wheeler's descriptions is that the use of wire as an obstacle depends, once again, on supply. It is seen as yet another resource you might, when lucky, have available to you. You reach your bivouac for the night, and what do you find? A wood nearby, perhaps, and so you build palisades. A dam, perhaps, so you can inundate the fields. Or at the least, you can dig a ditch. And now, say, you have found a piano in a deserted village house—wires for fortification! Such scenarios aside, my guess is that what Brackenbury and Wheeler primarily have in mind is the case where headquarters has supplied you with excessive amounts of telegraph wire—whichever way, as the nineteenth century progresses, wire is ever more likely to come your way. We can say, then, that wire became another feature of the landscape, and so we are still firmly inside the period of *natural* field fortification, where the obstacles depend on the accidents of nature (albeit, in this case, man-manipulated nature). We have not yet moved to the period of *artificial* field fortification, where nature itself is remade to conform to a military need.

Thus it appears that barbed wire was used, occasionally, in war, in the last decade of the nineteenth century. A mention is made of its use in Cuba in 1898, in the Spanish-American War (which I will return to in the next chapter); that war was very short, however, and was decisively won by the Americans.[50] It thus left little mark on future military thinking. The case was different with the Boer War.

This war, as we have seen already, used much barbed wire: nature came forth abundantly with barbed wire, and much experimentation was made. Baden Baden-Powell—whose more famous brother had founded the Boy Scout movement—also served in South Africa as a British officer, and his observations were remarkably prescient. "Barbed wire," he noted in 1903, "may be considered as an important innovation in modern warfare, and is likely to be largely employed in future wars."[51] His description of the evolution of barbed wire use is instructive. At first—inspired by the military manuals—a singe line of wire, or at best a net extending in depth, was drawn about one foot from the ground. Non-barbed wire was indeed preferred over barbed wire. The purpose was to rely on the near invisibility of wire from a distance, so that the physical delay of an obstacle would be enhanced by the shock of surprise. Clearly the inspiration is the favorite obstacle of the period, the *trous-de-loup*—narrow pits, almost hidden from sight, to ensnare an unsuspecting enemy (in particular, of course, an unsuspecting *mounted* enemy). The wire is a kind of trap, then: a device of ingenuity more than of sheer violence. This, as Baden-Powell explains, does not quite work: wire is "of little use except as a tripping wire for horses, [or] may cause a man to stumble on a very dark night."[52]

In general, there was a trade-off between surprise and effectiveness. The question of the posts used for keeping the wire in place may serve as an example: "If rough branches, with the leaves on, be used, they may look like natural bushes. But posts *must* be strong, else they are easily knocked down or pulled bodily out."[53] We briefly glimpse avenues that military history opened but did not pursue: barbed wire as a tool for camouflaged entrenchment—so that even field fortifications could merge into the natural world. But no—*posts must be strong*. Instead of merging into the natural environment, it is preferable to create a wholly new, artificial one.

As Baden-Powell saw it, barbed wire formed a new departure in the use of obstacles, so that surprise could be cast aside and all attention focused on effectiveness. The reason was that barbed wire proved to be effective in an unprecedented way. Its delaying power could be tantamount to actual blockage of movement: "Given the art, time, and material, [a fence can become] absolutely insurmountable, and could only be got over by being destroyed or bridged."[54] Now, why is it that such fences could not be built with previous materials? Of course, in principle, one could always have built a wooden wall, or even one of stone, that would be "absolutely insurmountable"—of course, "given the art, time, and material." So much was always the case, but this much was new to barbed wire: the qualifications of art, time, and material were drastically diminished. Barbed wire was quick to deploy and cheap to get. Thus even a very complex entanglement could, in principle, be built within the time and means available to field commanders.

This was true in principle and was noticed by observers such as Baden-Powell. It still was not true in practice, for a simple reason that Baden-Powell noticed as well: "It has often occurred that, though wire was plentiful, there were no posts available (all wood being required for fuel)." We return, then, to the basic consideration: even in the Boer War—with its enormous strategic use of barbed wire—its tactical use was still constrained by the limitations of natural availability. And since posts could not be found in the field, and were a heavy burden to carry, there was no point in assigning barbed wire itself as a tactical tool.

The best example is provided by Swinton's *A Summer Night's Dream: The Defense of Duffer's Drift.* This remarkable book from 1907 (a small gem both as literature and as a manual of field tactics) recounts not one dream but six. The hero, Lieutenant Backsight Forethought, keeps dreaming that he has been assigned the defense of Duffer's Drift, a desolate spot on the veld. Through the first five dreams, he prepares for the defense, is overwhelmed by the attacking Boers, and then, to his great relief, finds himself cast back into the same dream. He then corrects his previous mistakes, only to make other, no less fatal errors. The final dream, of course, has him emerge triumphant, whereupon he wakes and realizes he is still in his barracks. (The poignant point of the novel is that, in truth, he still has to fight in the waking world, and dreams will not guarantee success.) Swinton was an extraordinarily intelligent and original military thinker, and we will meet him again as one of the inventors of the tank. All the more remarkable, then, that in all six dreams, Backsight Forethought never once even considers the use of barbed wire. Yet this is not an oversight but a precise observation on Swinton's part: Forethought uses no barbed wire for the good reason that he *does not have any*. Barbed wire is still not part of the natural world available to a military commander.

The experience of the Boer War, however, already suggested to some officers that barbed wire might have significant tactical potential. Soon they had the opportunity to test this in great detail—half a globe away, in northeastern China.

The helplessness of the Qing dynasty was readily apparent at the beginning of the twentieth century, and the world's powers rushed in to assert their respective interests. A special source of friction was the control over the Qing's original homeland, Manchuria. Its main distinction for Russia and Japan was in its being, relatively speaking, nearby. The hypothetical future riches to be won from exploiting China were dependent—so these two empires reasoned—on gaining control of this barren, cold land. The Russians had rather the better Manchurian deal coming out of the settlement of the Boxer Rebellion in 1900; Japan felt excluded; so war it had to be.

The Japanese acted in 1904, in a surprise action disabling the Russian fleet at Port Arthur (the main Russian base in Manchuria). Immediately afterward, the Japanese launched their invasion. This was an important experiment: after a long lull in world history, there was finally a war between two fully equipped modern armies. Indeed, there was much excitement at the time among military observers. Much like soccer coaches who will sit in the stadium to follow a match between two foreign teams, foreign officers now made the pilgrimage to the Manchurian theater. This being still a gentlemen's world, they were, in fact, invited as guests of Russia or, more often, of Japan. The writings of these observers are instructive in showing the depth of new tactical developments, though, it should be said, their descriptions, as well as their interpretations, were often clouded by false presuppositions.

Manchuria, it turned out, was not a pleasant place to wage war in. There were vast areas to be covered. The land was poor then, as it mostly still is today, and the climate harsh. Both sides had to ship their soldiers a long way—the Russians, of course, much farther than the Japanese. In other words, the rapidity of modern weapons coincided with a relatively slow deployment of troops. The tempo of the war was thus characterized by long intervals of buildup punctuated by relatively rapid engagements. To give a sense of the proportions: the war started on February 8, 1904; the first major land engagement was fought on May 26, took less than one day, and claimed more than five thousand lives.[55] Swinton had allowed his fictional Lieutenant Backsight Forethought a day in which to prepare for each engagement: a literary demand, of course, to keep the Scheherazade-like nature of the narrative, but also a realistic depiction of the Boer War. In Manchuria, everyone had ample time, and so most engagements took the form of an attack on a well-entrenched army.

The abundance of cheap labor was another helpful factor. This, indeed, was an advantage of all colonial wars. Just as in South Africa the British barbed wire lines were constructed by African labor, so most of the work in Manchuria was carried out—to use the expression of the contemporary observers—by "Chinese coolies."[56] But while labor was easy to come by, transportation did present a difficulty. As an American observer pointed out, "The roads in Manchuria are abominable. . . . The natives make no effort to improve them. In the wet season the mud is bottomless, and in dry weather the drought and deep ruts almost make one wish for mud."[57] The preparation for battle therefore had to rely on easily transportable materials. This differed from the European situation: given three months of preparation in Europe, a general of that time would try to build a *fort*: heavy walls, towers, and all. In Manchuria, however, such lavish constructions were out of the question, and field fortifications came to receive the attention once accorded to permanent constructions.

Of course, with so much time on their hands, engineers tried to create all the textbook obstacles—especially the traditional *trous-de-loup* dug into the ground or, where wood was available, *abatis*. Remarkably, however, these were all now supplemented by barbed wire: barbs covered the pits of the *trous-de-loup*, and barbs were strung around the wood structure of the *abatis*.[58] But above all else, barbed wire came to be a central tool of the key structure of the war—the trench.

Captain Soloviev—Russians, too, made their observations—summed it up clearly: "It may be remarked about the late campaign that the spade takes its place side by side with the rifle. . . . [T]he spade has become a purely fighting weapon."[59] The spades went deep and wide. Trenches were dug from seven to eight feet deep (this gave good protection from shells) and ten feet wide.[60] They were, then, almost like a narrow street in nature, albeit dug in the ground, so that motion inside the trench was easy enough. Notice that these subterranean streets varied greatly in length but were on the whole *short*—between a few dozen to a few hundred yards. This is important to stress because, influenced by the imagery of World War I, we tend to think of trenches as a *continuous* system. This, however, was a later development. The trenches of the Russo-Japanese War were still conceived on the model of the fort. They were, in fact, the poor man's fort, made with an abundance of cheap labor and light materials, but with nothing else. This explains the fundamental shape of the trench—a lunette. A real fort is a circle, created in advance to prepare for all emergencies; the trench, which is an ad hoc, ersatz fort, is a segment of a circle, prepared to meet an attack from one definite direction. A sequence of such lunettes formed the basic preparation for battle: they were arranged to form the line of defense, in width and also in depth (a first line for reconnaissance and delay, a second line for the defense itself, and a third line to which to retreat if the second was to fall).[61] Each lunette projected a space of defense, and in their combination, they dominated an entire front. In other words, control over space was understood in the traditional sense of control being extended from unconnected points.

How does a trench define a space? This has several components. First of all, the three-dimensional geometry should be understood. We tend to think of a trench as no more than a hole in the ground, but a moment's reflection will reveal that digging sand from the ground is, at the same time, piling sand on top of it.

Using this principle, then, trenches tend to have a wavelike structure, rising somewhat in their back, falling into the trench itself, then rising again to the front. This creates the parapets from which a certain field in front of the trench can be brought under control. This is the first component of the trench's spatial control: its definition of a space that is right beneath it.

Now add two further components. The first is a machine gun, positioned in the trench itself or at a prepared position directly behind it (I will return later to discuss the precise nature and significance of this instrument). The machine gun, as well, projects into the same space dominated by the trench, now defined by its effective range (measured in the hundreds of yards).

The second of these components, finally—and the only one to be located in the dominated field itself—is the barbed wire entanglement. This was positioned at a distance of about sixty yards from the trench. The obstacle typically consisted of three lines of wire formed together in depth (reminiscent of the arrangement of the trenches as a whole). Under the same sign of three, we may note that the barbs were set very thickly together—three inches apart—and that the height of the entanglement was three feet.[62] No mere trip wire, that. With the complete structure in place—trench, machine guns, barbed wire—a very special space was constructed. A typical trench dominated a roughly rectangular area, say one hundred yards deep and three hundred yards wide: all visible, all vulnerable, all blocked. Thus both armies prepared, for months on end, by preparing and refining such spaces of defense.

Then the enemy finally came. For a few minutes, the space below the parapet would be animated. What happened then? Here is an example of a rare event: a successful attack (by the Japanese side) on the wire: "Volunteers were called . . . to cut the wire entanglements. The whole company stepped forward, but only 50 men were chosen. . . . [They] rushed up to the entanglements under an awful fire from rifles and hand-grenades. The men lay on their backs pretending to be killed or wounded and thus worked their way up to the wire, and succeeded in cutting it." Not all, however, had to pretend: "Of the 50 who started 28 were killed or wounded."[63] Notice the slow-motion, crawling action: to survive in this space that was created to stop all motion, one had to assume the immobility of death.

The observers quickly formed a consensus that attacks on a trench were most likely to fail.[64] Although they understood this fact, however, they thoroughly missed its consequence. The perfection of defense seemed to call, simply, for more effort on the side of the attackers. Even the failure of the cavalry could be misrepresented. Colonel Birckbeck was scathing: "The inaction of the Russian cavalry [in the war] is difficult to account for . . . [in the] open valleys. . . . [T]he river and streams were all frozen and passable anywhere. . . . [T]he country was full of *kaoliang* [sorghum], which is excellent forage." Cavalry officers always had to have an eye for nature, but Birckbeck failed to realize that what counted now was artificial nature. "Yet absolutely no offensive movement . . . to us this is incomprehensible, unless it be that the Russian dragoon has been so emasculated by his training as to have lost all the élan and enterprise of the true cavalry soldier." And here comes an amazing conclusion: "There is no more conclusive argument in support of the retention in our cavalry training of all that relates to *l'arme blanche* [lance combat]."[65] We are back in the dream world of spirit and élan. The alternative, after all, was to be emasculated—to be no longer a subject of violence but its object. How was your masculine pride to survive in a world where, in order to stay alive, you had to pretend to be dead?

This was a Boxers' revolt, with both sides insisting on boxing against a superior enemy. Russian cavalry failed because it lacked spirit; so Japanese infantry had to succeed because it had it. Japanese heroism in pushing against obstacles was often commended. Lieutenant Colonel Hume of the Royal Artillery report, based on a Japanese briefing, is revealing:

> Then a company of infantry (5/24th Regiment, 12th Division) got close to Ha-Ma-Tang on the north. . . . The captain commanding the company was shot, and a lieutenant assumed the command. He also was shot and another subaltern took com-

mand. About half the men of the company were killed and wounded and all their ammunition expended, but not a man flinched. At this moment the other companies of the regiment came up and shot down some three hundred of the Russians who had just begun a bayonet charge. The 5th Company of the 24th Regiment is now famous in the Army.[66]

The example is in fact typical. Through sheer determination, the Japanese army did manage to win most engagements—paid for by a massive loss of life. All victories became Pyrrhic. Consider the battle of Mukden—one of the decisive *victories* won by Japan during the war. It ended with perhaps as many as seventy thousand Japanese casualties.[67]

Let us try to understand this. Why was the barbed wire trench so effective? This question deserves careful consideration. As noted earlier, the prevention of human motion is in fact difficult (this is why we have *war*—instead of just having fences along our borders). We have noted the human ability to climb and crawl through difficult terrain. Further, humans move in unpredictable ways, cunningly working against the adversary's expectations. Added to this, humans are—while not quite in the same league as the horse—rather fast animals. Finally, humans are often imbued with fanaticism that will allow them to sustain an amount of violence that would stop most other creatures. Thus, to prevent human motion, it must be made smoother, more predictable, slower, and much violence must be exerted. Barbed wire admirably answers all these requirements. Aware of its presence, attackers must curtail their motion so as to deal with the difficulty of terrain, hence all we have wished for: predictability, smoothness, and slowness itself.

Above all other considerations looms the ratio of violence to motion: if you are able to exert more units of violence for less units of space traversed, you are more likely to defeat the motion across that space. Thus we can see how machine gun and barbed wire belong together: they fulfill the same task. Barbed wire gets the violence-per-motion ratio higher by reducing the space traversed in a given unit of time; the machine gun gets the ratio higher by raising the number of units of violence released in the same given unit of time. Compare a human running without obstacles, faced with a nonautomatic weapon. You can only attempt to hit him or her a couple of times, no more. Reduce the speed of the human, raise the speed of the weapon, and you have trench warfare.

The period, indeed, saw an important development in firearms: the machine gun itself. By loading automatically, it could quickly fire large quantities of ammunition.[68] This brings us to an obvious conundrum: which was the true killer—barbed wire or machine gun? The question is easily misrepresented. There are military books to read on the machine gun, a remarkable instrument in its own right, but—until now, that is—there is almost nothing to read on barbed wire. This is an ironic asymmetry, as the literature falls into a trap it condemns. Writings about the rise of machine guns invariably lament the failure of generals to realize, on the eve of World War I, the growth in significance of defense over attack. (The generals, as we have seen, were obsessed with increasing the power of attackers, failing to see just how much the power of defenders had increased.) In accounting for the increase in the power of defense, however, military historians then concentrate almost exclusively on the machine gun, ignoring the barbed wire, in this way reduplicating the generals' error: concentrating on the more exciting instrument, the machine gun, which extends violence forward offensively, and ignoring the much more humble barbed wire, which encapsulates violence in a static, defensive manner.

So how exactly to apportion death between barbed wire and machine gun? This conundrum is difficult to approach for the simple and significant reason that the two, in fact, were not tried separately. There were no lines of fortifications with machine gun alone, or with barbed wire alone. But we can note the following two pieces of evidence. First, in World War I, heavy bombardment designed to cut the wire entanglement was usually considered a prerequisite of any attack. Thus no one thought that an attack against intact barbed wire stood a chance. Such bombardments generally did not knock off all machine gun positions (nor did they always succeed in removing the wire), so that even when successful, they created, locally, a field with machine guns and no barbed wire. Typically, assaults at this stage were technically successful, in the sense that breaches in the defense were made. This first piece of evidence goes to show that machine guns alone do not raise the violence-per-motion ratio to the rate required to stop motion completely. Second, we should consider the Russo-Japanese War—especially in comparison to World War I—as nearly free of machine guns. In the greatest battle of the war, in Mukden, there were fourteen machine guns assigned to each Japanese division, that is, about two hundred machine guns overall.[69] Thus many positions were defended not by machine gun but with rifles alone. An example would be the engagement at the battle of Mukden discussed earlier: "50 men were chosen. . . . [They] rushed up to the entanglements under an awful fire from *rifles and hand-grenades*. . . . Of the 50 who started 28 were killed or wounded" (italics mine). Defense here is based on the combination of barbed wire and rifles. Indeed, it is probably for this reason that twenty-two men of the fifty remained unharmed. Without machine guns, the barbed wire trench was certainly less effective; but it was effective enough.

But of course the exercise is imaginary and largely meaningless. Barbed wire acted here—as it always did—as part of a system. In this new context of machine guns and an overall rising violence, the violence implicit in the barbed wire itself was, in turn, multiplied. Together with machine guns, it formed the perfect obstacle.

With such perfect obstacles, the Russo-Japanese War, if properly understood, should have been the war to end all wars. To Europe's misfortune, the war was not properly understood. This was primarily because—almost without deserving it—the Japanese did win the war. They did not win it in Manchuria, though. In spite of their superiority in management and in morale, the Japanese land forces won land battles, but not the land war itself.

When Russia sued for peace in 1905, Japan had no more money—or soldiers—to send to the war.[70] Victory came to the Japanese, in part, through naval successes, fought in an arena where motion and its prevention were radically different.[71] To an even greater extent, the Japanese victory came through the failure of Russia as a modern nation. Far to the west, a revolution was breaking out—the first Russian Revolution of 1905. To observers at the time, this seemed to signal the obsolescence of traditional Russia. In this, of course, they were right, and we will see much of this in the book ahead. But observers failed to see that the war also signaled the obsolescence of traditional war itself.

We are about to reach 1914, the defining moment of the coming of modernity—the moment barbed wire suddenly became a major feature of human experience. We have been following it for forty years now; its achievement could make Joseph Glidden proud. Now is the right moment to explain this achievement. What, ultimately, caused barbed wire to be transformed; why did it cross from animal to human history? I will recapitulate the order of causes.

We saw how the tactical application of barbed wire came about not through explicit planning but through the accidents of availability. That barbed wire was widely available in certain environments made officers consider using it. This happened primarily in South Africa; then, following the preliminary South African test, came the more thorough Russo-Japanese application.

We should next ask why barbed wire was so widely available for field fortification in South Africa. The answer is clear: because it was used for the great division of the veld to seal in the Boer commandos. And why was it chosen as the tool for this project? Here we can name three main reasons.

First, there were clear antecedents in peace for the protection of railroads by barbed wire. Second, the main goal of the exercise—to block the motion of horses—was demonstrably feasible with this animal-stopping tool. Third, and most important, the price was very cheap.

Why, finally, was barbed wire cheap? Here is the ultimate

cause: a quarter century of agricultural production had already pushed its price right down. Barbed wire would never have come to the battlefield otherwise. In retrospect, armies would realize how useful barbed wire was, but in the actual historical unfolding, it first had to become a natural part of the environment, something that could be picked out and used without much extra expense. To enter human history, barbed wire first had to reach ubiquity, which it naturally did, being a tool for the control of animals. This control, finally, was everywhere.

Humans lived in the years before 1914—without their realizing it—in a dangerous environment: a world where violence was everywhere used to prevent motion. A few advance guards of humanity had the warning—in South Africa, in Manchuria. Now it would be told in Europe itself: unwanted human motion was about to stop.

4. THE OBSTACLE TRIUMPHANT

It seemed as if it took very little to start the war. A few telegrams were exchanged between Vienna and Belgrade, with escalating threats. (Their subject is well known: on June 28, the Austrian archduke Francis Ferdinand was murdered, and his assassins—Serbian nationalists—seemed to have had their orders from Belgrade.) Other telegrams were exchanged between Vienna and Berlin (Germany would not object to Austria's policies against Serbia), and between Belgrade and Saint Petersburg (Russia would come to Serbia's support). Prudence called for mobilization.

Russia had a spatial problem: it had enormous distances to cover. Thus it had to run frantically to man its borders, and the Russian train transportation system (recently built on a large scale) quickly began to send troops westward. Then followed a simple domino effect of terror. With railroad transportation, quick mobilization was everywhere possible, so that everyone had to mobilize or else risk being caught unprepared.

Germany had a spatial problem of its own: it was likely to have war on two fronts. Thus the German war planners reasoned that they must quickly disable one opponent before the other could join in. This imposed a particular strain: once everyone was mobilized, it would already be too late for Germany to fight. Either take the preemptive action, or admit defeat. So, with the trains of Europe all carrying troops, Germany had no choice. On August 4, the German army crossed the Belgian border.[72]

So did it take little, after all, to start the war? This first impression is perhaps misleading. To start World War I, it took, in fact, the telegraph and the railroad. Verbal threats reverberated instantly and could be followed, with only slight delay, by the physical threat of massed troops. Now, in general, wars start not so much from actual grievances as from potential fears. With the railroad network, potential menaces multiplied across Europe. The worst part of it was that no one knew how this was going to work—Europe had never experienced a railroad conflict on a continental scale. This further multiplied the fears of potential mobilization by the factor of the unknown. There was the irony: for decades, Europeans had assumed they had become too interconnected to fight; yet it was the very network of connections that caused the war.

Following the telegraph and the railroad came barbed wire. The three technologies once again worked to form a single environment—with yet another irony built into it. The first two tools, the telegraph and the train, were extremely effective for facilitating motion, so that they forced a rapid pace of events and led Europe to its war. The third and final tool, barbed wire, was extremely effective for preventing motion, so that following the frantic motions of July and August 1914, a perfect standstill ensued. Europe found that it could quickly start a war—and then that it could not bring it to an end.

We recall Colonel Von Poseck, lamenting the slow pace of movement across Belgium and France in August 1914, with wire fences and industrial works everywhere. A first important discovery: cavalry was not going to achieve mobility in the modern landscape. Still, for a few weeks the armies did make considerable progress. The great forts of Belgium—on which much hope was pinned—quickly succumbed to heavy guns. A second important discovery: permanent fortifications could no longer prevent motion. (I will return to explain this failure, which highlights the effectiveness of barbed wire.) Then events transpired in a manner typical for such mobile engagements. The Germans, desperately marching as fast as they could to envelop Paris, had left a flank insufficiently protected. The gap was exploited, the Germans had to halt (they were even turned back), and the rapid march was over. There was a brief lull. Since, for the moment, there was nothing better to do, the soldiers dug into the ground in preparation for further action. All this, history had seen time and again.

Then, when battle was rejoined, something quite novel happened. This—the effectiveness of field fortification—was the third and final discovery. It descended on the western front in September 1914, and by November 1918, when the war ended, it was still largely occupying the same fields, dominating them with the same perfection of control.

In the Boer War, barbed wire played a strategic role, bringing huge spaces under control. In the Russo-Japanese War, it played a tactical role, designating small areas to become killing areas for machine gun fire. In World War I, the strategic and tactical roles came together. Essentially these were the trenches used in the Russo-Japanese War, only much more so. The individual lunettes joined hands to form a continuous line. (This is the usual topological transformation we are accustomed to: what was originally unconnected points becomes, in modernity, a connected network dominating space.) Of most interest to us, barbed wire defenses reached an intensity far outstripping that of the Russo-Japanese War. Thus was fulfilled Baden-Powell's prophecy of an insurmountable obstacle.

Returning now to the genre of military manuals, we may take a British manual published during the war. Here the description of obstacles becomes much crisper than in previous manuals: "Front trenches . . . must be protected by an efficient obstacle. Some form of barbed wire entanglement is the most efficient obstacle and is that universally used." This is how the author acknowledges the military writing tradition, with its manifold obstacles. No more shall we hear of *trous-de-loup*! "A wire entanglement must be broad enough not to be easily bridged or quickly cut through, must be under the close fire of the defense, and near enough to be effectively watched by night. The near edge of the entanglement should be about 20 yards from the trench, and it should be at least 10 yards broad." But this is only the beginning. "It may sometimes be useful to construct a second belt of wire beyond the first, with its outer edge some 40 or 50 yards from the trench." Not enough, though: "Good strong entanglements . . . should be constructed wherever it is possible. With proper training, infantry should be able to make entanglements of this nature as close as 100 yards from the enemy on a dark night," where, of course, they would be likely to reach the barbed wire entanglements laid by the other side.[73]

The Germans relied on barbed wire even more heavily, and Ellis reports that "their wire was hardly ever less than fifty feet deep, and in many places it was a hundred feet more. In [some German lines] every trench had at least ten belts of wire in front of it."[74] (A "belt" refers to a whole entanglement, consisting of many strands of wire.)

We should further note that the entanglements came to be produced to special military specifications: the barbs were spaced closer together, with longer barbs, almost twice the length of the agricultural variety. If the barbs of Russo-Japanese wire were spaced at three-inch intervals, the barbed wire of World War I was often a compact sequence of nearly continuous barbs. (Soldiers often mention in their memoirs how they would get accidentally cut while laying the wire: there was little non-barbed wire to hold on to.) In other words, barbed wire quickly made the backward evolution from "obvious" to "vicious," reaching viciousness that far exceeded that suffered even by the cow.[75] Needless to say, the industry had a boom, surpassing even the initial expansion into the Great Plains. While the space involved was limited, the depth and intensity of entanglements multiplied the mileage greatly, so that during the war, U.S. Steel produced 2.8 million miles of barbed wire.[76] Not all of it was for the western front, and not all of it was deployed. But the magnitude of the operation is suggested by such numbers. It would not be far wrong to say, as a rough estimate, that every day for the duration of the war, an amount of barbed wire equivalent to the entire length of the front was laid.

The static and symmetrical nature of this war makes it less relevant to think of the barbed wire obstacle in terms of the operations of a single side. In a broader perspective, we should see here a collaborative work, shared mostly by Germans, French, and British, defining a unique space. Millions of people lived inside it and served it directly. These in turn were supported by huge networks of supply leading from both sides. Most of the world economy was reorganized with this space as its effective center. All lines of connection, railroads and sea-lanes, led to the front; and all met there in a single line of disconnection—the open space—the no-man's-land.

So this is what the world now had as its center. A remarkable monument: a river of steel, 475 miles long (though usually no more than half a mile wide),[77] flowing all the way down from the Swiss Jura to the North Sea. The image of the river is useful in that it helps us think about the obstacle in the way contemporaries thought about it—as a permanent feature of the landscape. It was no longer a tool designed for a specific action; it was the premise of all activity. Here, finally, was a form of life organized around the single problem of preventing human motion, providing this problem with its perfect solution.

Consider the reasons for the success of this solution. The basic consideration is purely quantitative. As suggested already, the tools of the Russo-Japanese War were multiplied many times over. Thus barbed wire provided a nearly insurmountable obstacle, and machine guns threatened nearly inevitable death. We recall that the Japanese in Mukden had fourteen machine guns per division. At the end of World War I, the Germans had 350 machine guns per division, apart from many independent units that carried machine guns as well.[78] (Of course, the concentration of divisions per unit of space was far higher on the western front than it had been in the Russo-Japanese War, creating an even higher proportion of machine guns per unit of space.) Hence the infamous death tolls of the war. In all, Germany had lost at least 1,800,00 men, France 1,384,000, and Britain 743,000. The overall rate of death in the war was about 5,600 casualties per day, most of them sustained on the western front.[79] Of course, the average is misleading, as death was not evenly distributed. The kind of ratio we saw in the Russo-Japanese War—fifty soldiers running to cut the wire, twenty-eight killed or wounded—was often repeated on much larger scales. Thus on a single day—the first day of the battle of the Somme, July 1, 1916—the British suffered 60,000 casualties, of whom 21,000 were killed. Keegan, recounting this, goes on to compare the experience of trench warfare to that of the concentration camps; and being a careful scholar, he hastens to note that the comparison must be qualified.[80]

In fact it is hard to find exact analogues to the world of the trenches. Life in this world had a peculiar spatial structure, as survival depended on a drastic limitation of mobility to an unpleasant hole in the ground: a kind of open-air dungeon (complete with the swarms of rats of which all soldiers' memoirs complain). It also had a peculiar temporal structure, as long periods of boredom were broken unexpectedly by long periods of terror and death—heavy bombardments with their incessant shock, day and night—and then the fast-moving experience of massive death in battle. The closest comparison would be with the temporal regimes of interrogation by torture, where the victim typically undergoes long periods of inactivity and uncertainty, followed by long periods of deprivation of any normalcy, followed by the extreme infliction of pain. While, intentionally, no statistics were kept, it was widely recognized that many of the casualties, unsurprisingly, were caused by mental breakdown.[81] The major difference between the life of the soldier on the front and the life of the victim of repression was that the group feeling of fellow soldiers was encouraged. This, while keeping many people sane in the short run, ultimately had a dangerous effect. Life in the trenches could often be borne only through cultivating a hysterical devotion to a mystical union of military camaraderie.[82] The residues of this emotion would later be central to the appeal of fascism.

How did the leaders of Europe allow this to go on? Unfortunately, the brief description just offered—that, through mere quantity, barbed wire and machine gun created a perfectly impregnable obstacle—is not quite precise. This would have been too simple, and had breaching barbed wire been strictly impossible, even the generals of World War I would at some point have stopped trying. However, it did seem possible to pierce barbed wire, and in fact it was pierced time and again. This was the real reason for the carnage: not the strict impossibility of motion but the impression of motion it did allow. That this impression was a mere illusion was due to a more subtle, qualitative feature of the combination of barbed wire and machine gun, only very slowly understood.

The illusory solution was simple and was invariably adopted by all generals on all sides. Since—barring divine intervention—an intact structure of barbed wire and machine guns was, indeed, literally insurmountable, one had first to remove the obstacle and then to cross the front. Now, removing the obstacle was not a physical impossibility: given a sufficient quantity of explosives, any solid structure will ultimately disintegrate. Thus the solution adopted was straightforward: heavily bombard the no-man's-land and the front trenches and then attack. After all, it was this principle that brought down the Belgian forts. Heavy guns—heavier than ever used before—were brought, and the forts were punctured, losing their impregnability. There seemed to be nothing wrong with the idea of applying the same principle, so effective against permanent fortification, to field fortification as well.

There were two basic problems—economic and military—with this new application of artillery. Both had severe consequences. Here is the economic problem. Barbed wire is, in economic terms, very much unlike forts. This is because a fort is an extremely expensive structure to build, so that even with a large amount of explosives spent on its reduction, the attacker is likely to have spent less than the defender. Thus in a duel between guns and forts—one side building forts, the other gunning them down—the gunner can go on further than the fort builder. But in the duel between gunner and barbed wire manufacturer, the terms are reversed.

Compare the price of a shell to the price of barbed wire removed by it. How much barbed wire does a shell clear? Bear in mind that shells will remove anything, in time, but that barbed wire will take relatively more amount of shelling than other structures of similar weight, for three reasons. First, wire possesses great strength (especially in its steel variety). Second, because of its latticed structure, barbed wire is very difficult to hit. A barbed wire obstacle is made mostly of air, and many of the shell splinters are likely to pass between the wires rather than through them. Finally, even where cuts are made, these still do not annihilate the barbed wire but merely reduce its overall connectivity.

Thus a medium shell clears—at a very optimistic estimate—no more than a few square yards of wire. Further, to get the correct calculation, we must remember that there would inevitably be many misses. A more subtle point is that there would also have to be considerable overlap: it is impossible to have a neat grid of shells, each clearing a precise sector. Let us say, then, for the sake of this calculation, that each shell clears one square yard with perhaps ten yards of length of barbed wire.

Now we should remember that we consider top-quality, heavy barbed wire; furthermore, prices rose considerably in the period of the war, following the large rise in demand. In fact, this was the only period in the history of barbed wire when it consistently gained in price. Consider the data from Pittsburgh; the unit is one hundred pounds of barbed wire (about three hundred yards of length). This cost $1.62 in July 1914. About a year later, European demand began to spike the prices, reaching a peak of $4.10 in July 1917 (see figure 2, based on data from Stewart 1919). Still, ten yards of barbed wire would cost between five and fourteen cents, no more. An eighteen-pound shell (a typical shell to be used against wire) cost between one and one-half British pounds at the beginning of the war to half a British pound when production was

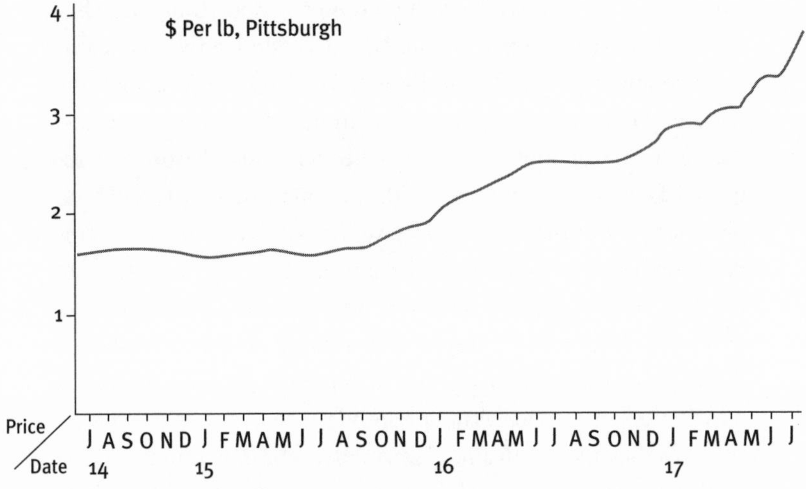

FIGURE 2 *Price of barbed wire, United States, July 1914–July 1917. Data from Stewart 1919.*

fully streamlined.[83] This is equivalent to a range from about seven to two dollars (the dollar got stronger at the time; as we will see, this was precisely because the British ordered so many shells, causing inflation). In short, it cost 15 to 140 times more to cut barbed wire than to replace it.

The duel was inherently unfair—for the same principle, repeated throughout the history of barbed wire. The tool is useful precisely because it is violence reduced to its absolute minimum. It is no more than a piece of sharpness fixed in space, nearly devoid of inherent structure. The shell, on the other hand, is an articulate mechanism, demanding precise manufacture with special tools and resources. This is why the war led to a drop in the price of the shell, but to a rise in the price of barbed wire. There was much room for improved efficiency in shell production, none in barbed wire production. Barbed wire was already as efficient as violence can be.

For this economic reason, we can say, in retrospect, that the clearing of barbed wire by bombardment was, after all, a miscalculation. Nor was it justified on strict military grounds. Indeed, it would have been worth spending even enormous sums had they been able to decide the war. But the method of heavy bombardment followed by attack could not and did not achieve any such decision. This method failed for a simple reason: it went against the principle of mobility itself. The heavy bombardments required took days, even weeks (with the consequent torturelike experience of the trenches). This gave the defender time to assemble reserves and prepare for the attack. The entire strategy of breakthrough and its exploitation was based on the surprise of mobility; but the heavy preparation of bombardment transferred the advantage of mobility to the defending side. By making its destruction into a necessary preliminary to attack, barbed wire turned attack itself into a fundamentally *static* operation.

When attack came, it had to cross through a terrain so thoroughly upset that negotiating the ground was still much of a problem. Further, sufficiently many defensive positions remained in place. Trenches provide excellent defense from shells, and even with a bombardment calculated to obliterate all life, defenders usually survived. Now, with the bombing coming to a halt, they had a precise notification of the impending attack. (It is a feature of the method of preparation by heavy bombardment that defenders have not only the general warning of an oncoming attack but also a specific warning for the precise moment of its start.) As they emerged from their trenches to dominate the no-man's-land, defenders inflicted severe casualties on the mass of attacking infantry. By the time the defensive line was breached—as usually it was—the defending side would already have begun to reestablish a new line of defense, a mile or two deeper (prepared beforehand in skeletal form), and that was all the attack gained.

One is reminded of another basic property of barbed wire. Economically, barbed wire was unbeatable because it was so cheap; militarily, barbed wire was unbeatable because it was so easy to deploy. It did not take more than a few hours to put in place a substantial barbed wire obstacle. The river of steel went momentarily dry, like the Red Sea; yet when the battle settled, it was already fully replenished. It merely meandered a little to change its course in a minor way—and it drowned the army that came through it.

Remarque, in *All Quiet on the Western Front*, describes this well, even if in a fictional narrative. I quote extensively from chapter 6. The German company has suffered through bombardment, and they await attack:

> Suddenly the nearer explosions cease. . . . The bombardment has stopped and a heavy barrage now falls behind us. The attack has come. No one would believe that in this howling waste there could still be men; but steel helmets now appear on all sides. . . . The wire entanglements are torn to pieces. Yet they offer some obstacle. We see the storm-troops coming. Our artillery opens fire. Machine-guns rattle, rifles crack. The charge works its way across. . . . The enemy as they run cannot do much before they are within forty yards. . . . They have already suffered heavily when they reach the remnants of the barbed wire entanglements. A whole line has gone down before our machine-guns; then we have a lot of stoppages and they come nearer. I see one of them, his face upturned, fall into a wire cradle. His body collapses, his hands remain suspended as though he were praying. Then his body drops clean away and only his hands with the stumps of his arms, shot off, now hang in the wire.[84]

The images of bodies hung from wire had a bad effect on soldiers on all sides. Even the imperturbable Douglas MacArthur—a major in the American Expeditionary Force—was haunted by "the vision of those writhing bodies hanging from the barbed wire."[85] Such haunting images aside, I will continue quoting from Remarque, to show further the technical effectiveness of barbed wire: "We are about to retreat. . . . We make for the rear, pull wire cradles into the trench and leave bombs behind us. . . . The forward trenches have been abandoned. . . . But the enemy's casualties increase. They did not count on so much resistance." Notice the great ease with which the preparation of new obstacles takes place *simultaneously* with the attack itself: we see the quick deployability of barbed wire in action.

Thus failed the method of heavy bombardment. The most important outcome of this failure, of course, was death on a massive scale. But there was yet another indirect consequence, of great historical significance, that arose from the combination of the economic and military considerations. Since shells were more expensive than the barbed wire they removed, and since they repeatedly failed in the goal of deciding the war, Europe was thrown into an uncontrollable cycle of shell acquisition. The steel of barbed wire, itself produced in unprecedented quantities, served as the trigger for the steel production, even more massive, of guns and shells. And then come all the other indirect consequences: for instance, with more guns in place, there would be greater need for guns to fight against guns, and then guns to fight against those guns in turn, and so on.

Barbed wire was put in place, bombed out of existence by shells fifty times as expensive as itself, and then quickly and easily replenished, leading to further steel production. Wars always involve heavy spending; they are always a gamble. But here governments bet, time and again, on the card of shells and were trumped, time and again, by the combination of barbed wire and machine guns; and then they went on betting until, finally, all were bankrupt. Industry had to be reorganized, and financial reserves everywhere had to be liquidated. This had two consequences, one local to each fighting nation, the other international.

Locally, that nations went on spending beyond their financial reserves meant that the gold standard of finance was over. States promised contractors money they did not have, and this was the end of financial stability and the beginning of inflation. Where the regime was already weak, this inflation served to destabilize it further: I will consider this later in more detail for Russia.

Internationally, all fighting European nations—Britain included—became debtors. Hence arose a considerable simplification in the world system. Before the war, the center of industrial production had been in the American Northeast, and the center of finance in London; now everything was centered in New York. Yet the transition was difficult. Following the war, European governments tried to wiggle themselves out of debt to America, mainly by trying to force defeated Germany to pay them as much as they owed America. As Keynes and many others following him have argued since, it was this constellation of debt and inflation that produced the economic instability of the 1920s and ultimately led to economic collapse in 1929. World War I, we can say, waited for 1929 to collect on the gamblers' debts.

One cannot help asking why governments kept on throwing away their soldiers and their money. But it did make some sense for them. At first, many still looked for the decisive breakthrough—where, through a perfect combination of tactics and good military fortune, the breach could be held for sufficient time, the cavalry would emerge through the breach to turn the entire enemy position; and at the start, who could have guessed how futile this hope was? This was especially true of the French and the British, where this illusion persisted for much of the war. Another strategy was to attack, mainly so as to provoke the enemy into its own attack—in full realization that the war had now become a battle of attrition. This strategy was tried by the Germans, especially in the battle of Verdun (without success: through the logic of attack, its failure, the temptation it created to counterattack, and so forth, the Germans finally lost as many as the French did).[86] Other, more subtle tactics gradually evolved and appeared promising. In particular, the armies realized that they could obtain a better result by replacing the heavy and prolonged bombardment of a narrow sector by a somewhat lighter and shorter bombardment across a wide front. In this way, reserves could not be so effectively assembled by the defender. The initial breach was still very costly, in shells and in human lives, but at least it could be sustained longer. This method was invented by the Russian general Brusilov in 1916 and was used again by the Germans, followed by the Allies, in 1918. By the standards of the war, it was a successful method: it allowed progress to be measured not in single miles but in a few dozen. But, after all, the front would always be reestablished, arguably even in November 1918 itself. The basic advantage of barbed wire and machine guns over attacking infantry could not be resolved.

Since the problem arose from new tools of defense, it was natural to seek a solution in new tools of attack. Two such attempts at solution were especially radical. We should consider these two attempts—the two children of barbed wire—as they reveal just how dramatically the field of battle was now changed and how precarious was the position of the human body in it.

The barbed wire and machine gun structure was based on two components: an effective obstacle, and an effective violence to back the obstacle. The first solution to the problem focused on the violence itself, the second on the obstacle.

How to remove the violence backing the obstacle? Clearly, if you succeeded in disabling all defenders, then you could pass across, barbed wire or not. Germany, in particular, had access to means of mass lethality. It dominated the world's dyestuff industry (its only serious rival in the field being nonbelligerent Switzerland),[87] and it was well known that many of the ingredients used by the industry were highly toxic. Chlorine, for example, exposes the lining of the bronchial tubes and lungs and blocks the windpipe with fluid, with the likelihood of death from internal drowning.[88] Germany now had nowhere to export dyestuff to, anyway, and throwing chlorine on its enemies came as a natural thought. In particular, such a weapon could create a breach without any need for long preparation, thus solving the basic problem of the war. It was a tool that could spread violence, quickly, over a determined area—an effective tool for controlling space.

The idea of using gas, then, was promising, and its first effective application—at Ypres (Belgium), on April 22, 1915—not entirely without merit. The weather was helpful: warm, with the breeze consistently flowing from the German to the French-British side. One hundred fifty tons of chlorine were released across a front seven thousand yards wide. An impressive cloud—white and then yellow-green—engulfed the landscape, reaching a height of some ten to thirty yards. (This height, caused by specific temperature conditions, was unfortunate in that it thinned the gas at ground level.) The cloud moved ahead at roughly half a yard per second. The defenders—French colonial soldiers from Algeria—had several minutes in which to watch the cloud approaching them. That they remained, transfixed, in their trenches, serves to remind us how deeply ingrained was the instinct that survival depended on the trench. But now this instinct proved false: the cloud reached the trenches, and soon the soldiers began to feel an extreme irritation in the lungs. Quickly thereafter, they were choking, blue in the face. Some fell where they stood, others tried to run back from the cloud—as it kept rolling, slowly, to the west. Following the cloud came the German troops. There was little resistance. Understandably, however, the Germans moved with extreme caution, keeping their distance from the gas. Of course, with such slow, deliberate progress, cutting the wire caused no extra delay.

In this respect, then, gas was a success—but it did not succeed in changing the equation of the war. It is sometimes suggested that a better exploitation of the breach at Ypres could have had far-reaching military consequences, but as a matter of fact, the attack at Ypres ultimately failed. Having made their breach, gaining a couple of miles in slow, methodical advance, the Germans tried to attack again during the next few days, but the line was now filled in by British and Canadian troops, who rapidly re-created a line of defense. By April 24, the German advance halted without any meaningful gain.[89] One may ask, then, why the Germans did not simply go on, in the spring of 1915, releasing gas day by day, attack by attack; but what if the wind blew to the east? Such uncertainties disrupted the best-laid plans. Consider, for instance, Loos—today, an hour's drive from Ypres—where, on September 15, the British tried to retaliate with a chlorine attack of their own. Along many parts of the front, the wind simply stalled as the cloud engulfed the no-man's-land. Now it was barbed wire below and chlorine gas above.[90]

Gas was often used in the war, and means of discharge—as well as of protection—were further developed. On the western front, gas accounted overall for some 500,000 wounded and about 72,000 dead—an insignificant fraction of the total. Gas failed, ultimately, for two reasons. First, as seen at Ypres, it could not take flexibility away from field fortification. Thrown back, an army could still quickly reestablish position. Second, gas failed because—in spite of its ultramodern appearance—it was a premodern tool for controlling space. It depended completely on the natural environment and was disrupted by the local detail of folds in the ground or changes in the air. What was required instead was a tool that could nearly ignore the natural terrain—that could extend control in an artificially defined way, across an artificially defined space. Something rather like barbed wire—only that it had to be offensive rather than defensive. This would be the second child of barbed wire: a tool used not so much to deny the violence behind the obstacle as to deny the obstacle itself.

We recall Swinton, the author of *The Defense of Duffer's Drift*. In July 1914—just in time—he received a letter from a Boer War friend, the mining engineer Hugh F. Mariott. This Mariott was interested in finding vehicles for mining ventures in remote regions. Here is Swinton's memory of the letter: "After having considered light railways, the mono-rail, aerial tramways, etc., he had in the course of his search found in Antwerp an agricultural machine of American manufacture called the Holt Caterpillar Tractor, which had surprising powers of crossing country. He thought that the army might be interested in this machine for the purposes of transport. . . . It could traverse narrow trenches or holes in the ground and was so powerful that it could drag a five-furrow plough, set at the maximum depth, through marshy soil."[91] Already by October, Swinton realized that this tractor could transform trench warfare. Whether in fact he was the mind behind the new invention—as he himself claimed—is of course a difficult question to answer, with so many Britons arguing, after the fact, to have been the first to conceive of the idea.[92] But we should take a look at the tractor: it will loom large in the following chapter, and it is another important reminder about the relationship between war and agriculture.

Whether tilling, sowing, or harvesting, farmers essentially

move across a field, carrying weight. Thus farming is basically a matter of *traction.* In the ancient Mediterranean, this traction exploited the muscle power of oxen, and in medieval Europe it exploited the muscle power of horses. These are powerful and enduring animals, and when shoed, a horse can cross even very difficult terrain. However, in America of the late nineteenth century, this was no longer satisfactory. The tools carried across the field—such as the plow—became more and more powerful and productive. You get more of your field if you use an iron plow instead of a wooden one, still more if you use steel. Special machines, such as the combine, that enhance productivity even further, became heavier still. Horses struggled to carry this new weight, and horse power was no longer the support for agricultural productivity that it had been in the Middle Ages. It became, instead, a limiting factor. This limiting factor could be removed, finally, with the internal combustion engine—mainly a development of the 1890s. On the well-prepared roads of the city, wheeled vehicles were a natural replacement for the horse; hence the automobile. In the countryside, one needed a fuller equivalent of the horse—something that could go wherever a horse's hooves went.[93] Benjamin Holt, from Stockton, California, found the solution: instead of wheels, use a revolving base. He called it the Caterpillar tractor and tested it in November 24, 1904, beginning production soon afterward.[94]

The tractor allowed space to be brought under a more perfect control: heavy tools could reach most places a farmer wanted to reach, so that fully intensified agriculture could become nearly universal. Once again we see that the problem of control over space is first solved as an *agricultural* task: agriculture is the place where space poses the most direct economic incentive. But already early on, the applications of the tractor went beyond agriculture itself. The problem of heavy traction across rough terrain would be raised in any attempt to control space, not least by the military. In 1916, for instance, Pancho Villa, a Mexican rebel, was troubling the American border. The American army had to operate in this difficult borderland, and tractors proved to be a useful addition to traditional draft animals.

The tractor's real breakthrough came with World War I. Armies demanded enormous amounts of traction, soon reaching the limits of power available from draft animals alone. This was beneficial to the tractor industry in two ways: first, in a direct way, as tractors were ordered for use by the Allies on the western front: almost 10,000 during the war (in comparison, in 1915 there were only 2,000 tractors in agricultural use).[95] Second, and indirectly, the huge military demand for draft animals limited their supply for agricultural application, and with America's eventual entry into the war, human labor itself became scarce. Farmers—even American ones—usually change their practices only in times of radical transformation. World War I was such a radical event: by greatly raising the price of labor (human and animal), it created the incentive for a massive accumulation of tractors, a form of capital that could replace labor. Some 150,000 tractors were produced during the war years.[96] The intensification of American agriculture reached an important threshold as iron and machinery finally replaced the productive role of animal bodies. Here came the tractors, removing the Kansan soil. The American plains—their animals kept behind barbed wire and their land plowed by tractors—would soon rise to the challenge of feeding a world exhausted by war.

The tractor was an impressive invention. But how to apply it to the military problem at hand—offense on the western front? Writing in December 1915, Churchill (whose powers of persuasion did much to make this new application a reality) saw the problem in clear terms: "If artillery is used to cut wire the direction and imminence of the attack is proclaimed days beforehand. But by this method [i.e., the military application of tractors] the assault follows the wire cutting almost immediately i.e. before any reinforcements can be brought up by the enemy."[97] The specific method Churchill had in mind at this stage had a markedly agricultural complexion: a fleet of caterpillar machines working *parallel* to the enemy's trenches, carrying wire-cutting implements—a sort of wire-harvesting team plowing the fields of the no-man's-land. This, of course, was actually redundant, as the tractors effectively crushed the entanglements without any wire-cutting tools (barbed wire was invented to stop cows, not heavy steel vehicles). Heavily armored as well, military tractors could resist machine guns while crushing barbed wire, neatly solving the problem of the front. In February 1916, the go-ahead was given for producing the military tractor, now assigned the code-name "tank."

So how was the tank invented? What we must realize is that when Swinton and other British officers began to discuss using the tractor as an offensive tool, they were considering a well-known agricultural tool. Indeed, even so, there was much skepticism concerning the wisdom of venturing into such radical experiments. By the time they came to fruition—so people reasoned in 1915—the war was likely to be over. It is clear that without the tractor available and functioning, the tank would never have been given any serious thought at all. Historians sometimes refer to H. G. Wells's 1903 story "The Land Ironclads" as an inspiration for the invention of the tank; but had it not been for the tractor, the British army would have been as likely to pursue the development of tanks as it would have been to pursue that of Wells's time machine. Just like barbed wire itself, the agricultural application of the tractor had to precede its military one.

American agriculture had developed two distinct ways of making iron control space: the brute violence of barbed wire, and the heavy but sturdy mobility of the tractor. The military application of the first necessitated the military application of the second. Barbed wire made the horse obsolete; agricultural technology had already come up with its replacement. Thus cavalry was remade, in the years 1916 to 1918, now based on iron instead of flesh.

Did tanks negate barbed wire? They did not, at two separate levels. First, at the strictly military level, World War I was not won by tanks. A tractor is a complex thing, and applying it for military purposes was not as simple as applying barbed wire. Early tanks were mechanically delicate and ditched in great numbers, often remaining stuck—like the chlorine cloud at Loos—in the no-man's-land. In the battle of Arras (April 1917), for instance, the

French sent a fleet of 128 tanks—of which *none* reached the German front line. While not an easy thing to destroy, a tank could be disabled by guns—and a tank did cost much more than an artillery shell and was much more difficult to replace. It was a mobile piece of permanent fortification, with all the entailed costs. Finally, the tactics of tanks in action had to be developed, and World War I was largely a period of experimentation.

Still, one of the important breakthroughs in the war occurred on August 8, 1918, when six hundred tanks broke through the German lines at Amiens. The Allies began to move forward, and the German army did retreat considerably. The newer tactics modeled on those of the Russian general Brusilov helped, as did the appearance of American troops in large numbers. Even so, at the strict technical level, the advance could perhaps still be stopped by the end of October, and the German surrender did not signify the overruling of new field fortification. Like Russia in the Russo-Japanese War, Germany was defeated through its naval and internal failures no less than its military ones. Its U-boat campaign—sending submarines to choke off supplies to Great Britain—did not starve England, while the British blockade did starve Germany; and there was an overall failure of nerve in the German army in October 1918. We will never know what would have happened had Germany found in itself the willpower to go on fighting. Many Germans were certain the war could have been prolonged, and they may have been right. The peculiar thing is that they actually *regretted* its end. This frustration—to repulse the enemy for four years and then to surrender—was the principal motive animating Hitler and his close followers. Soon they were seeking new battles, this time aiming to break through the enemy lines with unprecedented mobility. With heavy use of tanks (as well as of airplanes), this was, in a sense, achieved in World War II, and at this technical level, the total control of barbed wire was ultimately breached.

But here I will address the more fundamental question, of the tank as an agent in the more general conflict waged between flesh and iron. In this battle, barbed wire won a victory for iron that the tank merely confirmed. Tanks became necessary—to accommodate human motion inside the new environment defined by barbed wire and machine gun. They did not subvert the new environment but proved its domination. Just as animals had to be fenced in to survive in the new environment of barbed wire agriculture, so humans had effectively to be *caged* in, to survive in the new environment of barbed wire warfare. What the western front settled for good was the complete control that violence gained over the motion of unprotected flesh.

So here are two of the things the western front with its barbed wire had achieved. It achieved the domination of flesh by violence, and it achieved Hitler. The two were not unrelated, and in the following chapter, I will discuss their combination. But even before that, we must pay attention to another major conflict of the war, with its own important consequences.

The eastern front—where Russia fought against Germany and Austria-Hungary—encompassed much more land, much less intensively developed than that of the western front. Thus it allowed more mobility. Advances, in some spectacular cases, measured even in the hundreds of miles. But this did not matter, since the spaces themselves (particularly after the Russians were thrown back, far away from Berlin) had little strategic value. It made little difference whether an army had rebuilt its defensive line two miles to the rear, or two hundred miles, if those two hundred miles encompassed impoverished Galician villages or Belarusian marshlands. Thus the war was essentially similar, and where the lines stood—and they usually stood for many months before being breached—they were not much different from those on the western front. Soldiers died as massively as they did in the West, pointlessly rushing against barbed wire; guns and shells were produced in a similar spiral of increased production.

The crisis of ammunition production, however—in one way or another felt everywhere during the war—hit Russia especially hard. This had two aspects, political and economic. Politically, the regime was especially badly placed to weather the crisis. For decades, the members of the Russian elite had been disillusioned with a tsardom that they felt to be backward and oppressive. The tsars' only remaining source of legitimacy was as the focus of patriotic allegiance to imperial Russia. With the ammunition crisis came a sense that Russia had been betrayed by its own backwardness and that the imperial cause was mishandled—perhaps even treasonably—by the monarchy. (The idea of treason did not seem at the time so far-fetched; like all European royal families, the Russian, too, had more foreign than local ancestry. This intermarriage was supposed to ensure peace, but in a real crisis, it rather served to undercut monarchy itself.) The Russian elite believed that it could raise ammunition better than the monarchy could, and in the summer of 1915, the elite began to organize on its own. Local organizations of industrialists and noblemen—patriotic and liberal in their politics—became the real focus of economic and political life. Through the crisis of the war, this Russian elite now wielded real power; through the perceived failure of the dynasty, it was now confident that it alone was deserving of it.[98] There would thus be no support for the monarchy when the final crisis of the regime came; to the contrary, there was another group ready to assume power.

This final crisis was the economic outcome of the Russian crisis of ammunition. It resulted, paradoxically, from the success of civil society in restructuring the economy. The Russian ammunition crisis was, in fact, solved—in the narrow sense of shell production—by a huge expansion of production in the cities. This could happen because Russia already had a significant industrial base, as well as an effective rail network leading to the front—the one that had frightened all Europe into mobilization and ultimately led to the war. Like the railroad system itself, this industrial base was no more than a thin layer thrown over a premodern economy. It was built to support modern warfare, not modern economy: the railways led to the front, not to the countryside. Agriculture was based on an inward-looking village based, still, on the open-field system. (The government did try, in the decade before the war, to foster a homestead system with more intensive farming, one that was more closely integrated with the cities—but such efforts came to little.)[99] Thus the immense growth in urban production in the war years could not be based on an equivalent growth in agricultural production. Instead the worlds of the city and of the village diverged further. With industrial expansion came inflation and a constant rise in urban prices and wages. The peasants did not have the economic organization to benefit from growing demand and instead felt that they had little reason to exchange valuable grain for a ruble that kept diminishing in value. Their life was based primarily on subsistence farming, trade with the city being a relatively marginal activity. With the strain of broad structural changes, their natural reaction was to retreat even farther away from the city.[100] This was the fundamental reason for the Russian failure: the integration of village and city was so precarious that a crisis severed it altogether. American farmers reacted to the war by buying tractors; Russian farmers reacted to it by feeding grain to their horses. By 1916 there was less bread in the cities, and by 1917 there was hunger (if not quite famine). In February, when the first demonstrations came, it was soon realized that there was no one there to support the tsar. In a few days, Russia was a democracy led by its elite. It became a glorious land of unbridled freedom. Then, in the course of a few months, the elite discredited itself by its failure to deal with the impossible; hyperinflation, hunger, and the war, together with the revolution itself, brought total chaos. Very few supported the Bolsheviks in October 1917, but even fewer had any willpower left to resist them. Now had begun the process of bringing Russia back in order: but it was to be a new kind of order, much more modern than the tsar's. The Bolsheviks were to apply a new method of control based on centralized violence on a mass scale.

Thus—even with the horrors of World War I—we have not yet quite reached the culmination of the history of barbed wire. With the Bolsheviks bringing Russia under control and Hitler seeking his revenge, this culmination was yet to come. But before we can begin to discuss it, we must retrace our steps: we should first study the origins of the concentration camp. This brings us back to the turn of the nineteenth century.

3 CONTAINMENT

Barbed Wire in the Concentration Camps

Would barbed wire be useful for the problem of controlling civilians? At first sight, it might appear to be incongruously violent. Its very function was based on inflicting harm. This was quite appropriate for animals, with which humans always did communicate through the language of pain. But with humans, verbal threats are as effective, and so the control through actual violence can always be removed from sight. There is no need to put barbed wire in the way of civilians: put a sign saying No Trespassing, and ninety-nine out of a hundred will stop. But then again, sometimes they do not stop, and violence must be administered. The problem is exacerbated when fundamental loyalty is in question—when people do not agree with the No Trespassing signs. Suppose you conquer a foreign people, or suppose some of your subjects are citizens of a nation with which you are at war: how would you make them respect your rules? Violence must be used, then, on a large scale. An instrument for the deployment of violence on a massive scale would be very useful for this purpose, and this is how barbed wire enters political history—as a continuation of the history of war.

Note that this control over space displays an interesting duality—a microcosm and a macrocosm, so to speak. We find small spaces, within which humans are held, their motion brought under relentless control; and then these small spaces radiate a much larger space of more subtle control over the entire subjugated population. In other words, we have prisons, and we have an entire people, and it is the presence of prisons that pacifies the people. Prisons serve two purposes. First, they physically break up contacts and motions: leaders are taken away, families broken apart. In this way, the subjugated people are atomized and reduced to less than the sum of their parts. Second, prisons have an important moral role. Like many other animals, humans feel pleasure in motion itself and suffer when it is prevented. To be confined in a small space where motion is limited to a minimum is a punishment that humans dread almost as much as death itself. You can use this dread—so that the *threat* of motion prevented will suffice to control human motion outside prison itself. The microcosm radiates into the macrocosm.

Thus the colonization of space gives rise to small enclaves within it—settlements of a few squares miles, at most, within which human motion is heavily curtailed. While small in physical extension, these settlements have great historical significance: they are the key to the control over the entire space surrounding them. During the twentieth century, an important class of these settlements came to be surrounded by barbed wire. It is probably for these barbed wire settlements that the twentieth century will be remembered.

As in military history itself, so in the control of peoples: the introduction of barbed wire was gradual and serendipitous. The tool was available; the situations arose, and settlements of imprisonment were set up; barbed wire was used; and suddenly a new practice was enshrined. The parallel with military history is even closer. As in military history, barbed wire made its entry into political history in the Boer War, when the concentration camp was invented; the barbed wire settlement was then made routine in World War I. Then, however—in a development original to political history—barbed wire went on to evolve beyond World War I itself.

This new tool—the barbed wire settlement—was made routine in World War I. At that time, it merely solved problems that were largely predictable and that kept recurring in each conflict: enemy civilians, prisoners of war. It did not yet originate its own policy but served in the policies of the past. Then something new happened: certain political structures were built *around* this new tool, taking advantage of the new opportunities opened up by the concentration camp. This gave rise to the Soviet and Nazi experience, where the history of barbed wire reached its culmination.

The main feature of the political use of barbed wire was its asymmetry: on the one side an all-powerful government, on the other side a defeated, unarmed mass of people. This was a new stage in human history, but not so much in the history of barbed wire. In a sense, barbed wire reverted to its original function of controlling weak living beings, depriving them of their last powers so that total control could be gained. Unarmed humans, subdued and controlled by barbed wire, differ greatly from soldiers. They do not issue violence but are the passive recipients of violence. They are reduced to flesh and in a sense become a mere biological receptacle for pain and disease. To a certain extent, then, the concentration camp system was a recapitulation of the animal industry, now as *human* industry. It neatly sums up this history, bringing the ecology of flesh and iron in the age of barbed wire to its culmination.

In this chapter's first section, "The Control of Nations," we will see how, around the end of the nineteenth century, the concentration of entire enemy populations became an established practice, and how barbed wire came to be an effective tool in this practice. The second section, "Enemy People," considers the standardization of this practice, especially during World War I, with its many prisoner-of-war camps and internments of aliens. The third section, "Tractors to Ukraine," follows the first major application of this tool (by now standardized) as the foundation of policy: the Soviet Gulag. This is especially interesting, as, arguably, the main force driving this new application was the desire of the Soviet Union to gain control over its rural countryside. In this case, then, the questions of agricultural history are closely tied with those of political history.

The fourth section, "Trains to Auschwitz," finally reaches the most horrific use of barbed wire, in the Nazi death camp system, where the comparison between human brutality toward humans and human brutality toward animals is most obvious.

1. THE CONTROL OF NATIONS

Three colonial conflicts marked the turn of the nineteenth century: the Spanish-American War of 1898, the Boer War of 1899–1902, and the Russo-Japanese War of 1904–1905. We have seen how this nearly uninterrupted sequence of colonial wars, spanning the globe, signaled a realignment of colonial powers: America, Britain, and Japan on the ascent, Spain, the Boers, and Russia on the decline. The powers of modern colonialism beat the powers of old colonialism. So much was understood at the time. No one understood, however, that the most important legacy of this period was not military but political. In two of these wars—the Spanish-American War and the Boer War—history was being made not on the battlefield but away from it. Governments treated civilians with extreme ruthlessness. This was little understood at the time—considered, if at all, as if it were a throwback to a barbarism of bygone ages. In fact, this was not a vestige of the past but the first suggestion of an important future trajectory.

This starts on the island of Cuba, in 1895. Here was the last important stronghold of the Spanish Empire, and the Spanish were used to fighting fierce wars against local rebels. The last such war was a long and confused ten-year conflict, from 1868 to 1878; the island remained restless, the mass of its population angry not only about Spanish colonization but also about the social evils of a plantation economy. The countryside was strongly for revolution, and the authorities had to find ways to control it. The basic geography was helpful: Cuba is a narrow island, usually not much more than fifty miles wide, so that it seems straightforward to divide the land by lines cut across this width. In fact, the 1868–1878 war gave rise to just such a line, the Trocha, running from the city of Morón near the northern coast to Jucaro, on the southern coast. This was essentially a very long ditch. It had a system of blockhouses attached to it, as well as a railroad supplying it to its length. The net result was to divide Cuba into two islands, each easier to control, and in 1878 this system seemed to have been successful enough. (It was, indeed, one of the inspirations for the British blockhouse system in the Boer War.)

But in 1895 the island was in rebellion again, and popular support was such that the Spaniards could no longer contain it. Cuba has tropical vegetation, and while mostly flat, the island does have many hilly lands and, elsewhere, marshlands. Geography, then, was not wholly on the Spanish side. The Cuban guerrillas could appear unexpectedly, inflict casualties on the Spanish soldiers, and then disappear into the hills and marshes. With the support of the peasants, the guerrillas could even bypass the thinly manned Spanish lines. The rebellion started in March, in the East; by July, the rebels crossed the Trocha into the West. (It was like the Great Wall of China: a massive, inflexible fortification that proved useless once it was breached.)[1] By late 1895, Spain had not much more than Havana and a few other provincial capitals under its control. The commander of the Spanish forces in Cuba was sent home, to be replaced by General Weyler. Here was a commander notorious for his cruelty in war, and at this moment of crisis, cruelty seemed to be in order.

The basic problem was that the rebels had full control of the countryside—because they had the support of the people there. It was impossible to make the people pro-Spanish, but it was possible to remove them from the countryside. Thus the logic of the situation seemed to dictate the solution adopted by Weyler: concentrate the rural population into the cities. We can see this as the blockhouse system turned inside out—the topological inversion with which we are by now familiar. Instead of the Spanish soldiers going out to impose order on the countryside by setting up garrisons there, creating points of control across an uncontrolled plane, the countryside was now to be concentrated in the points where the Spanish could easily control it, the plane being made open for Spanish military maneuvers.

The policy, called "reconcentration," was gradually proclaimed across the entire island. The inhabitants were allowed eight days to collect their goods and animals; after that, it would be a crime to remain in the open. (It was essential that they took animals with them, as well: the main purpose was to deny the rebels food.) Special areas around the towns were given over for cultivation of food, and the hinterland was systematically destroyed. Meanwhile the refugees were sheltered in whatever accommodation could be found—old warehouses and abandoned buildings, now overflowing with people. Weyler, literally, had swept the ground from under the feet of the rebels.[2] He now counted on constructing new Trocha lines and beating the rebels against them—just as the British would do five years later in South Africa.

Things did not work out quite like this. Weyler did not calculate correctly for several nonmilitary consequences, biological as well as international. It was not just a matter of Spanish against Cubans: there were other agents involved. There were germs—bringing about dysentery and yellow fever; and then there was the United States.

The basic biological problem should have been predicted, as it was, indeed, a constant of military history. War always creates a disruption in the spatial arrangements of life. Normal lines of communication are broken; others are overwhelmed by immense flows of soldiers and refugees; everyone is on the move. With the disruption of everyday routes comes a disruption of the agricultural cycle: quite simply, many farmers cannot reach their land to till it, and hunger soon follows. At the same time, people assemble in great numbers. What is worse, they congregate with people they have never met before, carrying germs for which they are unprepared. They are probably hungry and weakened already, and so they are easily infected. Soon disease explodes into epidemics. The epidemics take their toll, once again, on the agricultural cycle itself—as the peasants are too weak to work—and so follows that typical human disaster: war in the midst of famine and plague. People, in sum, are not inert items in an inventory that can be moved and heaped together in this or that warehouse. They are biological organisms whose existence depends on a certain mutual arrangement with each other and with their environment. Disrupt this arrangement, and crisis follows. All of this was the normal consequence of war, from the Athenian plague described by Thucydides in the fifth century BC to the influenza pandemic at the end of World War I.

Weyler's method directly amplified this consequence. The towns—sites of concentration—now had half a million civilian inhabitants on top of the old ones, this without mentioning the Spanish troops who, as described at the time, "occupy so many buildings that no suitable lodging is left for excess people. The living quarters of the *reconcentrados* are little more than pigsties."[3] Further, food production was deliberately curtailed to starve out the rebels. All of this had two immediate outcomes detrimental to Weyler's plan. First, the reconcentration order was, in effect, an invitation to infect the army. Since the evacuees were forced to stay near the garrisons, it was a completely foreseeable result that, with the coming epidemics, the soldiers would become sick as well. At any given time, at least 50,000 of the 200,000 soldiers available to Weyler were sick, so that the army was pinned down to defensive duties.[4] Second, the reconcentration created terrible suffering, with pitiful sights of oppressed humanity, beggary, prostitution, and, above all, mass death. Tens of thousands of Cubans, perhaps as many as a hundred thousand, died in a little over a year.[5] Here enters Weyler's second miscalculation: he should have considered the United States.

Many Americans were always interested in Cuba: in fact, the same southerners who fought against Mexico always dreamed of further Caribbean conquests, particularly that of Cuba. At this point, imperialism and humanism went hand in hand. The realities of Cuban misery, reported sensationally (but fundamentally truthfully) by the popular American press, now made the American public as a whole eager to fight against the "Butcher Weyler." In what was to become a twentieth-century pattern, the United States was inching forward to intervening in a foreign humanitarian crisis. The USS *Maine* was sent to "pay a visit" to the port of Havana; on February 15, 1898, the battleship exploded at anchor in the harbor (for causes that will forever remain unknown); soon afterward the Spanish-American War began.[6]

The war was the first in which barbed wire was, if briefly, used for military purposes. It was also short and decisive. It started on April 11, 1898; on August 11, the same year, Spain agreed to the American terms. Spanish imperialism effectively ended, as Cuba, as well as the Philippines (another remnant of the Spanish Empire), were now placed under American control. This new American imperialism was clothed with the promise of future independence, and for long-suffering Cuba this now sufficed. The Philippines, on the other hand, started on its own insurrection, now against the United States, in 1899.

I now have to report an irony that is almost too crude: the U.S. Army, frustrated by the jungles of the Philippines and by the widespread support of local peasants for anti-American guerrillas, adopted by the end of 1900 a policy of concentration. We do not need to go into details, as the practice was explicitly modeled on that of Weyler: as a contemporary American put it, "We executed a 'Weyler' campaign, but did it according to military law."[7] In fact, the practice was not adopted wholesale as in Cuba but was used locally, which perhaps explains the relatively low mortality: about 11,000 Filipinos died in the concentration zones. Most important, the Americans succeeded. The insurrection itself was poorly organized, compared to the Cuban one—and there was no further America to intervene against America itself. By 1902, the Philippines were pacified.[8]

The failure of Spain in Cuba shows that the method of concentration was flawed; its adoption by the United States shows that it was, as it were, inevitable. There really was no other way to gain control over rural population. Indeed, there are clear historical precedents to show that the method is, as it were, "natural." Consider the White Lotus, a rural rebellion in China from 1796 to 1804. First, the Qing government was left without an effective response, allowing the White Lotus rebels to overwhelm large parts of Sichuan and other parts of inland China. Finally the solution was found: build forts across the land and force the peasants inside them, destroy crops in the field, systematically pacifying in this way the entire province—the whole sequence we are familiar with.[9] In all such cases, whether in Cuba, the Philippines, or Sichuan, we see the problem of a central urban authority gaining control over a recalcitrant rural population. The difficulty is that there are so many peasants, so widely scattered. How to extend control across this spatially challenging terrain? The solution we have seen was forced pseudo-urbanization: very rapidly, peasants were ordered to concentrate in large settlements, where they could be better controlled. The main failure of this method was that cities, indeed, are not built in a day. The construction of the structures to support large-scale settlements takes the time and resources that are lacking in wartime situations. Thus the method is really no more than an exercise in the massive killing of peasants.

This is one failure of the method. Another is that it does not ultimately achieve a real topological simplification of governmental control. The perimeters of allowed civilian presence were monitored, under this system, by troops patrolling the entire land. In other words, all such systems approximated the idea of the *curfew*, rather than that of the prison. Their foundation was the threat of violence against civilians found outside a defined area. To make the threat real, soldiers still had to inspect the countryside and punish—usually kill—civilians found there. In other words, violence had to be exerted everywhere and was not confined to a few points of control. This was because the central points did not have any infrastructure of control, or to put it simply, there was nothing to stop people from going out of the cities into countryside—except for the soldiers in the countryside themselves.

To put it simply: a prison is a way of economizing on prison guards. By getting the prisoners inside a single location, fewer people can look after them. A prison does call for a considerable preliminary capital outlay, so that there is no use building a prison for an ad hoc problem such as the control of nations in war. Thus the control of nations was, historically, extremely labor intensive and, in truth, was never fully achieved. But once prisons could be improvised with little capital investment, governments gained a new tool, flexible and effective. The control over entire populations could quickly be achieved. No one realized this at the beginning of the century; this new application of barbed wire, just like the military one, came almost by accident.

In the Boer War, the British were determined to treat civilians humanely. This gave rise to the concentration camp. As noted in the preceding chapter, subduing the Boer guerrillas involved two sets of policies: a civilian policy and a military one. I have discussed the control over space gained in the veld by the system of blockhouses and barbed wire. The British system of military control—through barbed wire lines and prefabricated iron blockhouses—was far superior to the Spanish Trocha in Cuba with its fifty-mile ditch. The British system of control over civilians, too, was superior to Weyler's; this was gradually achieved.

The basic distinction between military and civilian was difficult to make. The Boers fought as a nation, and once the war had reached its guerrilla stage, there were no clear fronts. Once again, part of the problem was that this was a farmers' community, with the consequent spatial spread.

We should consider this community in greater detail. It was a conservative society with clear demarcations of race, ethnicity, and gender. Race and ethnicity defined the Boers on the outside; they used black labor, essentially as slave labor (and the black members of their communities would share in the full horrors of the war when it came), and shunned any non-Boer, white intrusion—which was of course at the root of the war itself. Gender defined the Boers on the inside, specifically in terms of motion. Fundamentally, this was a society where men moved about a lot. As a rule—when not too young or too old—they rode on horseback. Women stayed homebound. These gender roles were a precondition for the guerrilla war. The men were used to living in small masculine bands away from home, counting on their homes as stable bases for their pastoral life. Come the guerrilla war, Boer society became bifurcated. On the one hand were fighting men with their horses; on the other hand were farm-bound women, together with children and the old, the black servants, and cows and sheep.

The basic problem for the British was that while they had to supply themselves through long and vulnerable lines (in this case, the railroad), the Boer commandos could resupply themselves simply by visiting the farms. The farms were clearly a military asset to the Boers. Nor were the women really any better than the men, as a British publication of the time complained: "Many of the women had been guilty of acts of treachery; they constantly shot at isolated patrols, trusting to the immunity which their sex gave them in the eyes of even the worst of our men, and at all times they assisted the Boer forces with food and ammunition."[10] Naturally, then, during the summer of 1900, the British policy was reached: to destroy Boer farms when they were suspected of aiding Boer commandos.[11] This quickly amounted to a great part of the Boer settlement (by the end of the war, nearly all Boer farms were destroyed—their roofs, incidentally, often used to roof British blockhouses).[12]

By spring 1901, the piecemeal destruction of individual farms had reached the limits of its usefulness. Punitive destruction made the British even more intensely unpopular while failing to prevent the remaining farms from supporting the guerrillas. Besides, the mass dislocation of Boer civilian life began to create a crisis.

The British perception of the situation was as follows: on the one hand, they were forced, quite against their better instincts, to resort to farm burning; on the other hand, this policy resulted in a massive problem of dislocated Boers. The setting up of refugee camps was dictated by the crisis itself. Thus arose the fiction—which the British government never fully gave up—that the British were engaged in some sort of humanitarian crisis management, as if they were simply trying to solve a refugee problem. Their policy was seen as the expression of a kind—though stern—concern for civilians in wartime. Thus, unlike the Cuban and Philippine evacuation (where civilians had to fend for themselves), the British had gradually created an entire apparatus to provide the Boers with accommodation, medical care, education, protection, and, most important, food. It all came about through British improvisation in the face of crisis. A camp was founded near Mafeking as early as July 1900; others were set up later in the summer; and by March 1901, the entirety of the civilian Boer population was relocated to such camps.[13] But instead of the Cuban and Philippine concentration zones, the British system relied on small temporary settlements, originally called "refugee camps" or, later on, "concentration camps."[14] Thus the concentration camp was invented.

The numbers of camps and inmates were constantly shifting, but altogether there were about fifty camps for Boers (their black servants were kept apart, in their own camps). The total number of inmates was about 100,000,[15] and an individual camp had a few thousand inmates. Most of these inmates, as we have seen, were women and children. Consider the Johannesburg camp—probably an extreme case: it had 382 men (in all likelihood, old), 967 women, and 3,740 children.[16] In other words, the population of the camps was easy to control: mostly children—and then their mothers, preoccupied by the need to care for those children.

These mothers had soon much to worry, and grieve, about. The entire Cuban scenario was replayed: forced congregation in crowded, unprepared spaces, coupled with the shocks of dislocation, and then disease and a catastrophic rate of mortality. Perhaps as many as thirty thousand died in camps during the war, that is, almost one-third of the inmates.[17] (The very high number is perhaps explained by the fact that most inmates were young children.) This led to an outcry. Lloyd George—then a young Welsh MP—now came into national prominence by his outspoken views against the Boer War, declaring in Parliament that "in this war we have gradually followed the policy of Spain in Cuba."[18] But in this he was not quite right. In some ways, the British concentration camps were more modern than their immediate antecedents. The rail network in South Africa was extensive (relative to those in Cuba or the Philippines), so that the camps were sited according to this network. The inmates were counted and provided with food according to rations. The camps had an architecture of sorts: essentially, a vertical and horizontal grid arrangement of tents, each housing a large family, with a few special tents (sometimes more permanent structures) for central functions such as baths, latrines, kitchens, hospitals, et cetera.[19] In short, the modern tools of planning and rail transportation provided the camps with the appearance of something like government custody rather than that of government punishment. This was not Cuba.

Violence took place on the veld: British soldiers would reach a farm, order the women and old men found there to collect their children, and whatever belongings they could carry, and then send them away on a wagon. Carried on the wagon, the Boer family would see, from a distance, their house dismantled and burned. All of this was the standard violence of the concentration method, familiar from Cuba or the Philippines—enacted on the field itself. But once people reached the camps, little violence was required. The problem of control was simple: since the inmates were so weak, and since they were totally dependent on the authorities for all provisions, they had little opportunity to form resistance. It was thus the practice, at first, to leave camps unfenced, further sustaining the fiction that these were refugees enjoying British protection. A local police was created, manned by volunteers from among the few men; these were instructed to arrest individuals trying to enter the camp or to leave it without authorization.[20] In short, space was defined symbolically and was supported by the enormous asymmetry of power between the British army and the Boer civilian population. The only thing that went obviously wrong with the camps was that people kept dying there. We will soon see how the British tried to account for that embarrassment, but for the immediate purposes of the history of barbed wire, it is crucial to note how important it was for the British to maintain the fiction of the camps as benevolent custody, with the initial lack of fencing.

This fiction, however, was hard to maintain during wartime.

Let us follow Kendal Franks, a British official inspecting the camps. In his visit to the camp of Standerton in the Transvaal, for instance, he tells us that Boers raided the camp on August 11, 1901, carrying away with them 157 cattle. (As was done in Cuba, farmers were concentrated with their animals, so as to deny them from the guerrillas.)[21] Reacting energetically to the challenge, the camp superintendent, Frank Winfield, ordered the inmates to erect a barbed wire fence surrounding the camp. A solid structure, comprising two rows of fences, sandwiching entanglements, it was in place by August 29. We are not given the physical size of the camp, but it contained 550 tents for accommodation, with 3,329 inmates, so we see here a rather large structure.[22] I follow this in detail, since we begin to see here a new phenomenon: a human settlement whose boundaries are defined by barbed wire. In this case, the barbed wire appears almost as an afterthought and represents the old need to prevent cattle from motion, as well as continuing its more recent use to repulse mounted Boers on the veld. But notice the revolutionary significance of this construction: while raised to prevent motion of Boer men from outside the camp to its inside, the fence immediately served also to prevent the motion of Boer women from inside the camp to its outside. They were no longer under curfew: they were now imprisoned.

Barbed wire fences were built everywhere throughout 1901, surrounding most camps. A new geography of barbed wire came about. As we saw in the previous chapter, the land as a whole was crisscrossed by the blockhouse lines. We now see that within the cells created by these lines, smaller cells were added—settlements defined by barbed wire fences. In both geographic scales—the macrocosm and the microcosm—the Boers were now surrounded and controlled by barbed wire.

Let us consider the microcosm. We may follow Emily Hobhouse—an English woman who threw herself into the cause of the camp inmates—writing back from the camp of Kimberly: "The tents, too close together, and the whole enclosed in an 8-foot high barbed wire fencing, which is supposed to be impregnable, and cost 500 Pounds. Sentries at the gate and walking inside. . . . Overcrowded tents, measles and whooping-cough rife; camp dirty and smelling; an army doctor, who naturally knows little of children's ailments."[23] The misery is obvious: but notice that Hobhouse's estimate of the price of fencing was clearly too high. We have already seen that a mile of barbed wire on the blockhouse line cost a mere fifty pounds. True, it appears that the barbed wire fencing described by Hobhouse was more intensively deployed than the military one, as its goal was not merely to slow motion but to prevent it completely. Still—especially since the space enclosed was so small—Hobhouse's estimate must have been exaggerated. Probably her wish was to impress upon the British public that the concentration camps were wasteful.

But that was the whole point: the concentration camps, and barbed wire in particular, were in fact very cheap to build. For this reason, above all, they were built everywhere. We may return to follow Kendal Franks, now visiting the camp Volksrust: he mentions that the camp (which has more than five thousand inmates) is entirely surrounded by double barbed wire fence, which he warmly recommends: this makes a local police *superfluous* (so the fence, pace Hobhouse, is actually economical).[24] It is clear that Kendal Franks has by now become something of a barbed wire fencing enthusiast, and on September 7 he notes, with great dissatisfaction, its *absence* from Heidelberg. The danger—he explains—is not merely military in nature; more important, the inmates tend to use their excursions out of the camp to "buy quack remedies which interfere very much with the efforts of the medical officers."[25]

Barbed wire—as a medical implement! Here we begin to see the British response to the mortality crisis, which was essentially to blame it on the Boers. Emily Hobhouse's reports created a tremendous political problem, at home and abroad; as a countermeasure, the British government had now sent a Committee of Ladies to inspect the camps and to offer constructive suggestions. (It is fascinating to see how the gender division went right through the Boer War, setting apart a masculine, military confrontation on the veld, and a feminine, civilian crisis in the camps.

Thus, in order to trump Hobhouse's sensitivity to Boer female pain, the British government had to draw on its own pool of feminine sensitivity.) The Committee of Ladies proved to combine the right balance of sensitivity and realism. Producing its report in February 1902—by which time it hardly mattered, anyway—the committee thoroughly supported the concentration camp system. One of the strongest recommendations of the report was to make sure all camps were fenced (or, as they delicately referred to this, "defined"): "The presence of . . . infectious diseases in either town or camp often makes a strict quarantine absolutely necessary. It is obvious also that a defined area is desirable from the point of view of cleanliness. It is much easier to ensure attention to sanitary regulations if the camp area is properly defined."[26]

To understand all this, one must bear in mind the extraordinary British view that traditional medicine and backward sanitary practices were at the root of Boer death rates. "In estimating the causes of bad health in the camps it is necessary to put on record that every superintendent has to wage war against the insanitary habits of the people. However numerous, suitable, and well-kept may be the latrines provided, the fouling of the ground . . . goes on to an extent which would probably not be credited except by those who have seen it. Constant vigilance, kept up night and day, is necessary to keep this pernicious habit within bounds." Hence the Boers are sick; even then, proper care must be forced on them: "Boers, not unlike the more ignorant of the English poor, strongly object to hospital treatment. . . . [They have] extraordinary notions regarding the treatment of disease. . . . [A description of quack medicines follows.] The dung of cows mixed with sulphur had been literally [liberally?] administered by mothers to their children. . . . A large number of cases in which the dung of cows, goats and pigs was being used . . . sometimes it is made into a poultice, and sometimes a horrid drink is made of it. Dogs' blood is in great request."[27] There is something truly upsetting about this haughty manner of the British ladies, describing what —we sense through their description—must have been a scene of terrible chaos and anguish. But we should understand the situation from their perspective—through which, indeed, it all made sense. The Boers really did not have British education or habits. It was typical that the ladies referred to this particular problem under the heading "Questions of Health and Morals": health was an ethical issue, representing the moral backwardness of the Boers. British superior science and civic practice now had to be imposed on the Boers, for their own good. The net result of the Committee of Ladies' report was to come up with a new justification for the concentration camp. Now the practice of the quarantine could be invoked as a new argument justifying the barbed wire settlements—even though the health crisis was, in truth, the *product* of concentration.

All the while, however, the original justification for the camps, as voluntary refugee camps, was never quite discarded, with an obvious resulting tension between the two kinds of justification. At the same time as the ladies issued their recommendations, in February 1902, some British camp administrators felt that the drive to fence camps was counterproductive and asked for exemptions from such fences: "Without a fence the people unquestionably feel more free and do not look upon themselves as prisoners. . . . [W]e have not had a single desertion. . . . [T]he health is excellent and the people are contented."[28] (This, incidentally, shows that barbed wire fencing had by that time become a routine practice.) The war ended soon after, however, and the question became moot. Not that it was really important to decide quite what the concentration camps were—refugee camps or quarantines. The important thing was to obfuscate their real function, which was, quite simply, control over an entire nation.

But we should not be carried away in criticizing British hypocrisy. It is probably fair to say that British plans were, up to a point, well meant. At any rate, there was no hidden plan to get thirty thousand women and children dead. The British were driven to the concentration camp solution by the logic of fighting a guerrilla war. Even the fiction of Boer consent was not a mere propaganda tool: it was necessary for the British themselves, so that they could feel they were in the right while pursuing a war whose methods they would themselves criticize, when followed by other nations.

The point must be stressed. When we note the surprising fact that the concentration camp was invented by Britain, in 1900, this is an indictment not of Britain but of 1900. The concentration camp was called forth by the times themselves. War was total, so that the enemy civilian population had to be dealt with. The planning and the transportation of a modern government made sure that this would result not in a directionless flow of refugees but in prepared settlements next to railroads. Then, with barbed wire being so cheap and easy to deploy, the construction of a barbed wire perimeter came as a natural conclusion. To enclose civilians inside barbed wire: what else could be done? As in the military sphere, so in the political: the very availability of cheap barbed wire led, almost without any further deliberation, to its gradual application.

Nor, finally, should we simply ignore British hypocrisy. The hypocrisy itself seems to have a historical significance. Was there ever a concentration camp without a hypocritical lie to justify it? Hypocrisy seems to be of the essence of the tool. The main function of a concentration camp is to control people by separating them from one another and by terrifying them—everything calculated to prevent people from organizing against the conquering power. The author of the concentration camp obfuscates and dissembles, so that the asymmetry of power is multiplied by the asymmetry of knowledge. In this way, the victims do not know quite what they are up against (animals, too, are so powerless, in part, because they do not understand what is being done to them).

The hypocrisy itself was a harbinger of things to come. But it was primarily at the basic material level that the British concentration camps were a watershed of history. An entire nation was controlled inside makeshift prisonlike structures, with physically defined obstacles—barbed wire fences—at their perimeter. This barbed wire fence localized control in a clearly marked "inside." The British had moved beyond Weyler's reign of terror, spread across the whole island of Cuba. The topology, finally, was inverted. In 1899 the British looked at the Boers from the insides of military camps, looking outside at a veld that was held by the Boers; now, in 1902, the British looked at the Boers from the outside to the inside: from the blockhouse lines to inside the cells in which the Boer commandos were hunted; from the perimeter of concentration camps to inside the camps themselves. Everywhere they would look through barbed wire—the tool that made this topological inversion possible.

The Boer War was an experiment: it groped for new applications of barbed wire, in the military as well as in the political sphere. To move from experiment to established practice—to make the barbed wire settlement a routine phenomenon—barbed wire had first to be replicated many times over. At the beginning of the twentieth century, the barbed wire settlement was still no more than a possibility, suggested by the Boer War. For this settlement to become standard, there would have to be a major crisis, calling for the mass-scale control over populations. Then came World War I.

2. ENEMY PEOPLE

The concentration of populations in South Africa—as in the Cuban and Philippine cases—came about as a result of war and was justified in terms of martial law.[29] War, after all, is when the violent control of humans is legitimate. To quote again the Committee of Ladies, "Under martial law the ordinary civilian is required to provide himself with a pass before he can go freely about the town in which he may have lived all his life. . . . Why should unrestricted right to come and go as they please be extended to the inmates of the concentration camps . . . ?"[30] Why indeed? The ladies have identified the essence of it. If you are in the business of controlling your enemies, then there should be no halfway control. Have their motions *restricted*.

We have seen how this problem applies to the civilian population. Whoever is against you, armed or not, is dangerous: hence the need to control enemy populations, seen in the preceding section. The same problem arises with the enemy troops themselves, as soon as they throw down their guns. You have succeeded and rendered your enemy harmless—and then what? No longer armed, he is still your enemy. In fact, the problem of prisoners of war is even more difficult than that of enemy civilians. The captured soldiers are young and organized men, and they are trained to cooperative action. Thus careful control must be established immediately. To make things even worse, you now have to establish this control while surrounded by the confusion of war. Prisoners of war are a permanent source of military crisis. The effective solution to this problem—obtained during World War I—is a tribute to the success of barbed wire.

There are many historical examples of the crisis posed by prisoners of war. Take a notable case from the American Civil War, for instance—a little before the invention of barbed wire and therefore a useful comparison. As defeat loomed, the South needed hastily to evacuate its Northern prisoners of war. Many were moved from their prisons in Richmond, Virginia, to a new location near the village of Andersonville, Georgia (chosen, of course, for its proximity to the railroad). The architecture of this prisoner-of-war camp is instructive. This being the Atlantic seaboard, wood was taken as the basic material (it would have been used for penning any other animals). A flat area was chosen and deforested; then a rectangle was traced by a deep ditch surrounded by a high stockade. (This is clearly an extension of the typical tactical obstacle of the time, ditch and stockade.) As a further precaution, a "dead line" was finally built, with a lower stockade, fifteen feet inside the main one: anyone reaching beyond the dead line, moving toward the main line of the stockade, would immediately be shot at by the sentries—themselves positioned on embankments along the stockade.[31] The overall size of the rectangle was about 1,500 feet by 700 feet, where, incredibly, as many as 41,000 prisoners lived.

The trouble with Andersonville was that it lacked any resources. Even timber was hard to come by in late 1864, and labor was in short supply. (Of course, the camp was built by slaves, but even they were now an expensive resource.) Hence the very small size allotted to the camp. But even worse, aside from the pen itself, nothing could be prepared. The prisoners were crammed inside a small rectangle, supplied with tents; the construction of barracks was planned but never went beyond a few buildings. The situation of humans left to the elements in such conditions can by now be easily imagined, and of the 41,000 inmates of Andersonville, 13,000 died during its period of operation—a little over half a year.[32] Essentially, we see that to construct a prisoner-of-war camp in the field was rather like constructing field fortifications and was just as expensive and labor intensive. It just failed, with the new flood of prisoners.

In fact Andersonville was recognized as a unique atrocity, the result of unique military pressures. There were very few installations of its kind in history. Of course, one can find a few other cases of prisoner-of-war camps based on the stockade principle—for instance, Camp Ford in Texas, set up in 1863. (This had especially built wooden huts, located inside a square wood stockade.) But the more usual practice was different, based not on the equivalent of field fortification but on the equivalent of *permanent* fortification.[33] This may be represented by the original prisons at Richmond—whence the inmates of Andersonville were taken—tobacco warehouses and a small island in the river.[34] The standard practice during this period, then, was to use whatever available structures there were, artificial or natural.

To build new structures was expensive; the temporary nature of the prisoner-of-war problem discouraged the construction of a specially designated camp; finally, up to the American Civil War itself, the numbers of prisoners of war did not, traditionally, justify large-scale building. Even the Napoleonic Wars were manageable: Britain, for instance, handled most of its French captives in a single prison at Dartmoor, which had the capacity to contain seven thousand inmates.[35] The point is quite simple: before the invention of the railroad, it was impossible to organize truly large numbers of people. This is why the American Civil War signaled a new era. With its millions of soldiers, it had new levels of human concentration on the battlefield; and this necessarily led to new levels of concentration in the prisoner-of-war camps. This war had nearly *half a million* prisoners of war on each side. A little later, in 1870, the spectacular French defeat in the Franco-Prussian War yielded the extraordinary number of 724,000 French prisoners. Their accommodation was still based on available structures, primarily military barracks (as it were, the German soldiers on French soil vacated their lodgings for the benefit of their French captives).[36] The war was short, and by winter's end the French prisoners went home, avoiding a crisis. But what would happen in a massive and *long* war?

World War I—with its huge armies and four years of fighting—was, of course, just that. The western front had more than a million prisoners on both sides; the eastern front (with its greater mobility allowing for more conclusive victories) had more than 5 million. But now the problem could be addressed satisfactorily. We may follow Solzhenitsyn as he describes, with a literary eye, the Russian prisoners of August 1914, taken by Germany—the first massive capture of prisoners of the war.

> The column of footsloggers is marched into a compound with a temporary, almost a token fence of barbed wire stretched between temporary poles in the open field. The prisoners scatter to lie or sit on the bare ground, holding their heads, or stand or walk around, exhausted, bedraggled, bandaged, with bruises or open wounds. Some, for whatever reason, in their underwear, others without shoes, and all, of course, unfed. They stare at us through the barbed wire, forlorn and sad. A novel idea! To keep so many people in an open field, and make sure they don't run away! Where else could you put them? A novel solution! The con-cent-tra-tion camp! The fate of future decades! The harbinger of the twentieth century!"[37]

Solzhenitsyn exaggerates the novelty of the idea: it is by now forty years old and very well tested, but it is true that it was only little used to guard humans, until now. Now it becomes the standard equipment of prisoner-of-war camps, as built by all belligerents.

From their temporary barbed wire pen (where they might spend a few hours, or even days), the prisoners would be quickly moved—usually by train—to other, more permanent camps. These were at first the traditional structures used in previous wars: the available warehouses, castles, churches. But already in 1914, almost all prisoners would reach a barbed wire settlement. James Farrant, a British soldier, recounts a typical prisoner's progress: First he was guarded in a church. Then he was moved to a barbed wire camp in Doeberitz, near Berlin; then to another barbed wire camp in occupied Russian territory, near Riga.[38]

Barbed wire camps quickly became the standard. It is typical that even where standing structures were used, these were now surrounded by barbed wire, for instance, the Vohrenbach camp in the Black Forest, which was "a recently completed [1916] school, a large two-storey building with a very large attic . . . surrounded by an eight-foot high double barbed wire fence."[39] Surround a school with barbed wire—and you have a camp. In fact the recipe could be given precisely, as the architecture was becoming uniform. The most common form was this: "enclosures surrounded by barbed wire fence about ten feet high; in some camps a single fence, in others an extra fence about fifty to seventy five feet outside the first fence. To be caught in the space between the two fences meant death."[40] Inside these enclosures would stand simple barracks, usually made of wood, arranged in a grid pattern. (It should be noted, incidentally, that camps were typically sited in plains with simple topography, which would have obvious advantages in controlling the prisoners, and this, too, favored the tendency to base the architecture on simple geometric patterns.)

I have already described the double stockade in Andersonville, and we see that the principle of a *double* layer of fences has now become established in the standard architecture of camps. This is an interesting new use of barbed wire, which we will see in all similar structures in the future. It reflects the fact that, in a prisoner-of-war camp, everyone assumes that the prisoners will try to escape. If you allow the prisoners to reach as far as the perimeter, this will give them the opportunity to work on breaching that barrier. Thus the perimeter is enhanced to define not only the obvious two spaces—the "inside" and the "outside"—but also a third, special space that we may call the "in-between." This was a forbidden zone separating the inside from the outside. Control over motion in the camp was now based mainly on the following principle: if you were in the in-between area, you would be killed. Thus the life of captives, on the inside, was hermetically sealed from the life of free people on the outside—by setting up a lifeless, lethal buffer zone separating the two areas of life.

To make this buffer zone lethal, one needed armed guards—which gave rise to a further element in the architecture. Once again, we see the two technologies that seem to go hand in hand: barbed wire and machine guns. Guards with their machine guns would be positioned around the perimeter, inside guardhouses. The goal of these guardhouses was to allow perfect visibility, not so much of the camp itself as of the forbidden zone between the internal and external fences. This was panopticism, to use Foucault's term: the guard, in principle, had a certain area where everything was visible so that total control was reached. (For this purpose of visibility, the semitransparent nature of barbed wire made it an ideal material.)

We have repeatedly seen a similar pattern, which we may now unpack: trenches and barbed wire in the Russo-Japanese War and in many wars since; blockhouses and barbed wire in the Boer War; and now guardhouses and barbed wire. There must always be (1) a central location where soldiers with rifles or machine guns guard the space that is brought under control, and (2) barbed wire to slow down motion in that space. The difference between trenches, blockhouses, and guardhouses is that of the different equations of power holding between the two sides. Faced by a well-prepared enemy, the shooter must entrench, giving rise to the Russo-Japanese trenches; faced by the lightly armed Boers, visibility becomes somewhat more important, defense somewhat less important, and blockhouses—prefabricated, relatively light forts—are the natural result. Finally, faced by unarmed but deeply hostile prisoners, visibility is all-important, but no defense is required; thus guardhouses are erected. But notice the continuity: the guards in a prisoner-of-war camp are, after all, in a state of war with their inmates. The guardhouse is a triumphant trench.

The architecture described so far defined the nature of the major drama of the prisoner-of-war camps, namely, the *escape*.[41] Of course, this can easily be exaggerated: most prisoners never attempted escape. But it is true that many captives and captors were obsessed by the notion—and so is the popular imagination of the prisoner-of-war experience. The great majority of literature on prisoner-of-war camps deals not with life *inside* the camps but with escapes *from* them. These—almost without exception—took the form of the tunnel. A group of prisoners would dig a way out, from a barracks, going beneath the surface of the camp, reaching out (when all went well) beyond the external barbed wire layer. (We would not know how to do this, but then, we have never dug trenches, either: during World War I, an entire generation was taught to *dig*.) The hold of the notion of escape on the popular imagination of prisoner-of-war camps is itself instructive. When engaged in an escape attempt, the prisoner of war has to a certain extent regained his autonomy. He is no longer a mere object of regulations made by his captors but instead assumes the status of a subject, making his own decisions. This—even more than the very achievement of escape—is why many prisoners of war did attempt escape: it was a way of regaining their humanity.

But were they fully human? The real life issues were not the semimilitary adventures of escape, attempted or prevented, but the biological realities of food and disease. For the captors, the prisoners were mere receptacles of organic material, to be preserved somehow till the end of the war.

Most governments made a genuine effort. Starvation was not a problem of the prisoner-of-war camps, and unlike the case of the British in South Africa, the problem of disease was addressed in a rational manner. By now, medical science understood the role of lice in spreading typhus, and camp administrators set up practices to deal with this particular menace. Prisoners' memories linger on the moment of passage into a camp, when they would be washed and inoculated, their hair cut, their clothes fumigated (this fumigation was designed, of course, to kill lice).[42] We should pause here to anticipate the end of this chapter. This method of biological control would come into prominence later in the history of barbed wire settlements, when it would be turned against the inmates themselves, in the Nazi gas chambers.

The comparison may seem preposterous, but it has important historical significance. The Nazi gas chambers were based on a received idea: that the entry to a camp should involve a process of biological preparation. We cannot fully understand Auschwitz if we do not grasp this assumption that made the idea of the "showers" plausible to start with: the perpetrators of Auschwitz were used to a world where people were moved inside barbed wire settlements and, upon entry, submitted to biological control. The basic issue in all such camps was that within the perimeter of barbed wire, humans became mere biological objects. They were no longer full people, responsible for their own destiny. Instead they became mere flesh, to be taken care of by their captors, whether, on the whole, benevolently, as in the prisoner-of-war camps of World War I—or with the sadism of Auschwitz.

With all good intentions, prisoner-of-war camps did sometimes become death traps. Many epidemics did break out. In what was probably the worst case—Totskoye Camp, near Samara, Russia—out of 17,000 prisoners, more than 9,000 died in a typhus epidemic in the winter of 1916–1917.[43] (But then again, Russia was soon to inflict similar catastrophes on its own people.) Epidemics were the usual danger of a prisoner-of-war camp; a new development of World War I was the concept of prisoner-of-War *labor*. With so many young men dead or at the front, all belligerent nations experienced labor shortages. It was thus a natural thought to make the prisoners work: to bring those young men, as it were, back into the cycle of production. Take an example: in Silesia, the Germans put prisoners of war to work in the salt and coal mines. The inmates worked under the same conditions as free miners, but unlike free miners, the prisoners' treatment when sick would be "Aspirin und Arbeit"—aspirin and work.[44] Other prisoners were put to work in factories; still others were loaned out to rural farms.[45] This caused relatively little concern at the time, especially since all sides participated in the practice, which, indeed, was not lethal in character. But we see here an important new principle: coerced labor based on barbed wire camps.

The barbed wire settlement for prisoners of war was becoming routine, and in this context of mushrooming barbed wire settlements, it also became standard to enclose *civilians* inside barbed wire. World War I thus repeated, on a grand global scale, the experiment of the Boer War. There were many cases of internment of alien citizens, merely suspected of being potentially dangerous.

Once again, Britain may have led the way. London, a bustling port city, was full of people of every nationality, posing confusing problems. Consider, for instance, an Austro-Hungarian citizen, who is also Polish speaking (say, from a Galician village). Shall we assume that he is faithful to his country of citizenship? Or can we rely on his word that, as a Pole, he has no sympathy to the Austrians? On the other hand, will he not be as much anti-Russian as he is anti-Austrian? The Russian are our allies: how would he feel about us, then? (Finally, isn't he actually Jewish?) Mind-boggling complications! Special committees had to be formed for each national shade, screening aliens person by person.[46] At the end of this screening, about 60,000 aliens were still considered dangerous —about 50,000 of them German citizens and 10,000 Austrian citizens.[47] It is reported that they were mainly "waiters, barbers, cooks, bakers, tailors and clerks." Not trained soldiers, then; still, they were mostly young men. Sending them back home would clearly help the German war effort, while keeping them in Britain without supervision would pose obvious dangers. So what else could be done? A concentration camp system was set up to house this army of waiters. Some were placed in the usual assortment of disused structures—a deserted skating rink in Southampton, a former factory at Lancaster—but most were put in a couple of barbed wire camps on the Isle of Man, thus combining the safety of an inner island with that of barbed wire.[48] The barbed wire fences were built up quickly, but inside them there were only tents to start with. Fortunately, the war began in summer, so this was not so much of a problem, and by the end of autumn 1914, the usual architecture of the evolved camp was already in place on the Isle of Man and elsewhere: barbed wire outside, wood barracks inside. This being Britain, a committee was formed to write a report—this time a delegation of MPs. They were sent on inspection in April 1915 and concluded with satisfaction that the internees' accommodation was "infinitely more comfortable" than what British soldiers had experienced during the previous winter (which was likely enough). Indeed, one of the committee members added, the treatment of internees was "not only considerate and liberal but generous to a point sufficient to attract a certain amount of criticism."[49] At any rate, it is fair to say that the British did take great care to prevent a humanitarian disaster: they imposed a strict biological regime. The regulations are worth quoting from in some detail: "1. . . . It should be the aim of each prisoner to co-operate in . . . sanitation. 2. Prisoners should make a point of taking baths . . . as frequently as possible. 3. Prisoners should keep their hair cut as short as possible. . . . 4. Prisoners should lose no opportunity that may be offered of being vaccinated. . . . 5. After clothing has been washed it should be wrung out in a five per cent solution of boracic acid. . . . 6. Every prisoner should do his utmost to keep his hut as clean as possible, and free from refuse."[50] The lessons of the Boer camps were taken.

The real purpose of the MP delegation visit was to impress on the world the contrast between civilized British conduct and German atrocities—the story being put forward was that British civilians in Germany were victims of "horrors and tortures." There was not an ounce of truth in this. But naturally enough, British civilians of military age were interned. There were about six thousand of them, and most were now concentrated in a disused racecourse in the town of Ruhleben (that is, "peaceful living") near Berlin. This provided a good array of structures—stables, huts, the racecourse itself—that could be used for accommodation (naturally, everything was surrounded by barbed wire). Conditions in the camp were, in this case, genuinely better than on the outside: while Britain blockaded Germany as a whole, the inmates of Ruhleben received food sent by their families through neutral Holland.[51] But it would be pointless to give marks to this or that kindly establishment—which really makes us parties to the crime. Let us concentrate on the crime itself, not on its benevolent perpetrators. Here is the crucial point: it now became routine to imprison people simply because of their *suspected* loyalties. Preventive mass-scale imprisonment became routine.

This routine was immediately globalized. In Australia, for instance, there was a sizable German community. Thousands of miles away from Europe, patriotic Australians were eager to do something, and quickly, for the empire; so Germans were carted away to concentration camps. The Australian authorities were selective and concentrated on those they considered, rather impressionistically, as especially "dangerous" (that is, basically, prominent citizens). Overall about seven thousand people were interned, and the usual concentration camps set up.[52] Across the globe from Australia, Canadians were building their own concentration camps in the Rocky Mountains. Altogether there were twenty-four camps in Canada, housing more than eight thousand civilians (the choice of inmates was particularly absurd, as most were Ukrainians of Austro-Hungarian citizenship, hardly harboring any enmity toward the British Empire). The Castle Mountain camp may be taken as an example: a clearing in the forest in a level area between the mountains; a rectangle of barbed wire; rows of tents inside (see map 6, based on a sketch by a Canadian officer: the outlines of the standard rectangular concentration camp are neatly visible here). It should be noted that clearing the woods was done mainly by the prisoners themselves.[53] Compare this to the Australian case: the main concentration camp there was at Holdsworthy, not far from Sydney. We happen to have a detailed description of its construction, which follows a familiar pattern. When the first inmates were brought, no more than a small area was cleared in the bush. This was surrounded by a triple barbed wire fence, and a few tents were thrown inside for accommodation. The inmates had to do the rest of the building of the camp: clearing

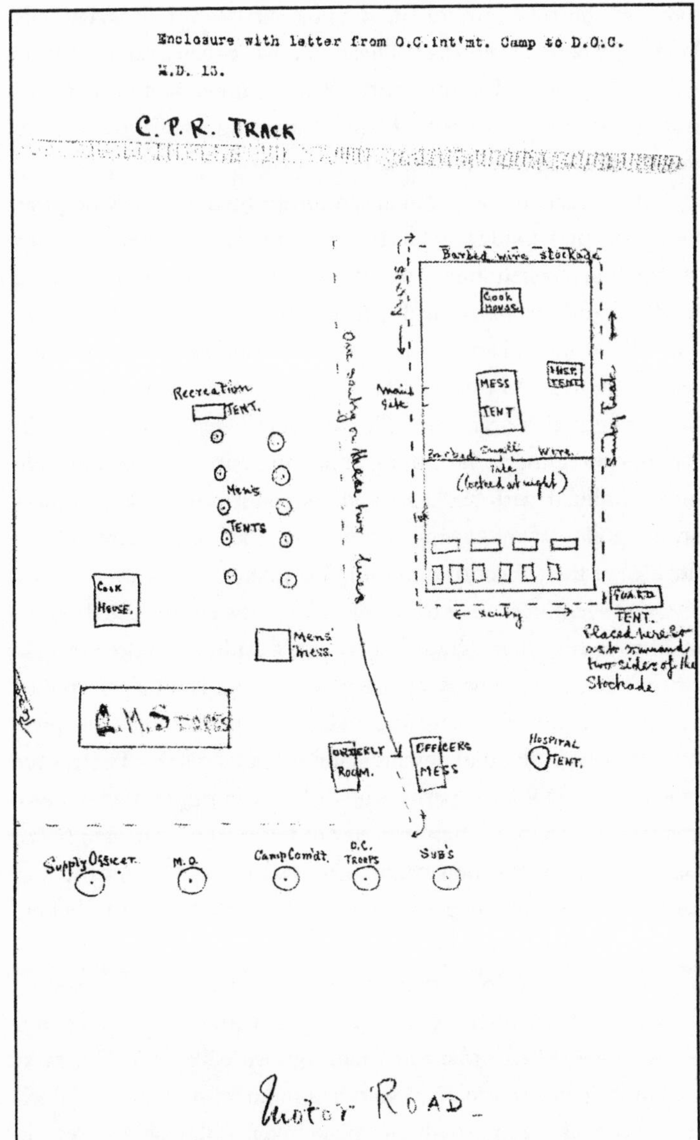

MAP 6 *Castle Mountain Internment Camp, Canada, World War I. Reproduced from Kordan and Melnycky 1991, 9. Reprinted with permission, Canadian Institute of Ukrainian Studies Press.*

more of the bush around it, digging ditches for drainage, and building wooden barracks.[54] This may now be seen as an important cost-saving method in the concentration camps. Not only do you rely on the cheap materials of barbed wire and wood; you also rely on the cheap labor of inmates.

I claim that this was now taken for granted as a routine practice. The best evidence for this routinization comes not from World War I itself but from World War II: we should glance briefly ahead, chronologically, to see how the internment of enemy aliens was taken as an obvious precaution, almost without second thought, in this war itself. This is particularly striking, as the Western democracies explicitly fought that war against the tyrannical regimes of arbitrary imprisonment. That nations genuinely imbued with such high ideals could nonetheless embark on the policy of mass concentration is a measure of how natural the idea of the concentration camp became.

Once again, Britain had to set up committees for the discernment of enemy aliens' loyalties. In fact, it had even more German citizens this time, mostly Jewish refugees. Nazism being a political phenomenon, the committees faced a difficult subjective question. Was an individual person genuinely anti-Nazi? (These were called *Class C*.) Was he perhaps an ordinary immigrant who might therefore be no more than *suspected* of German nationalism (*Class B*)? Finally, was he downright pro-Nazi (*Class A*)? As the war started, there were no more than a few hundred found to belong to Class A—and interned straightaway—while the few thousand in Class B had restrictions imposed on their motion (they were not allowed to travel more than five miles without previous police permission). Then, in spring 1940, France collapsed. The invasion of Britain itself loomed, and in a moment of panic, the decision was made to intern all German citizen males aged sixteen to sixty of Class B; furthermore, in coastal areas, simply all German citizens—A, B, and C—were interned. Thus Britain was now managing concentration camps for, mostly, Jewish refugees. We need hardly follow the familiar details—transit camps in disused factories surrounded by barbed wire, then the permanent barbed wire camps on the Isle of Man.[55] It was as if Britain was destined to repeat in exact parallel the internment experience of World War I, now vastly more absurd.

Equally absurd—and much better known—was the American experience of internment in the same war. As in Britain, this too was the product of panic. In the wake of Pearl Harbor, the notion of a Japanese landing on the Pacific coast did not seem so wildly implausible as it now appears, in hindsight. The American Pacific coast had a substantial Japanese American community. That these were closely integrated into American life only made matters worse. Alarmed officials noted that Japanese could be found next to all strategic locations: "San Diego County: Thirty miles of open coast broken by small water courses with a Jap [*sic*] on every water course. . . . Alameda County: Japs in vicinity to Holt Caterpillar Tractor Co., San Leandro."[56] Internment was the natural conclusion, and already by March 2, 1942, the process of concentration was begun. The policy was extraordinarily draconian, so that the entire Japanese American community—110,000 men, women, and children—was sent into barbed wire settlements.

The settlements themselves are familiar—wooden barracks surrounded by barbed wire and guardhouses. It is only fair to add that the barracks offered a relatively high standard of living compared to other concentration camps. They were the same as the temporary barracks now built everywhere to house GIs. (Of course, GIs did not come with entire families.) Rooms ranged in size from 16 by 20 feet to 20 by 24 feet, with a family in each, which made for crammed living conditions. Most difficult was the climate. As is typical for such reallocations, the Japanese Americans were sent to remote parts of the country. Britain used the Isle of Man; America had the entire Rocky Mountains and the Midwest open to it, and camps were built in remote areas from Arizona to North Dakota.[57] This is especially interesting for our history: barbed wire, as it were, came home. The American West was suddenly—if briefly—the site for barbed wire structures alternating between imprisoned animals and imprisoned humans.

All of this is useful to bear in mind, in that we are reminded of how natural, by 1942, the concentration camp had become. But we are pushing ahead of the story—and, needless to say, concentration camps, by 1942, could be infinitely worse than those housing Japanese Americans. In the prisoner-of-war camps, as in the civilian internment camps, the hypocrisy of benevolent governmental care was not completely without substance. In the place of concentration itself, it would be perceived by both sides—concentrated as well as concentrator—as a necessary evil, whose discomforts were to be mitigated, as best as possible. This, then, was still a preparation, no more, for the main historical role of the concentration camp. The tool was made routine—but only as a response to the extreme conditions of war. It was not yet applied, in peacetime, as a preemptive tool meant to ensure the control of a government over its civilian population. For this to happen, war and peace had to approximate each other even more closely than they did in World War I: this would happen first in Russia. We should follow this development with special interest: surprisingly, we will find that it highlights the relationship between human and animal destinies. The Soviet experiment pretended that the two can be taken apart, and the price paid was the Soviet catastrophe.

3. TRACTORS TO UKRAINE

The Bolshevik coup was not a revolution but a counterrevolution. The Bolsheviks took great pains to conceal this fact so as to clothe themselves with the red flag of revolution—a successful concealment that became the foundational lie of their regime. Even now, when the words "the Russian Revolution" are mentioned, what comes to mind is the picture of sailors and workers storming Saint Petersburg in October 1917 to free it from tsarist reaction. In fact, by October 1917 Russia was a democracy, the product of the revolution of February 1917, in which the people of Saint Petersburg did away with the tsarist regime and created a free land. So free that by October, no control was exerted anywhere by anyone. The troops lost their discipline; the outlying nations of the empire were preparing to secede; bread stopped reaching the cities. It fell to the Bolsheviks to reassert power over the Russian Empire, to recolonize it. They called it the Soviet Union, and they claimed to protect it from a tsarist restoration, but in fact they themselves were the imperial restorers. The "Whites" who fought against the Bolsheviks almost all aimed to protect some version of the free Russia of the revolution of February. The goal of the Bolsheviks was the exact opposite of such freedom: they intended to assert full control from Petrograd (or later from Moscow) over the entire land.

The reason no monarchist restoration was attempted in Russia was that no monarchist could muster the ruthlessness required to achieve control in the face of an anarchic country. People were moving without constraint: soldiers from the front, back to their homes; workers from the cities, back to their native villages (where food could be found). Hence the army and the economy ceased to function. Someone had to bring a stop to all that motion, to restrain people, indeed to retrain them back into submission. The Bolsheviks, alone of all Russians, had the fanaticism of Leninist ideology to justify, in their minds, the use of terror for this retraining.

Thus it must be stressed that terror—and the concentration camps—were the tool of Soviet Communism right from its inception. Of course, there was nothing surprising in that: given the times, it would have been outstanding had there been no concentration camps. After all, there was a civil war going on, so the natural thing was to set up barbed wire settlements for captured or potential enemies. The war, however, was extraordinary in nature, and so would be the camps.

Even apart from their ideology, the Bolsheviks faced a special problem, that of a civil war. Quite simply, parties to a civil war do not issue passports: the definition of "enemy" is based purely on the perceptions of the sides. Hence terror would have to be particularly arbitrary. Typical to this were such vaguely defined policies as the proclamation of August 31, 1918: "Anyone who dares to agitate against Soviet authority will be arrested immediately and confined in a concentration camp." In practice, this would most often be the camp of Kholmogory (set up in 1919 on the river Dvina, not far from the northern town of Archangelsk). Malsagoff identifies the camp inmates: "captured White officers . . . Kronstadt sailors" (The sailors of Kronstadt, among the first supporters of the revolution, rebelled against it in 1921), "peasants from the Tamboff government who had belonged to Antonoff's bands" (a peasant rebellion against the Soviet regime), and "members of the intelligentsia of all nationalities and religions, Kuban and Don Cossacks, etc."[58] We see here a mix of the prisoner-of-war principle (White officers, rebellious sailors, armed peasants) and the preventive internment principle (intelligentsia, Cossacks): the blurring of the line between actual and potential resistance would be a constant feature of Soviet terror.

In terms of living conditions, the inmates were put up in unheated huts where temperatures could reach as low as minus fifty degrees Celsius, and they were offered as food "one potato for breakfast, potato peelings cooked in hot water for dinner, and one potato for supper. . . . These people, driven by the pangs of hunger to eat the bark of trees, unable to stand from exhaustion, were compelled by tortures and shootings to perform hard labor—digging up tree stumps, working in the stone-quarries, floating timber."[59] Once again, some of the practices of Kholmogory had precedents. There were many previous cases in which men were thrown into improvised barbed wire settlements with inadequate housing, and there were also precedents for putting such men to forced labor. The deliberate starvation of the inmates, however, was already a new departure, suggesting a radical difference between this camp and previous ones: now, the lethal potential of the policy of concentration was made into an intentional outcome. Kholmogory had the usual outbreaks of typhus and cholera; on top of them came starvation, overwork, and mass killings (a typical practice was to tie stones to inmates' necks and then throw them into the Dvina River).[60] It was effectively a death camp: no statistics are available, but certainly at least a few tens of thousands of inmates died there between 1919 and 1922.

In 1922, when the Russian Civil War was definitely over, the Soviet concentration camp system was relatively small: 24,750 persons were detained in fifty-six camps. The next year there were only twenty-three camps.[61] For a brief period, the Soviet camps were actually contracting. In general, control was reestablished over the old Russian Empire. The democratic forces were all destroyed, most non-Russian nations were brought back into the empire, and normal economic life was somewhat resumed. One could envisage a Russian future without concentration camps. But here the special character of the Soviet conflict was revealed. Even after the Civil War itself, camps were not dismantled but transformed. The Civil War, in a sense, never ended: for the Communists, existence was a war—"class struggle"—and they were determined to seize the initiative and win this war, waged against their own citizens.

An important decision was made already in 1922: to finish with Kholmogory and rebuild the system with its center at the Solovetsky Islands, not far from Archangelsk. Since medieval times, Orthodox monks had lived in these small islands in the harsh White Sea. They succeeded in founding a self-sufficient community away from the mainland. It was probably this self-sufficiency that had attracted the Soviet authorities: Kholmogory, even at the rate of a couple of potatoes per person per day, cost more money than could be made by lumbering there. The new experiment was made to set up a fully self-catering—indeed, profitable—concentration camp. Also, Solovetsky was promising for reasons that are by now familiar to us. Small islands are easy to control—we may compare this with the British use of the Isle of Man—while monastic structures could often develop a secondary use as prisons. Thus Solovetsky made good sense as a concentration camp. In the autumn of 1922 it was refitted. The monks were removed, the wooden buildings burned; then barbed wire was put around the main cathedral.[62] On its floor were laid wooden boards, and this was now the barracks. The old frescoes were painted over; instead of them, the walls were covered with slogans such as "Without education and cleanliness there is no road to Socialism" and "Work strengthens a man's soul and body."[63] A secondary concentration camp was built on Popov Island, nearer

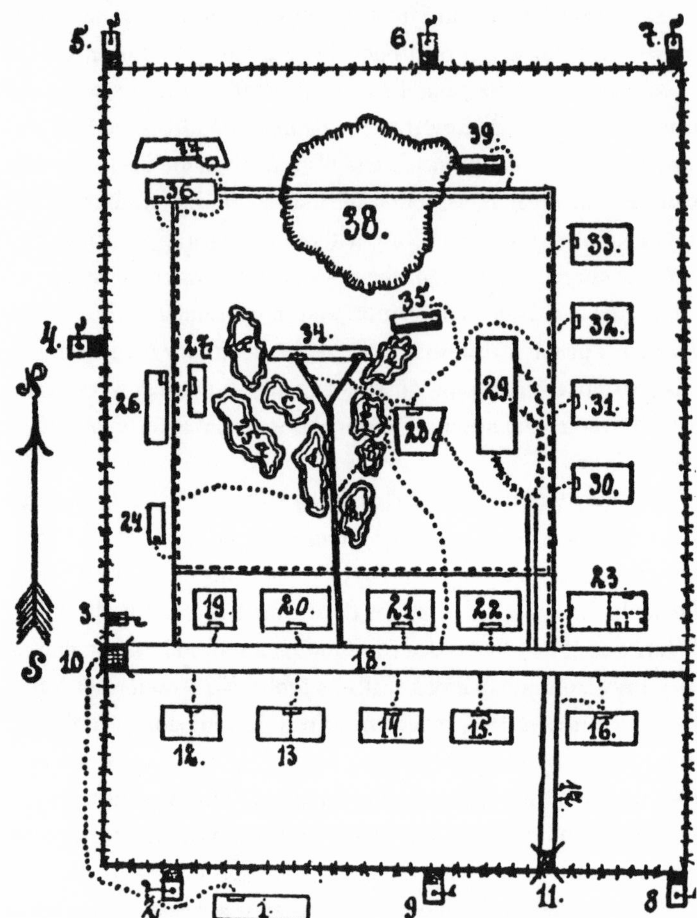

MAP 7 *The camp on Popov Island (part of the Solvetsky complex, White Sea), early years of the Gulag. Reproduced from Malsagov 1926, 80.*

the coast—the usual structure of a barbed wire rectangle enclosing wooden huts (see map 7).[64] This duality of two concentration camps, on two islands, had a practical significance: inmates were constantly on the move, either brought in via Popov Island or lent out along the same route to various economic projects in the mainland. Agricultural production in Solovetsky should have made the camp self-sufficient, while the work on the mainland should have made it profitable. This seemed to be a success, and from 1926 onward, more and more prisoners were temporarily imprisoned not in the Solovetsky Islands themselves but on the mainland, so that the original two camps were giving rise to new camps built on their model.[65] The number of prisoners, too, was on the rise: starting from three thousand in 1923, there were fifty thousand in 1930.[66]

This Solovetsky success—a self-sufficient concentration camp system—was an important discovery: the forced labor of the concentration camps could now become an economic resource, to count in Soviet planning. Still, the Solovetsky Islands were primarily a place of terror, where the enemies of the regime could be killed and tortured. Many of the inmates were the survivors of the repressions of the Civil War, and others were common criminals.[67] It was still a time when, exercising prudence, a Soviet citizen could have a reasonable certainty of staying out of concentration camp.

We have now reached the end of 1920s. The Communist Party had resolved its internal struggle that had followed Lenin's death in 1924. An unchallenged leader—Stalin—had emerged. Now, finally, the essential problem of control over the Russian Empire was to be addressed head-on. Let us concentrate on this moment. It is the beginning of the barbed wire camp as a tool of mass terror; it is also the moment where modernization is deliberately planned and thrown over an entire land. We remember the system seen in the first chapter—an urban center gaining profits from control over the produce of a land. Total control over space, based on violence deployed on a mass scale: the same formula adopted in the American West was to be followed in the Soviet Union. This was achieved, in America, by free enterprise; now it was to be achieved by state fiat, based on state violence. The tools were different, but the goal was similar. In a very real sense, the Bolsheviks set out to colonize the Soviet countryside. And barbed wire—once again—would be a crucial agent. This time, however, it would be used not so much against animals as against humans.

At the end of chapter 2, I mentioned the basic Russian problem, when discussing the Russian failure in World War I. Russia did not have the central control to meet the challenge of modernization imposed by the war. The transportation network was thin; economically, town and countryside were badly integrated. With their Marxist training, the Soviet planners had a clear sense of the problem. To modernize, one needs investment—so as to build mines, railroads, factories. Someone must pay for the investment. In other words—and here Marxism is useful—someone must be *exploited*. This notion of "exploitation" is not moral but economic. Every accumulation of capital is ultimately based on a worker who gets less compensation than his labor is worth, so that the gap between the value of labor and the compensation for it represents surplus value, or capital. For instance, a farmer deserves ten rubles for his grain; you give him, say, seven rubles. Suppose now you sell the grain again (e.g., export it to western Europe) for its full ten rubles' worth. You have gained three rubles, which you can now invest as capital (e.g., by buying western European machines): a small step gained in the march toward modernity. The entire problem for the Soviet regime was that under the tsars, the Russian peasants had been underexploited. The peasants lived miserably, but no one really lived *of* the peasants. The extreme backwardness of the Russian village defeated all efforts to make it into a basis for capital accumulation. Russian noble families accumulated debts, instead, trying to live off the shrinking rents from their landholdings. The cherry orchards were gradually sold, as in Chekhov's play, and little came out of prewar efforts to introduce modernized agriculture into the Russian countryside.[68]

Following the February Revolution of 1917, the villages took over the land still owned by the nobles. This was the only fruit of the February Revolution that the Bolsheviks did not immediately annul. In fact, it was this land policy that gave them the edge in the Civil War. (The peasants suspected, correctly, that the various Whites might respect the noblemen's titles to land.)

Everywhere, the countryside reverted to its oldest practices. It was the European medieval synthesis, as described in chapter 2—set in the twentieth century. Land was cultivated by the open-field system. The strips were reallocated to families from time to time (hence little incentive to improvement); the animals were pastured together. There was little differentiation between families, almost no investment in agricultural tools, and little trade with the towns. The villages retreated inwardly. Before the war, 50 percent of the grain was grown by such smallholding, traditional peasants, who then consumed 60 percent of their own produce; in 1927, 85 percent of the grain was grown by them, and they consumed 80 percent of that. The grain Russia had once sent for exports now no longer left the village.[69]

In practical terms, the regime had two distinct goals: to make the peasants produce more, and then to move as much of that produce as possible out of the villages. The crisis was due to the obvious tension between these two goals. What repeatedly frustrated the regime was that the peasants *resisted* exploitation.

Naked exploitation was tried during the Civil War itself, and this experience still marked Soviet attitudes. The Bolshevik regime, after all, was born out of the food crisis of World War I. Quite simply, the Bolsheviks lived in towns and therefore needed —in order to survive—to get hold of the grain. Thus by 1920 a simple solution was adopted: troops went out to the countryside and expropriated grain. (This is part of what was called "War Communism.") The result was often peasant rebellions—such peasants, remember, were among the inmates of the death camp of Kholmogory—but even more dangerous for the regime, the peasants now saw no reason to go out and cultivate their fields. What's the point if grain is to be expropriated anyway? During World War I the peasants retreated from the cities, to sell less and less of their product; now, with the Civil War, they retreated from the fields, confining themselves to minimal subsistence farming. Then the climate turned against them, and in the drought year of 1921 came the great famine. It was the worst Russia had experienced until that year (worse was to come under Stalin). In the Volga region—which saw the extreme of the disaster—peasants resorted to baking flour made from acorns, sawdust, clay, and horse manure. Cannibalism was frequently reported; in some places, soldiers were mounted to protect cemeteries from corpse thieves. Villages were deserted, and typhus and cholera decimated a weakened population. In all, 5 million people died. Under these conditions, the Soviet regime agreed, in 1922, to accept food from America. The American Relief Administration, led by Herbert Hoover, had already fed Europe in the aftermath of World War I. Now it was feeding 10 million people in the Soviet Union, sending in the tools and seed that finally ended the long crisis of food production. By 1923, the Soviet agricultural system was stabilized—shored up by the grain of the American Great Plains.[70] So much for the dream of Soviet export of grain as a foundation of capital accumulation. It was clear that grain expropriation had failed. Lenin—much to his own disgust—accepted the principle of NEP, the New Economic Policy, whereby market forces were largely allowed to control the flow of foodstuffs. This was an interlude. The peasants were lulled into a complacent sense of false security, and the Communist regime was considering how to regain full control over its domain.

The villages, as we have seen, were thus in a world apart, and this is why speaking of "colonizing the countryside" is appropriate: the Soviet towns really did not have control over the Soviet villages, and so these villages had to be conquered—in a kind of internal colonization. The alternative—to offer the peasants incentives to produce more, and to wait for this process to make the countryside more prosperous—would obviously entail capitalism with all its evils. This was NEP, a compromise, an intermediate palliative until a better solution could be found. No—what was required was a fundamental change—one that went much beyond the mere requisitions of the Civil War. The very structural relation between town and country had to be altered. Quite simply, a way had to be found to keep the peasants in the fields, working for the towns, whether they wanted to or not.

To make things worse, this was not just a matter of townsmen gaining control over peasants; as is typical of such colonial conflicts, an ethnic dimension was added as well. The most fertile area of the Soviet Union, the bread lands of the South, was the land of Ukrainians and Cossacks. They were only grudgingly part of the Russian Empire before and, obviously, were now even more hostile to the Soviet regime. Further east, in central Asia, Muslim nations never ceased fighting against European colonialism. Although Communist in title, this was still a Russian empire—the empire of Saint Petersburg (renamed Leningrad) and, above all, the empire of Moscow. Muscovite control had to be gained, everywhere, in a direct continuation of Russian imperial practices. Thus those unreliable nations of the South and the East were especially targeted—in their case, the dangers of an "enemy class" (peasants, nomads) were multiplied by those of "enemy nations" (Ukrainians, Cossacks, Muslims). So this would be the theme of Bolshevik colonization. Everywhere, peasants were to be *brought under control*; in a long arc leading from Ukraine to Kazakhstan, they would be *destroyed*. Let us see how this unfolded.

By 1929, Stalin began to apply the new policy of collectivization. Collectivization had two pillars: barbed wire, and tractors. Both served the same purpose of subduing the peasants. First, barbed wire. Inside each village, the stronger peasants—as well as many others, picked almost at random—were arrested and sent into exile and concentration camps. The theory—never shared by the peasants themselves—was that the traditional village had a class structure, with simple peasants exploited by richer "kulaks" (literally, "fists"). Hence this terror went by the name "dekulakization." (It was at this moment that the Soviet concentration camp system was rapidly enlarged to reach its full, massive scale, which it was to maintain for a quarter century.) As for the peasants left behind in the village, they were forced to give up their belongings and to become workers in a state enterprise (theoretically "theirs"), the collective farm, or *kolkhoz*. By 1934, nine-tenths of Russian agriculture was concentrated in about 240,000 such collectives across the entire Soviet Union.[71]

Above the level of the individual village, the main instrument of state control was tractors. *Kolkhozes* were brought, at least in theory, under the control of a machine tractor station: essentially, a tractor depot. A cluster of *kolkhozes* would be made dependent on a single central tractor station, their fields now cultivated with the aid of these tractors. By the end of 1932, 2,446 machine tractor stations were built with (official numbers) 75,000 tractors.[72] The machines were supplied by the state; the *kolkhoz* would pay for tractor service with its produce, and being dependent on tractors, they could be extorted to pay extravagantly. Hence the tractors would serve to get the grain, first from the land and then from the peasants.

In short, modernization and centralized control were to be established simultaneously, all based on the conquering power of iron. It was assumed that cultivation with tractors would expand production. Then, terrorized by dekulakization, the peasants would be forced to serve the command economy of the *kolkhoz*. Furthermore, since they were dependent on the machine tractor stations, a larger part of their produce could be taken away. This exploitation would now serve as the basis for Soviet capital accumulation, allowing the state to buy more machines—such as tractors—and so the circle would be complete.

The modernity of the West would reach the lands of the Soviet Union—and the desire to emulate America was everywhere (only later would it be muffled by the Soviet paranoia we are familiar with). Trotsky could tell a visiting U.S. senator—in all truthfulness—that "the words 'Americanism' and 'Americanization' are used in our newspapers and technical journals in an altogether sympathetic way and by no means in the sense of reproach." The phrase "In America they have invented a machine" (as Jeffrey Brooks notes) became standard in promoting new technology. The foremost of those machines was the tractor. Such new technologies—associated with the image of America—were to transform the Soviet Union. "We are becoming a country of metal, a country of automobiles, a country of tractors," said Stalin in 1931.[73] And who was more appropriate as a vehicle of this new poetics of metals? After all, the very name 'Stalin'—the name Iossif Vissarionovitch Djugashvili had chosen for himself as an underground Bolshevik—meant "the man of steel." Stalinism, quite literally, was the cult of steel. A basic Soviet trope (typical for this culture of the hackneyed phrase) was "the steel horse," referring, of course, to the tractor. And indeed it was around such steel horses that, in the years of collectivization, the Soviet dream was dreamed. It was the dream of the European steppe—Ukraine and southern Russia—becoming a mirror of the American Great Plains, teeming with tractors, large farms, and modern agriculture supporting a modern state.

In reality, Ukraine and southern Russia were now the scene of genocide, in part planned, in part the result of a miscalculation. This massive miscalculation is extremely interesting because it shows certain limitations of the modernist imagination. Modernism—of which Marxism is a species—imagined a world where technology governed nature. Soviet Communism attempted to gain this control by state fiat. Nature was disrupted—and a catastrophe ensued, from which the Soviet Union never recovered.

The genocide was achieved by two means: deportation and famine. I will consider them in turn. One can wonder whether the famine was fully planned; as for the deportations, there is no doubt that they were planned from the center. The Soviet Union had now entered its first Five Year Plan period, and everything was dictated by quota, including mass exile and prison. The original quota given to the police was the arrest of 60,000 families of kulaks, but—the same would happen in all other industries—the quotas kept being raised. The deportation of 1,803,392 people is recorded from 1930 to 1931. They were transported across thousands of miles by special trains (by regulation, these were made of forty-four cattle trucks with forty deportees apiece, so that it took about one thousand round-trips to complete the evacuation).[74] A crude selection based on previous wealth defined certain peasant families as first-, second-, and third-category kulaks. Those who were classified as second or third category would be sent to a distant rail terminus, forced to walk hundreds of miles to a desolate spot, and there made to work for the state. These were called "special settlers," and a certain fiction of freedom pertained to these exiles (in this case, the thin transportation system of the Soviet Union could serve to isolate just as effectively as strict imprisonment did: if you put someone in the taiga, three hundred miles away from the railroad, he is not easily going to get back to Ukraine). First-category kulaks—those who might have owned, say, a couple of horses—became prisoners outright and (when not killed on the spot) were sent to the concentration camps. The concentration camp system now began its numerical, as well as geographic, expansion. We have now moved to the realm of the full-blown Gulag (a Russian acronym: Central Administration of Corrective Labor Camps and Colonies). In 1929 the concentration camp system consisted largely of Solovetsky and its offshoots on the shores of the White Sea. By 1932 there were already fifteen separate camp complexes, with dozens of camps in each. Besides Solovetsky itself, I can mention complexes such as the White Sea–Baltic, Ukhto-Pechorsky, Svirsky, Temnikovsky, Vishersky, Kungursky—all of these were still in northern European Russia. Here—north of Moscow, and west of the Urals, usually not far from the White Sea—was still the focus of the Gulag. But other complexes were already established farther away in the Soviet Union, with complexes in central Asia, Siberia, and the Far East. In 1929 there were about 50,000 prisoners; by January 1932, the Gulag had 268,700 inmates (this of course represents much more than the implied 220,000 new prisoners, as many prisoners were dying all the time).[75]

This initial period of growth had a crucial significance. One can say that as the Soviet Union as a whole was entering a period of capital accumulation, so was the Gulag itself. The basic infrastructure had to be put into place. After all, to have millions of prisoners housed inside thousands of camps—as the Soviet Union would soon have—called for a construction work of staggering proportions. Where would all the labor come from? Obviously, from the camps themselves. Memoirs of prisoners always refer to the first task in a new camp—which was to build the camp from scratch. I quote a survivor, Zurichenko:

> After a compulsory trek of two months through Peniug, Kotlas, Archangel, and Narayan-Mar, we approached our goal—

> the Pechora shipbuilding project. [The prisoners are left on an empty shore, where they are addressed by the camp commandant.] "You are now in the location of the future shipbuilding project on which we will start working tomorrow. The limits of the camp are indicated by signs and guard posts. It is strictly forbidden to go beyond those limits. Violators of this rule will be considered runaways, and guards will shoot without warning . . ."
>
> "Where are we to sleep?"
>
> "Right where you stand!"
>
> Only a month later were we able to sleep under a roof. Until that time we dug deep dugouts, covered them with tarpaulin tents and slept in three tiers on plank-beds.
>
> We had no bathhouse, no laundry, no kitchen. The administration was in a hurry to build a punitive isolator for "refusers," a house for the guards and for the camp GPU.[76]

Zurichenko does not mention the building of the camp perimeter; no doubt this was built as soon as the materials became available.

For the year 1937, for instance, T. A. Pechenyuk describes the construction of the camp, picking up the narrative from the point at which Zurichenko left it: "In this manner we constructed the restricted area [*zona*]: we dug out the position for setting down posts, then dug in the posts, and strung along barbed wire, making it with a slight incline toward the inside of the camp." (This was a typical practice in all camps, designed to make climbing the fence more difficult.) "We have constructed all the dugouts for living, and the other necessary objects."[77] Notice the order: first a barbed wire perimeter, then dugouts (not even barracks) for daily life and the rest.

But even this represents the relatively established patterns of 1937. Earlier on, materials could be in extremely short supply. Here is a description of Vorkuta, a major camp in the northern Urals, in 1931: "The words 'camp' and 'camp site' call up an image of barbed wire, but it was difficult to obtain in Vorkuta, and during its first years [the camp] was surrounded partially by wire, partially by plank-fencing, and in places by nothing at all except a row of meter-high stakes with signs on them saying 'restricted area' in red paint."[78] In the early 1930s, the Soviet Union was starved for barbed wire.

As, of course, it was starved for bread. As mentioned already, part of the destruction of the countryside came from the deportation of the more successful peasants, while those who were left behind were now dying in a terrible famine.

It is not at all far-fetched to suggest that to a large extent, the famine was planned. It should be remembered that besides the economic task of gaining central control over agricultural production, the Soviet regime also had a political task. The goal was to subjugate a disloyal population. This might be compared, say, to the problem facing Weyler, trying to subjugate the peasants of Cuba. How to bring an entire population into submission? Weyler starved the peasant population by relocating it to the cities. In Soviet experience, however, the memory was still alive of another, more direct method of starving peasants: forcibly taking away their food. In short, the famine of 1921 was now to be repeated, but this time without meddling Americans to save the peasants.

This would teach the peasants submission. That is, they should learn that from now on, the grain was considered state property, and they were to be fed according to the state's goodwill. A naive peasant might perhaps otherwise think that if all he produced was the minimum for his own subsistence, then at least this would not be taken away. It was imperative to dispel such illusions (otherwise such illusions might act as a disincentive for production). To make the point clear, the state now took away *everything*. This policy was fundamentally preconceived, but its actual consequences were not clearly foreseen. Here comes the essential miscalculation of the Soviet regime.

The sequence of events went like this. In the aftermath of collectivization, production plummeted (I will immediately return to consider why this was the case). This, in itself, was seen as a form of resistance against the regime; hence the official assumption was that the peasants had simply *hidden* their grain. State representatives were therefore sent to take away whatever grain could be found—in particular in the suspect lands of the South. After a while, there was nothing left to take: "In 1931 there were still a few instances of hidden grain being discovered, usually about 100 pounds, sometimes 200. In 1932, however, there was none. The most that could be found was about ten to twenty pounds kept for chicken feed. Even this 'surplus' was taken away."[79]

Let us pause to consider this surplus chicken feed, as it provides the key to the entire catastrophe. For, after all, now that their feed was expropriated, what would happen to the chickens? Here was the problem: one dealt not with abstract economic forces but with the concrete patterns of life: seed giving rise to grain; one animal generation giving birth to the next; humans, born and dying. At this biological level, a cataclysm now shook the Soviet Union. It was like a meteorite hitting the countryside, disrupting its fundamental ecological complexion.

This started immediately with collectivization itself. Consider central Russia, an area that was not especially targeted for repression. During the first three months of 1930, as collectivization was introduced there, the peasants slaughtered 25 percent of the cows, 53 percent of the pigs, 55 percent of the sheep, and 40 percent of the chickens.[80] Across the Soviet Union, from 1928 to 1933, the slaughter and starvation of domesticated animals led to the following loss: cows, from 70.5 million to 38.4 million; pigs, from 26 million to 12 million; sheep and goats, from 146.7 million to 50.2 million (all according to official record, the reality being probably worse).[81] Nothing could be simpler: now that these were no longer peasants' property, there was no point in keeping them alive. This slaughter was going on everywhere: the kulaks were deported, and the animals were killed. To quote Chernov—in charge of grain collection in Ukraine—"For the first time in their sordid history the Russian peasants have eaten their fill of meat."[82]

Collectivization turned the peasants against their animals; stripped of their agricultural meaning as *property*, animals reverted to their primordial status as *prey*. A more subtle point—

another indication of the new relationship between human and animal—was that the competition for food between humans and animals changed its meaning. The animal has been expropriated: why let it eat the food you might otherwise eat yourself? Why grow food for horses when you don't know what you yourself might eat tomorrow? Horses received less and less fodder. Peasants—at this stage not yet mad with hunger—often took pity on such starving horses and let them loose to fend for themselves. The story goes that herds of starving horses ran wild throughout Ukraine—a new, strange feralized species. But mostly the horses simply died.

In an unpublished memoir, N. A. Panarin tells of collectivization as seen by the peasant. The following moment is framed, in his memoir, as the crucial dramatic transition.

> I walked next to the horses, guided them. I see—our mare was as if soapy all over—she swayed, I idiotically whipped her with the knout, which has never happened since her birth, and there she fell. I approached her, she wheezed, her eyes grew dull and rolled underneath her brow, foam bubbled on her lips—she shook and went dead. I fell involuntarily on my knees, started to caress and hug her on the neck, crying like a baby. She was our most beloved horse, big, strong, fine. We two were as one, we understood each other . . . and suddenly she was no longer.[83]

Panarin goes on to express his suspicion that the mare was poisoned, and he notes that "this is how began to grow the poisoned seeds of the speedy collectivization." Crucially, then, his narrative contrasts the instinctive, intimate relation between man and horse before collectivization to the breakdown of all social relations in the village following it; and he sees this social breakdown of relations as the cause of the death of the horse. In all of this, he is certainly right. The organic ties of care, binding together humans and animals, ceased to exist, and the animals died.

According to official statistics, there were 32 million horses in the Soviet Union in 1928, and only 17 million in 1932; that is, more than 15 million horses were by now dead.[84] Most of the slaughter must have happened during the earliest days of collectivization; the animals that survived were in bad condition. In other words, traditional European agriculture was finished, for who would now pull the plows?

The plan was for tractors to do the job; it was soon discovered that the Soviet Union had, so to speak, put the cart before the horse. The hypothetical surplus of advanced agricultural production was to buy machinery—bringing in tractors and all the rest that America had; but meanwhile there simply were not enough tractors to go around. The Soviet Union had tried hard enough: 53.9 percent of the entire Soviet output of quality steel went, in 1931, to farm machinery (hence the lack of barbed wire, as noticed, for instance, in Vorkuta). But to bring this into perspective, one must realize that by the end of 1930, machine tractor stations served a mere 13.6 percent of the *kolkhozes*.[85] The ideal of reaching the entire land, centrally, through iron failed to materialize. Meanwhile there simply was not the power to work the fields. If we believe the regime (which we should not), even by the end of 1932 there were only 75,000 tractors—but there were 15 million fewer horses. In reality, the gain of tractors was probably lower, and the loss of horses higher (even without mentioning the loss in horses' health and vigor). Thus each tractor should have substituted, say, for three hundred horses. Now, in 1934, American producers offered, for instance, the Silver King tractor—which came with an impressive, for the time, 17.35 horsepower engine.[86] In sheer energy terms, then, the tractors could replace, at best, no more than a million horses. But the gap was even worse than that. The Soviet countryside did not evolve gradually in anticipation of the tractor, from small horse teams to bigger ones, as America did. The tractor was invented to solve an American agricultural need, of expensive horses, heavy agricultural machinery, and large farms. But here tractors were thrown into fields that had previously been arranged for the plow carried by a horse or two. The fields were too small and too widely spread. Thus there was a mismatch between tractor power and terrain. The tractor—created for America's open plains—was sent to find its way through the Russian marsh and forest. Tractors spent much of their time not actually carrying plows but instead getting into position to carry a plow: Robert Conquest mentions a machine tractor station near Kharkov where, in September 1933, the sixty-eight tractors spent 7,300 hours just getting to their fields (this is over three hours per tractor/day).[87] In real productive terms, then, each tractor was probably worth no more than a few horses.

Hence the plummeting of production following collectivization, with the ensuing cycle of state expropriation. By 1932, this cycle reached the point that, in Ukraine and southern Russia, not even the seed was left for next year's sowing. Just as the continuity of the life cycle had earlier been disrupted for horses, it was now disrupted for wheat—a biological as well as political chain reaction leading from one species to the next. Finally this chain reaction hit humanity itself. The year 1933 saw unprecedented total famine. The domesticated animals had it easy, as it were: they had people to kill them, early on in the famine. For the people themselves, this was horrific agony. Villages were deserted as everyone died or fled to beg for bread; swarming, skeletal beings tried to reach the cities, lying dead by the wayside; the bodies were no longer collected. A good clinical description of the effects of famine, as witnessed by a survivor, is worth quoting in some detail:

> The skin assumes a dust-grey tinge and folds into many creases. The person ages visibly. Even small children and infants have an old look. Their eyes become large, bulging and immobile. . . . Motive power is lost, the slightest motion producing complete fatigue. The essential functions of life—breathing and circulation—consume the body's own tissue. . . . Respiration and heartbeat become accelerated. The pupils dilate, starvation diarrhea sets in. This condition is already dangerous because the slightest physical exertion induces heart failure. It often takes place while the sufferer is walking, climbing the stairs, or attempting to run. . . . The patient now cannot get up,

nor move in bed. In a condition of semi-conscious sleep he might last about a week, whereupon the heart stops beating.[88]

In fact, it is clear that in 1933 much of Ukraine and southern Russia resembled the appearance—of which we are more familiar—of the liberated Nazi camps from twelve years later. Robert Conquest estimates that 11 million peasants died as a result of collectivization.[89]

Another difficult comparison, which I cannot avoid, is that between human and animal suffering. The main point is not moral but ecological. Consider the numbers: in 1928 the Soviet countryside had about 110 million people, 70.5 million cows, and 32 million horses. In 1933 it had about 100 million people, 38.4 million cows, and 17 million horses. The land was now completely pacified into submission, and grain would be allowed back for sowing for next year; but whereas the wheat cycle could quickly be resumed, human populations, together with the populations of domesticated animals, took much longer to revive. The shock of the loss of animals was not merely numerical but moral; the peasants felt alienated and lost in a new world, so different from that of the human-animal relationship that was the only one that made sense to them. P. S. Altonets, in an unpublished memoir, describes this eloquently—evoking, based on family tradition, his grandfather's life in exile following collectivization: "Grandpa could not find his . . . place. . . . [H]e woke up at nights, turning and sighing, again and again remembering his life. He remembered how he returned [to the village] and took care of the farm, how they bought four calves. The two small calves grew up and became fine steers, and the two small heifers—good cows. 'They were fine cows,' Grandpa said . . . aloud. . . . Pain and inescapable despair hit the . . . heart."[90]

Altonets's grandfather—who died soon afterward—never did return to live a life surrounded by cows. Nor would the entire Soviet Union. Finally, it did not get its hoped-for agricultural surplus, and the agricultural sector remained, instead, a major drag on the economy as a whole and one of the crucial factors hampering Soviet economic growth.[91] There is no doubt that this, at least, was not intended by Soviet planners. What was their mistake? This brings us to the heart of the question of the relationship between economic and environmental history—a relationship central to this book.

It is often suggested that Communism was such a failure in the countryside partly because Marx, a bookish townsman, was not attuned to the needs of agriculture.[92] This is true enough, but the real issue goes deeper than that. Marxism was lacking not merely in the understanding of agriculture but in the understanding of ecology and therefore of history itself. Marxism was primarily a theory of history—but of human history alone, whence—to a large extent—followed its failure. It was an extreme case of the modernist failure to understand humanity's place in nature.

Two assumptions regarding the countryside dominated the thinking of Soviet planners. First, the village—just like everywhere else—was a scene for class struggle, in this case between rich and poor peasants; second, nature and humanity were two separate domains, whose relationship could be reduced to the technical problem of gaining useful products from nature to serve humanity. (The first assumption was Marxism's original observation, and the second assumption was carried over into Marxism from the European Enlightenment.)

From these two assumptions, combined, the following project was shaped for Soviet agricultural policy: first, remove the richer peasants, and second, arm the poor with the technology that would allow them to conquer nature. This was the basic outline for collectivization.

Both assumptions failed to face the complex multispecies society of agricultural life. As Panarin's horse and Altonets's cows remind us, domesticated animals are not quite like machines—a mere property owned by humans. Animals are social beings; in short, they are like laborers themselves. The reason for this is that they are alive, and so they wish to go their own way. And so to make them do as their masters wish, some sort of social relationship has to be established. The sociology of the village encompasses not only the grandmother telling the grandchildren an old fairy tale, or the father giving his daughter away as bride. A human provides a mare with a lump of sugar; he strokes her; he beats her—all such acts are part of the social network that binds the village together, part of the daily exchange that sustains the power structure within the village and allows its continuing economic life. In short, the village is a multispecies society. This society is indeed based on an asymmetrical relation: animals either work for humans or are eaten by them. And yet, while asymmetrical, the relationship is not one-sided: in return for their labor and eventual death, the animals are given, while alive, some food and shelter.

Seen from this perspective, the absurdity of the notion of a "class struggle" in the countryside becomes obvious. There was nothing of the kind, in the Soviet village of the late 1920s. Quite simply, peasants did not exploit each other's labor. To see this, let us imagine two peasants, one somewhat successful and the other thoroughly poor. In Marxist theory, the successful peasant should have been doing better than the poor one through some exploitation of the poor's labor, but in fact, the poor did not work for the successful peasant. What in reality made the successful peasant do better was that he had access to more *animal* labor. The peasant made his living not by the surplus value produced by humans but by the surplus value produced by horses. The issue is simple: a horse could be made to make more grain than it ate itself, and this was where peasant surplus came from. This human/horse relationship was based on exploitation—but it was only through this relationship that the horse, too, could be provided for. It had no place in human society unless it was socialized into this regime of exploitation. This was the most significant social and economic relationship in the countryside, and it involved not simply humans with each other but humans with animals.

Considered purely as a human society, and abstracted from the multispecies society in which it was embedded, the village could no longer make sense. The Bolsheviks—who in all their reading of Marx and Engels had read nothing about the exploitation of horses—therefore saw a phantom village. An imaginary class struggle was superimposed on the village, with some peasants arbitrarily cast in the role of "kulaks." And what next? In typical Soviet brutality, the so-called kulaks were sent to exile and to the concentration camps. Further, it was imagined that animals, just like all other commodities, could simply be redistributed, and horses were taken away from their owners. This was understood as a policy of leveling property, but it was in reality a policy of destroying labor—animal labor. Taken away from the social institution of the peasant family, the horses simply died; they had no existence otherwise. And in this was precipitated the catastrophe of the Soviet village.

To be fair, this criticism of Soviet planners might perhaps be misplaced. In some ways, the catastrophe of the village did not trouble Soviet authorities so much. While the depth of the economic failure was probably not planned for, the genocide itself was planned or at least tolerated, and it did indeed frighten the countryside into submission. The overall outline of Soviet society emerging in the mid-1930s was basically that desired by Stalin. I will now move on to discuss this society—essentially founded on the concentration camp.

The essence of Soviet society was government control over space. The big towns, primarily Moscow, definitely succeeded in conquering the Soviet Union. It was for this reason that collectivization, if an economic disaster, was still a political success. The peasants came to live under the control of party officials in the *kolkhoz*. Even the destruction of horses became useful: it made the peasants less mobile. Even when some relaxation of the collectivization regime was allowed, so that peasants could have a small plot in their garden, typically with a cow (now an enormously valuable property), one strict rule remained: the peasants were never allowed back their horses. Thus the peasants had to beg the *kolkhoz* officials for the access to horses. Fitzpatrick reports a typical complaint by a peasant—that, in three years, the *kolkhoz* chairman never allowed him to use one of the horses to go to the hospital or to bring in firewood. (This was wrong, because according to the rules, peasants had to pay to use a horse for purposes such as going to market or visiting other villages, but to get to the hospital, they should get the horse for free.)[93] In short, the confiscation of the horses drastically limited the geographic horizons of the peasants; furthermore, it made them depend, for their mobility, on the representatives of the regime.

The destruction of the horses was just one aspect of the Soviet project of pinning the peasants down. The most important tool in this project was that of the internal passport. Here was another example of the Soviet regime as counterrevolution. Under the tsarist regime, one had to have an internal passport to register legally in a town; this was canceled by the democratic February Revolution and finally, in December 1932, reinstated. Everyone who could prove permanent residence and employment would get an internal passport, *unless he or she were peasants*. Without a passport, it was illegal to live in a town.

The two immediate consequences of the policy of internal passports were an exodus of the unemployed and the homeless out of the cities (300,000 from Moscow alone) and a future ban on any peasant mobility.[94] This was especially important now that famine had hit the countryside. Special vigilance was required, and the roads from Ukraine to Russia were blockaded to prevent the starving peasants from seeking food.[95] The system of internal passports, however, was not just a local response to the crisis of famine: it was a central feature of the regime. Every Soviet citizen, from now on, had his or her own special geography, specifying the places he or she was allowed to be in. The concentration camps existed as the limiting points of this new topology: the microcosm as the extreme form of the macrocosm.

A few, at the top of the regime, had access anywhere, but most citizens were limited to the village or (when fortunate) towns they were registered in. More than this: the permit to register as a resident in any given type of locality would be the very essence of Soviet life—a precious right, given and taken away according to the regime's pleasure. Exile was the basic punishment—a preliminary to more serious ones—and it was often imposed in a topological escalation. As an example, we may follow Osip Mandelshtam, some would say Russia's greatest poet of the age. Mandelshtam had written a poem that was explicitly against Stalin, and it was considered a miracle that he was not killed immediately. Instead he was exiled in 1934 to the distant northern settlement of Cherdyn; then suddenly this was commuted to the most lenient form of exile, the "minus twelve," where the exile could choose a town to register in, as long as it was not one of the largest twelve. (Mandelshtam chose Voronezh, a small town south of Moscow.) Then in 1937 came a brief period of confusion—was the sentence over? Mandelshtam went back to Moscow and was immediately transferred to the "one-hundred-mile radius"—that is, not allowed anywhere in the one-hundred-mile radius of the city. There was, in fact, an entire ring community of exiles just a hundred miles away from Moscow. Mandelshtam settled in the small village of Savelovo. This lasted a year, until 1938, when finally the logical conclusion was reached: exile was transformed to prison and concentration camp. Mandelshtam was sent to the Far East and died, apparently, not far from Vladivostok.[96] The topology is of the kind we are familiar with: first, the controlled have to themselves the plane, with the exception of the central points (this is the "minus twelve" stage), then the points reach out (this is the "one-hundred-mile radius"), until finally the controlled one is reduced to a single point, no more, where he is allowed (the concentration camp). Most often, victims of the regime did not move directly from freedom to concentration camp but, like Mandelshtam, passed through a regime of spatial limitation. The regime was shuffling people around. This "solitaire," as Solzhenitsyn calls it,[97] was replayed a million times.

Since everyone lived under the passport system, and since the passport system easily shaded into the restriction and exile system, which in turn easily shaded into prison and concentration camp, there was no clear gap between a world of the "free" and a world of the "imprisoned." To the contrary: everyone participated in this system of topological constrictions, so that everyone was enmeshed in a web whose center was in the camps. This microcosm and macrocosm duality was clearly perceived, and the camps' inmates used to refer to the "zone," meaning the compound area of an individual camp, and the "big zone," meaning the Soviet Union.[98] Both belonged to the same topology.

Let us consider again the smaller zones. There were, one will recall, 268,700 camp inmates in January 1932, already more than five times the number of three years before. The numbers were to rise much further, never to retreat until after Stalin's death in 1953—by which time there were 2.75 million inmates, in approximately five hundred labor colonies and some sixty large networks of labor camps.[99] What else could be done? The failure of collectivization and the accompanying Five Year Plan left the regime with many potential enemies, and few justifications. There was nothing left but terror. As it were, the tractors had failed, and barbed wire had to fill the breach.

V. E. Sollertinskiy, in an unpublished memoir, describes his arrival at the camp of Samarlag, a description that could be repeated millions of times over: "a high fence made of two rows of barbed wire [that is, there is an 'in-between' area between the outside and the inside of the camp], guard towers at the corners of the fence, barracks made of wooden boards and tarpaulin roofs, double beds along the walls of the barracks, pressed earth between the barracks—the place for existence [*mesto sushchestvovaniya*]."[100]

Rossi offers the general recipe for these places for existence.[101] Indeed, as in all such camps, inmates lived in wooden barracks. These had two-tier beds—either separate bunks, or sometimes simply a continuous wooden board through the length of the barracks. A typical barracks housed in this way between 120 to 240 prisoners, with about sixteen square feet per person. (This is typical of the Gulag: personal space is very constricted, but it does barely exist.) These barracks were surrounded, obviously, by barbed wire rectangles, though it should be mentioned that inside urban centers—there were camps there, as well—it was considered useful to hide the camp itself somewhat, and so wooden planks were added outside to cover the barbed wire perimeter.

The barbed wire perimeter itself was usually built of wooden posts with one-third of their length in the ground (the lack of iron posts is typical of the second-rate quality of the structures, even in this finished form). Those are from 2.5 to 6 yards high—depending on local conditions—and about 6 yards apart. Seven to fifteen rows of barbed wire are stretched horizontally between the posts; to these are added two diagonal strands between the two adjacent posts. It will be obvious that here, too, there is considerable savings on resources, with considerable gaps left between the strands of barbed wire. With, say, ten strands across the height of three yards, one can even envisage a very thin inmate—inmates would eventually become very thin—slipping through. Not that this would ever happen: as we have already seen in the prisoner-of-war camps, the inmates never actually got as far as the fence. There was a "prohibited strip" of up to sixty-six feet inside the fence, usually defined by a low barbed wire on posts about thirty inches tall: entering the area, as usual, would be punishable by shooting. In each corner of the camp there would be a guardhouse; usually built of wood, once again, it would be some three to four yards tall, roofed and enclosed chest high, but allowing unrestricted vision in all directions. When the corners were more than two hundred yards apart, there would be extra guardhouses built in between. The guards, as usual, would have machine guns. To make sure that the prohibited zone was clear from any motion, its surface had to be pristine; therefore it would be raked occasionally by inmates (given a special dispensation to enter this deadly zone). Typically—Russian climate being what it is—the prohibited strip would be covered with snow, which provided an ideal background for the detection of motion. Outside the perimeter, finally, there was a smooth wire line—here may come the only truly original architectural contribution of the Gulag—along which the chains of guard dogs would glide. Otherwise the structure is essentially the one made standard in World War I.[102]

The subject of dogs calls for brief comment. Dogs, indeed, may have been the only domesticated species to have benefited from the Soviet system. Solzhenitsyn titles the chapter of *The Gulag Archipelago* dedicated to the camp guards "The Dogs' Service," hastening to add, "Their service is the same as that of guard dogs, and their service is connected with dogs. . . . [T]here are whole officers' committees which monitor the *work* of an individual dog, fostering *a good viciousness*."[103] By day, guard dogs were constantly at the side of guards, accompanying prisoners to work and back. Robert Conquest reports that in Kolyma, "dogs—wolfhounds—were a constant presence. . . . They accompanied all marches and were trained on command to attack people in prison clothes. There are many tales of prisoners savaged, and sometimes killed. Their [i.e., the dogs'] rations were extremely good, better than that of the guards let alone the prisoners."[104]

In fact this was not a new use of dogs. Let us very briefly examine the practice. We have seen the cow, brought under submission, and the horse, cunningly exploited. Dogs are different, and more than any other domesticated species, they truly share in human practice. This does not reflect well on either dogs or humans. Wolves are predators with a keen sense of social hierarchy. In other words, they are as similar to humans as any animal can be. Violence and submission to authority are the ties that bind wolves and humans together. And so men have domesticated wolves, and they became dogs—humanity's accomplice in the control of species. Dogs serve either as hunters of prey (to be shared between humans and dogs) or—a role more important in agricultural societies—they serve as guards over other domesticated animals.[105] Essentially, then, the dogs in the concentration camps continue this role, with no more than a transformation in the identity of the herded animal: not sheep or cows but people. This is the significance of this excursus on dogs: they provide another example of the way in which, with the new asymmetry of power, prisoners in concentration camps approximate domesticated animals.

Dogs may have been the more expensive piece of investment in the Gulag; barbed wire, too, was difficult to get, at first. But, after all, we are dealing with the microcosm, the small spaces of the small zones, so barbed wire, ultimately, would not be a limiting factor. A small camp—say, the minimal square of 200 yards by 200 yards—would have a perimeter of 800 yards and so could be fenced in by, say, 10,000 yards or six miles of barbed wire (or about as many tons). In practice, of course, camps could be much bigger. We have a report of a request for barbed wire for the construction of fifteen special regime camps, in the middle of 1948, which called for *eight hundred tons* of barbed wire.[106] (These being special regime camps—for political prisoners alone—they might have required more barbed wire than usual.) Clearly the Soviet Union, with five hundred labor colonies and sixty labor camp complexes,[107] not to mention small subcamps and transit structures, would have had overall tens of thousands of tons of barbed wire in the Gulag. This may be compared to the fifty thousand tons laid across the American West and dramatically altering its face between 1874 and 1880; in both cases, continental areas came to be reshaped by barbed wire.

In this way, again, barbed wire was a tool of colonization. New spaces were opened up for human settlement—based on the barbed wire camp. The geographic significance of the Gulag must be stressed. Its forced labor served the basic project of the Soviet system—to bring Soviet space under control. First of all, as I have mentioned already, the prisoners had built the Gulag itself; and then, above all else, they were put to work on vast projects of *transportation*. Here was another dream of modernization thrown on the Soviet landscape.

As we have seen, in 1929 the Gulag was largely confined to a complex of camps around the Solovetsky Islands in the White Sea, and in its first years, northern European Russia, near the White Sea, was still the Gulag's geographic focus. Thus it was natural that the first major project of the Gulag—and the most famous of them—was the White Sea–Baltic Canal. The canal, in fact, neatly connected the Solovetsky with the city of Leningrad. It was built from 1931 to 1933, with as many as 140,000 prisoners working on the project simultaneously. (Many more were involved, as mortality was very high.) The goal of the experiment was to make prisoner labor profitable: that is, as little as possible was to be spent. The Soviet Union was to catapult itself into modernity, with the extreme exploitation of forced labor serving as the basis for capital accumulation. Thus the prisoners simply had no tools, not even wheelbarrows to carry the dug earth. Hundreds of miles of frozen earth were removed by the sheer labor of human hand and shoulder. Naturally, accommodation was completely improvised, and we are not surprised to hear that prisoners were sometimes left to sleep on the snow.[108] Following that came the Moscow-Volga Canal, the Volga-Don Canal, the Main Turkmen Canal, the Volga-Ural Canal, and others.[109] While there are exceptions to this, the canals were essentially cartographic achievements. That is, although real earth was moved, and, say, a picture from space would reveal a canal dug from sea to sea, this spatial picture was an illusion, a kind of Martian canal. The White Sea–Baltic Canal, for instance, was not only made on the cheap; it was also planned on the cheap: sixteen feet deep, which is just not enough for most vessels.[110] On the map, at least, one could show the Soviet Union transformed into a massively connected land, well ahead on the path to a modern economy.

Connecting lines had to be found everywhere to colonize space. It is reported that in 1947 Stalin had remarked—no doubt staring at a large map—that the "Russian People had long dreamed of having a safe outlet to the Arctic Ocean from the Ob River." So that was it: the dream was to be transformed into reality. Along the 800-mile stretch of this projected railroad (the Salekhard-Igarka line) more than eighty concentration camps were built. In the years leading up to Stalin's death, the inmates of these camps worked in temperatures as low as minus fifty-five degrees Celsius in winter, and the summer months teemed with mosquitoes.[111] (From Solovetsky times till the end of the Gulag, swamps and mosquitoes in summer seem to have caused the prisoners of the North even more anguish than the winter cold.) Yet the line was never completed. Today the taiga has overgrown the rails and the camps.[112] The area has a population density of 0.02 people per square mile.[113] In short, the abstractions of connecting lines were thrown on the map, regardless of realities such as climate, vegetation, and human geography. To say that Soviet planning was crazy is true but misses the point that, more essentially, the Soviet Union was engaged in *imitative modernization*. The Americans had tractors—so the Soviet Union had to have its own fleets of tractors, crossing the steppe. And since it was seen that modernization was everywhere based on a network of transportation, the imitation of such a network—regardless of its actual usefulness—came to be a goal in itself.

In truth, interconnecting the lands of the Soviet Union was a real challenge. It was not for nothing that tsarist Russia was left behind: the land is rich in resources, but they are scattered in space and hidden away in cold, wild lands. It was difficult to colonize such a space. I quote, for instance, from a British study published in 1934:

> In respect of Gold resources the Far East is practically a virgin country. Little serious prospecting has been done in this vast, wild and thinly populated area, and there is every reason to believe that a large number of rich gold-fields and lode deposits will be discovered there in the future. . . . It is obvious that the rich gold resources of eastern Siberia cannot be developed unless they are linked up with the industrial and agricultural centres of the Soviet Union by means of railways and roads. In present circumstances the heavy cost involved in the transport of foodstuffs, machinery, equipment, etc. allows only of the working of exceptionally rich alluvial deposits.[114]

Unknown to the British, the Gulag was already addressing this very problem. The main mining area was in the land north of the island of Sakhalin—a faraway land of permanent frost that could nowhere be reached by train. Prisoners would be sent as far as Vladivostok, then, and there carried by sea—packed into the holds of freight vessels—to this new land, Kolyma. I have mentioned already several migrations prompted by gold—to California, Alaska, Australia, and South Africa. Kolyma surpassed all previous such migrations. Three million people, perhaps more, were sent there as prisoners. Almost all died there (Mandelshtam, apparently, died en route).[115] Fundamentally, the work resembled that seen already: building camps and roads, and then turning up masses of frozen earth in search of gold. (The British study was wrong in this respect: little machinery was required, as much of the gold of Kolyma is in fact no more than a few yards below the frost, so that digging by hand was quite sufficient.) It took a few weeks in the mines to destroy the health of a strong man.[116] The usual structures were set up in this alien landscape: at least 125 camps, sometimes each with more than one site, so that Kolyma, overall, had hundreds of barbed wire settlements.[117] It should be stressed that in Kolyma (as in many other places in the Gulag) barbed wire served not so much to prevent escape as to simplify daily control. There was nowhere to escape to. This part of the earth was not yet prepared for any human life except that of the concentration camp.

It could equally have been a prisoner colony on the moon. It is typical that the few escapees had to live by scavenging on the outskirts of the Gulag, stealing into camp stores or from passing trucks; naturally, all were eventually captured.[118] Here was a human settlement where life—such that it was—was limited to the space within barbed wire fences.

Where did the Gulag inmates come from? The fundamental structure is well known: terror is contagious. Recall the fundamental principle, that imprisonment was *preventive*. This in itself was merely a continuation of the method of civilian internment, where enemy citizens were imprisoned by their host countries, not because they had done anything harmful but because, being alien, they could be suspected of harboring the *wish* to do something harmful. Enemy civilians are a clearly defined group; but once the same method is extended to the class war, it can no longer be contained by the realities of alien passports. For how would you know where to draw the line of suspicion? A handful of Soviet citizens—no more—were city workers, sons of city workers, and were themselves politically active; and they of course would be especially suspicious, for with their political activism, who knows what views they might have formed for themselves? Everyone was suspicious, then, and this was *logical*—for who was it, indeed, who wished the regime well?

Suppose, then, that you work for the secret police, and that you receive a denunciation against some chance person. Can you really ignore it? This would cast the shadow of suspicion on yourself. So the person must be arrested, and thereby—by the very fact of being arrested—he is certain to have become a potential enemy of the regime. Hence interrogation can yield nothing short of confession and incarceration. Confession gives rise to one new set of suspicions: all those people who were implicated in the prisoner's statement (a credible confession—the goal of both prisoner and interrogator—must involve not a single person but a full *conspiracy*). Incarceration gives rise to another new set of suspicions—everyone who can be assumed to sympathize with the prisoner, that is, his family and friends. Just as the confiscation of horses served to atomize peasant society, setting one village apart from another, so the terror atomized Russian society as a whole: the best defense was to have as few friends as possible (and to distance yourself—to the point of denouncing them—from your own family members, when they were tainted by suspicion). For example, it was known that if your name appeared in the address book caught among a prisoner's belongings, you would be imprisoned yourself; so prudence called for refraining from any correspondence. But even with all the prudence in the world, such an epidemic—transmitted, as it were, by human speech itself—could not be contained.[119] It could be fed by the slightest exposures: any contact with a foreigner, for instance, would be an immediate cause for suspicion, so that (this was one of the most amazing facts of the Soviet regime) the returning prisoners of war, liberated after World War II, were sent directly to the Gulag. They had seen the outer world![120]

It was at this moment of military crisis—during World War II and in its aftermath—that the function of control over nations became more important to Soviet repression. Russia, for instance, always had a large German community, in many ways closely integrated into Russian life. In 1941, of the 1,427,000 Soviet citizens of German ancestry, 1,209,430 were deported (an operation dwarfing, of course, the American internment of Japanese). Later in the war, as the Nazi armies were pushed back from Soviet territory, entire suspect nations were rounded up: first it was the Chechens, the Ingush, the Crimean Tatars, the Karachai, the Balkars, the Kalmyks, and then the Greeks, the Bulgars, the Armenians from the Crimea, the Meskhetian Turks, the Kurds, and the Khemshins of the Caucasus.[121] Prominent people were arrested, the rest put into exile in the Urals, Siberia, or central Asia. Essentially this was an operation of ethnic simplification. The Caucasus and the shores of the Black Sea had always had a complex mixture of peoples, which made them more difficult to control, and in 1943 and 1944, Stalin—himself a Georgian and therefore familiar with the area—set about to solve this ancient problem. Then the Soviet armies reached the Baltic countries and the West of Ukraine (areas that had only briefly come under Soviet control previously, following the pact between Stalin and Hitler in 1939). With their dangerous exposure to democracy in the interwar years, harsh measures were required: hundreds of thousands were imprisoned from these newly conquered lands.[122] In short, while sheer terror against the Soviet population as a whole always remained central to the Stalinist system, this new ethnic emphasis came to be more and more pronounced. Having accomplished the subjugation of the countryside as such, the regime was now reaching out to colonize the periphery—which, of course, included now a newly occupied Eastern Europe, as well. The "big zone" was now defined by the Iron Curtain—while still controlled from the zones of the concentration camps.

This project of controlling ethnicities—just because of their being different—reached its natural conclusion as the ethnicity of difference par excellence, that is, the Jews, became the main target. The last years of Stalin's life saw an anti-Jewish campaign, and it is often thought that Stalin was planning a mass deportation of the Jews before, on March 5, 1953, he died.[123]

Soviet leaders, fully aware of the contagious nature of terror—that had so often touched the leadership itself—now worked to contain it; they gradually achieved a retreat from Stalinism, and by the mid-1950s, the Gulag was so downscaled that it no longer was a major presence in the Soviet world. There were only eleven thousand political prisoners on January 1, 1959—fewer than at any previous time in Soviet history (though, of course, still many more than under the tsars).[124] In the years of its full operation, from 1929 to 1953, the Gulag had claimed some 12 million lives. I have hardly touched in this section on the horrors that preceded death through hard work, exposure, torture, and starvation.

The survival of the Soviet regime—mocked and hated by its subjects—for almost four more decades serves to mark the effectiveness of the Gulag as an instrument of control. Soviet society had been trained, by shock, and the very memory of barbed wire was sufficient to frighten it into submission. Barbed wire, then, could serve in the subjugation of people just as effectively as it could serve in the subjugation of animals. This, however, was not yet quite the most horrific achievement of barbed wire. While the concentration camps of the Gulag were often, in practice, death camps, they were not yet instruments designed primarily *for* slaughter. This final use of barbed wire—the most perfect approximation between human and animal histories—was left to the Nazis.

4. TRAINS TO AUSCHWITZ

Here is how the Nazis saw it: People were divided into races, struggling for space. This struggle reached its climax with the war between two antithetical races, Germans and Jews.

Germans were the landed people par excellence. They fought for their land and cultivated it. The main inspiration for the Nazis was, indeed, a historical fact: in the course of the Middle Ages, German-speaking people had gradually expanded the area of European agricultural cultivation eastward, often fighting for newly won lands. The Nazi aim for the future was to repeat this expansion so that, in the plains stretching east of Germany, a living space—Lebensraum—would be created for present-day Germans. I will begin, then, by stressing that Nazism was essentially a *colonizing* ideology. The goal—a typical twentieth-century goal—was to bring a certain space under complete control.

Here is where the Jews come in: control over this land could not be complete as long as it still harbored Jews. Since this people did not have a proper relation to a space for which it had fought and cultivated, it followed that their existence must have been parasitic upon that of the primary occupants of space. This biological metaphor of the parasite was articulated in myriad ways. Jews could be like bacteria, like maggots found inside wounds, like vermin, like rats, like wolves preying on sheep, like vampires feeding on blood, and so forth. In short, the Jews consumed and destroyed their host organism.[125] Thus a German space would ultimately be Jewish, unless the Jews were prevented from exercising their power of parasitic control. In other words, to obtain a German space called not only for a spatial push *outward*, toward the German Lebensraum, but also for a spatial push *inward*—making this space somehow *Judenrein*, clean of Jews. Thus these two Nazi catchwords, *Lebensraum* and *Judenrein*, represent the two sides of the same spatial exercise—the outward and inward pushes of the same drive.

We can immediately note that the Communists and the Nazis faced a similar problem. Both had to tackle enemies—either capitalists or Jews—that were not, to start with, limited to a single space. Hence, for both kinds of regime, the operation of concentration had a major importance. But we are pushing ahead. First of all—how did the Nazis get into a position to get their ideology into practice in the first place?

This is a difficult question. That an ideology as crude as Nazism could come to inspire a nation (and Nazism in Germany, unlike Communism in Russia, was truly popular) serves to show the extent that the German obsession with space had at the time. Indeed, the sense of borders—of struggling against external restriction—was palpable in interwar Germany. In World War I, German soldiers had pushed German control across borders—into Belgium, France, Russia. They stood there for four years of trench warfare. Then, for economic and strategic reasons—which were not visible to the ordinary soldier in the trenches—Germany collapsed. Instead of expansion, the war brought on contraction.

In 1919 the Treaty of Versailles redefined borders at Germany's expense. Germany's very spatial contiguity was lost: a Polish corridor to the Baltic Sea divided East Prussia from the rest of Germany. The Nazis' primary appeal was to those ordinary soldiers—the generation of Hitler himself—who felt cheated by Germany's failure to expand through their sacrifice.

The Versailles treaty, fully aware of the German potential for revenge, put Germany under a system of external controls: its army limited; part of its remaining land under temporary occupation; a regime of indemnities to tax its economy. Those indemnities were effectively imposed to pay for French and British war debts. Hence the curious global arrangement of finances throughout the 1920s. France and Britain paid the United States for their war loans; they collected the sum back, as indemnity, from Germany; Germany, in turn, financed its payments by borrowing from America. Financial arrangements are always a tightrope act, but this time the players were especially nervous: they knew how to play the system, assuming a stable London center, but now British finance itself was in disarray. It was a crisis of transition when the London-based system no longer worked, and the New York–based system was still being built. Thus when the New York stock market crashed in 1929, faith in the system failed. Panic set in; banks—beginning in Central Europe—went bankrupt as investors demanded their cash back. By 1931 the world economy was in collapse, and the ruling establishments were everywhere discredited.

In Germany this meant that the liberal and conservative parties lost all support; on the left, the Communist Party became dominant, and a Bolshevik-type takeover seemed a possible outcome. The one non-Communist alternative to the establishment was the Nazis themselves. The voters of the Right had always shared the Nazi desire to reverse the contraction of the Versailles treaty, and now, with the menace of the Great Depression on the one hand, and of Communism on the other, the extremism of the Nazis was no longer perceived as a drawback. The Nazis became the natural party of the Right, and by 1932 they were the dominant party in German politics.[126] On January 30, 1933, Hitler came to power.

The Nazis, unlike the Bolsheviks, entered power with genuine democratic legitimacy; like the Bolsheviks, the Nazis' primary goal was to establish strong centralized control on a permanent war basis. In many ways, the Nazi program was directly shaped by the experience of World War I. They were now, as they saw it, in the quasi-military emergency of a fight against the left wing. In World War I, the practice in Germany was to put dangerous civilians into "protective custody," or *schutzhaft* (as was done to the British citizens in Ruhleben). Now the same policy was adopted again, used systematically against the enemies of the regime.[127] On March 20, 1933, the first concentration camp of the Nazi regime was built near Dachau: it was a munitions factory, disused as a consequence of the Versailles treaty. (We see the usual reliance, in the initial stages of improvisation, on available structures such as empty factories.)[128] It took several weeks for the barbed wire to be found, finally, to enclose the new camp.[129] There was in general much improvisation as local Nazi authorities set up their own more or less private prisons and concentration camps, arresting tens of thousands of potential enemies of the regime in the spring and summer of 1933. (There is an official record of some 26,789 in protective custody on July 31.)[130] The prisoners were mostly left-wing activists, but it is difficult to generalize: since Germany did not reach its dictatorship through civil war, there were no prisoners of war, and all arrests were of the preventive kind with the typical outcome of the arbitrary definition of the "enemy," greatly differing from one place to the next.[131] Basic questions were left up in the air. For instance—this was typical of the Nazi takeover of power—there was a fundamental confusion about who had control over the prisoners. Did they fall under the control of state institutions, such as the police, or did they fall under the control of the party? By 1934, this debate was cleared: the camps belonged to a party institution, the SS, led by Himmler. Not that these camps, at this stage, were such an important element in the Nazi system of power. The

Nazis were successful, indeed popular. Terror was largely redundant. After the first onrush of arrests, inmates were gradually released, until by the end of 1936 there were only some 7,500 prisoners in the entire German concentration camp system. By August 1937 there were only four camps: Buchenwald, Dachau, Lichtenburg, and Sachsenhausen.[132]

The concentration camps had largely achieved, at this stage, their goal of subduing the enemies of the regime. Over the same years, Germany was refining another system of control over space. The problem was to prevent the Jews from having any influence inside Germany—to deny them access to all goods and all power. It was a massive project, and its implementation was once again largely based on local initiative. Friedländer quotes a Nazi report from the summer of 1935, when the process was already well advanced: "Bergzabern, Edenkoben, Hoeheinoed, Breunigweiler, and other places prohibit Jews from moving in and forbid the sale or real estate to them." (They were on the way to becoming *Judenrein.*) "Bad Toelz, Bad-Reichenhall, Garmisch-Partenkirchen, and the mountain areas of Bavaria do not allow Jews access to their health resorts. . . . [I]n Apolda, Berka, Blankenstein, Sulza, Allstadt, and Weimar, Jews are forbidden to attend cinema." Jews were prevented from the libraries at Magdeburg, from the tramways in Erlangen; and most of all, they were everywhere barred from the swimming pools (the sight of naked flesh was of tremendous concern to the biology-driven Nazi imagination).[133] We see here the first stage of topological exclusion, where the victims are barred from given points on a plane—the first step toward the ultimate exclusion inside limited points.

Even apart from explicit bans, social exclusion itself had geographic consequences. The Jewish community was gradually moving inside itself. Suppose your German customers boycott you: it would make sense to move to a neighborhood where there are more Jews. The Jewish community was always distinctly urban; now it was largely confined to a few urban centers. By 1939—when Austria was already part of the German Reich—more than half the Jews lived in just two cities, Vienna and Berlin.[134] Hence many small towns could become *Judenrein*, and in effect the topology began to be inverted against the Jews. They were no longer excluded *from* defined places, but, effectively, excluded *into* defined places. Furthermore, violence against Jews was endemic, so that prudence would dictate self-limitation to the areas considered safe. Violence on a local initiative was finally taken up on a planned, large-scale level, in the Kristallnacht (November 9, 1938). A centrally planned pogrom was launched against all Jewish communities; in its wake, Jewish life was made much harsher. On December 6, 1938, for instance, Berlin Jews were barred from *all* theaters, cinemas, cabarets, concert and conference halls, museums, fairs, exhibition halls, and sport facilities, as well as from (obviously) public and private bathing facilities; so far, enclosed spaces, so that the plane as such was still open, but then Jews were also barred from the center of Berlin: "the Wilhelmstrasse from the Lepizigstrasse to Unter den Linden . . . the Vossstrasse from the Hermann-Göring-Strasse to the Wilhelmstrasse, the Reich commemorative monument including the Northern pedestrian way."[135]

It almost seems more logical to move, at this stage, to the positive definition of a limited space to which Jews are still allowed. However, as Göring had complained to party members as far back as 1935, "We do not have any island to which we could transport them. We have to take this into account."[136] In other words, German spatial poverty was so acute that it did not allow even for the setting apart of some reservation for the Jews. Thus two possibilities seemed to be open: either to acquire much more space, where even the Jews could be accommodated in some kind of reservation (this apparently was still the ultimate goal), or in the meanwhile, one could get rid of the Jews. Jewish emigration was encouraged —this, indeed, was one of the main goals of the exclusion system. Germany and Austria had, in 1933, some 750,000 Jews; by 1939, 330,892 remained. This mass migration—especially in its highly accelerated stage in 1938 and 1939—led to pressures elsewhere. One consequence was especially noteworthy. The Swiss police, finding it difficult to monitor the nation's borders against refugees, was asking German authorities for some way of identifying German Jews (otherwise they could pass as Germans and pretend to be tourists). Responding to the Swiss request, all Jewish passports were marked in October 1938 by the letter *J*. Here begins the process of branding the Jews to define them, symbolically, away from European society.

The range of German operations was now, indeed, European: the outward push had already begun. The sequence of events is familiar: on March 13, 1938, Austria was annexed to the Reich; on October 6, Germany took over (with French and British agreement) parts of Czechoslovakia; and on March 15, 1939, it took the rest. Now, finally, France and Britain committed themselves to the defense of Poland, should it become the next target—which of course it did. Hitler demanded the restitution of contiguity between Germany and East Prussia; Poland resisted; Stalin quickly agreed to participate in the dismemberment of Poland. So on September 1, 1939, World War II started, and by the end of September, the western part of Poland was under German control.

At this point, the basic tension between the two Nazi goals —Lebensraum and *Judenrein*—came to the fore. Four hundred thousand Jews were pushed out between 1933 and 1939; and 2 million Jews were now acquired, in three weeks of fighting, in the part of Poland occupied by Germany. They were spatially spread out, in a network reaching from Warsaw itself (with 400,000 Jews) to many small towns and villages. Thus the spatial problem was posed in a much starker form than previously—and now this problem had to be addressed at a time of war. Thus even more drastic measures were called for, of spatial control over a population perceived as hostile and dangerous. Plans were improvised from September 1939 onward. A part of Poland was to be annexed to Germany straightaway: all the Jews were to be expelled from there into the remaining western part of Poland, called the Generalgouvernement. (This expulsion applied to Poles as well: the Nazis were creating a purely German Reich, and all non-Germans were affected.) Gradually the Nazis decided to add to this the expulsion of Jews from Germany itself, with the aim that the entirety of the Jewish population would be concentrated in the Generalgouvernement. So far, this was concentration on a large scale: inside the macrocosm of German-controlled territory, only a small segment was to allow Jews. But then, even in the remaining segment, the Jews had to be controlled somehow. In Poland, unlike Germany, Jews had a significant presence in the countryside, posing the usual difficulty, for their oppressor, of controlling a population spread across an entire domain. Hence another act of concentration was called for, now on the small scale of the microcosm. Inside the Generalgouvernement, all Jews were to be concentrated inside ghettos, or small enclaves inside a few urban areas. The order was that these must be situated at railway junctions, which suggests perhaps a plan for future evacuation, but would also make sense for facilitating the concentration at hand (most internment camps in the past were situated according to the railway).[137] Indeed, the policy would be depicted by the Nazis as continuous with past internments, and the secret order for setting up the ghettos stated that "the reason to be given for the concentration of the Jews in the cities is that Jews have played a major part in ambushes and plundering [against the German army]."[138] That is, the ghettos were to be presented as a standard policy of control over enemy population in wartime.

The sheer numbers involved made relocation to concentration camps, Boer-like, impossible, hence the concentration *within* urban areas. This is reminiscent of the Cuban evacuation of the rural population into the towns; but here, unlike Cuba, the concentration was to have a clear spatial definition. Ghettos were physically defined inside the towns. The concentration camp practice was simply moved into an urban setting. For instance, in February 1940, 160,000 Jews were moved into the ghetto of Lodz (set up in neglected districts of the town, whose non-Jewish population was in turn evacuated); a barbed wire fence was set up to surround the ghetto, and from May 1 onward, the police were ordered to shoot Jews approaching the fence.[139] Materials—and especially labor—were plentiful, and so the ghettos would typically be surrounded with more permanent structures, usually a brick wall with barbed wire on its top.[140] It should be noted that with more than 2 million inmates in all the ghettos, the system reached, immediately, the scale of the Gulag. And this system was qualitatively different from the Gulag: now, barbed wire encompassed an entire human group.

Everything was done to mark and isolate the Jews. At the same time as the ghettos were being set up, the Jews were also more explicitly branded: on November 23, 1939, they were required to wear a band with a Star of David. This somewhat absurd redundancy—concentrating all the Jews in a single space, and then marking them all—was in fact typical. The Nazis simply used any kind of violence and control they could envisage, so that the Jews were persecuted many times over.

What would happen inside these new areas of concentration? The danger was obvious—epidemics, which, indeed, were a major concern for German planning. This, incredibly, was a reason adduced *for* setting of the ghettos. After all, the entire persecution of the Jews was perceived as a kind of public hygiene campaign. Since the Jews were understood on the model of the "parasite," it was natural to conceive of them as carriers of disease. To cordon off the Jews was not merely an act of military control but also an act of *biological* control. The ghettos were understood, in this context, as a kind of preventive quarantine, set up to make sure that the Jews would not cause a wider epidemic. Once again, we see barbed wire as a medical implement, though in this case—unlike the British practice in South Africa—it was designed to protect the outside of the perimeter from disease emanating from the inside, rather than to protect those who are on the inside the perimeter. So that was the policy: the Jews were thrown inside the ghettos in conditions of extreme overcrowding (7.2 persons per room in the Warsaw ghetto).[141] Hygiene failed: in Warsaw, for instance, the sewage system collapsed in the winter of 1941–1942, so that human excrement had to be dumped in the streets.[142] The Jews were made destitute and totally dependent on minuscule shipments of food from the outside: for example, a daily shipment of one-third of a pound of potatoes per person—potatoes being the major source of nutrition—in Lodz, in February 1942.[143] Soon enough, typhus, typhoid fever, dysentery, and other epidemics became common—as if to justify the original German fears.[144]

Compared to other structures of mass internment, the Polish ghettos persisted for a relatively long period, about three years (the system was extended to certain areas occupied from the Soviet Union and came to hold most Jews from the Reich itself). In this period, about one-fifth of the Jews in the ghettos—roughly half a million—had died.[145] Since the conditions were much worse than in any previous structure of this kind, it might be asked why mortality was not even higher. Perhaps the relevant consideration is that the inmates—unlike the Cubans or the Boers—were mostly urban and thus already exposed to the diseases endemic in Poland. Much should be said for the efforts of the Jewish community itself; if nothing else, the Jews had plenty of physicians. At any rate, while mortality in the ghettos was very high, it could not in itself answer the Nazi need for getting rid of the Jews.

Alternatives were constantly being discussed. The main idea remained that of the Jewish reservation, and there was even thought that perhaps now, with the new Polish domain, a space could be found in which to cordon off the Jews. An area south of Lublin was briefly considered for such a Jewish reservation, and in 1940, some 95,000 Jews were transported there, but then the program was dropped—this, after all, was still too close to Germany itself.[146] Indeed, concentrations of enemy populations could not be allowed along dangerous borders, and the Nazis were already considering future plans against the Soviet Union. So where could the Jews be sent?

At this point, a certain misconception has to be cleared: the Nazis never did like the idea of concentrating the Jews in Palestine. Since so many Jews wanted to go there, the Nazis reasoned that there had to be some catch. Generally speaking, the standard anti-Semitic assumption—from *The Protocols of the Elders of Zion* onward—was that the Jews were planning to take Palestine as a center for some plan of world domination.[147] So, no: the Jews had to be sent somewhere they did *not* want to go. We recall Göring, bemoaning in 1935 the absence of an island to which the Jews can be deported: this was a consequence of the Versailles treaty, which had removed Germany's colonial possessions (Göring would have known: his father was the administrator of one of Germany's colonies in Africa, that of present-day Namibia.) One of the Nazi war aims was to rebuild this colonial empire, and with France defeated in the summer of 1940, this aim seemed within reach, with a suitable Jewish island as a bonus. The plan was formed to have all European Jews deported to the (as yet) French colony of Madagascar. Enormously distant, surrounded by ocean, this island seemed to offer sufficient protection from the Jews, even to the Nazi mind. Here, however, the German outward push began to hit the barrier of reality. The victory over France did not end the war. Britain was still fighting—and was still in control of the seas. The great naval evacuation to Madagascar was impossible, and other solutions had to be found.[148]

The outward expansion—frustrated by Britain—was now resumed in the East. On June 22, 1941, the German army invaded the Soviet Union. Many scholars believe that the Nazis, at this stage, waited for the breakdown of Soviet resistance, so that in the vast areas opened up, a Jewish reservation could finally be formed. Thus the solution of the Jewish problem was near at hand. In many other ways, this was the climactic moment for the Nazi imagination: the East was opened in the great battle waged against the forces of Bolshevism (supposedly the essence of the Jewish menace). This extreme war called for extreme ways of dealing with a conquered enemy.

At first, indeed, vast territories were taken, together with millions of prisoners of war. For this, the German command was prepared, issuing the appropriate commands in advance: "The members of the Red Army—including prisoners—must be treated with extreme reserve and the greatest caution since one must reckon with devious methods of combat. The Asiatic soldiers of the Red Army in particular are devious, cunning, and without feeling."[149] Hence the prisoners of war had to be put under a very strict regime.

World War I had standardized the procedure of controlling prisoners of war, and the first stage would be to herd the newly captured prisoners into a temporary pen: a field surrounded by barbed wire. Signaling the radical new departure of this war, the German army now made this structure permanent. The prisoners of war were left—without any shelter—inside a simple barbed wire perimeter (surrounded, of course, by guards armed with machine guns). This was the simplest barbed wire structure possible. An eyewitness describes a camp near Chelm (Poland) with some 150,000 prisoners: "Thick mud, in which the prisoners must sleep, without even a handful of straw. Food is worse than poor. The prisoners are actually dying of hunger and eat grass, straw and odd bits from the refuse heap. An epidemic of dysentery is spreading."[150] (Do remember, incidentally, that those prisoners who managed to survive and finally return to the Soviet Union were, without exception, sent to the Gulag.) Meanwhile the Jews in the newly captured areas fared even worse. Once again the theory was promulgated that the Jews would be the primary instigators of guerrilla war against the army of occupation, and so they were to be killed in a *preventive* act of antiguerrilla warfare. Mobile killing units reached the towns and villages as they were captured. The Jews were picked out of the population. For the guerrilla fighters that they were supposed to be, the Jews were phenomenally naive. Essentially, they were simply told to congregate—and did so. (The Soviet experience taught submission—while leading to believe that anything, even the Nazis, would be better than the past.) Then they would be marched off to some area just outside town, made to dig a ditch, stand next to it, and then were gunned down. When all were dead, the ditch was covered.[151] Certainly more than a million Jews were killed in this way.

So far we see a gradual escalation of violence, tied to a gradual escalation of the German war effort. At this stage we reach a certain turning point, marking the beginning of the Final Solution itself. The sequence of decisions and events is shrouded in mystery, but the fundamental outline is clear. First of all, the outward push against the Soviet Union failed. Large areas were conquered, but the Soviet army continued in its resistance. As usual, the invaders found that the Russian plains were too wide, too underdeveloped, to be effectively controlled. On the other side, even though Soviet losses were indeed immense, the Soviet regime did, in a sense, prepare for just this crisis. It had attempted the modernization, however poorly conceived, that had failed Russia in World War I. If nothing else, the Soviet Union did have all those tractor factories—which were now turning out tanks. And by the fall of 1941, the German army was blocked. So what was to be done with the Jews? The East, still a war zone, could not accommodate a Jewish reservation. Furthermore, with such a dangerous turn in the front, the rear had to be controlled with even greater strictness. In short, since the Jews of Europe could not be removed *out*, they had to be removed *away*: killed.

Now, an obvious option could have been to shoot all the Jews. This would have been an extension, inside Central Europe, of the method adopted in the areas conquered from the Soviet Union. The advantages of this method are obvious. It called for very little labor: there were altogether four mobile killing units, with about six hundred to one thousand members in each; that is, altogether less than one-tenth of a percent of the German army of invasion was purely dedicated to the killing of the Jews. Few resources were required, as well: the violence being so naked, there was no need for any special construction, the main tools being those of mobility and violence—trucks and machine guns—all widely available. So why did the Nazis not follow this method for the Final Solution? This is a difficult question, which I will try to address later on, but the main reason seems to be clear: the Nazis did not set up a new apparatus for controlling mass populations, because they had one in place already. By the time the Final Solution was decided on, in late 1941, the SS concentration camp system was already well developed, and it was in a position to claim its place in the new project of genocide. Once again, barbed wire was used, primarily, because of its very availability.

Let us return to follow the history of the SS camps. When we considered them last—in 1937—they were at their lowest point: four camps, with a mere population of 7,500 inmates in "protective custody" (this term, incidentally, was never dropped). The terror regime in Nazi Germany itself was relatively relaxed then—as it would remain almost until the end (only in the summer of 1944, as the war was obviously lost, did the Nazis lose their popularity, and real terror was started). But already in 1937, Himmler saw ways of developing the SS camps. By late 1937 a new policy was put in place of using the camps as bases for forced labor. Their main function would be the excavation of building materials for the new construction projects of Nazi architecture. Brickyards were founded in Sachsenhausen and Buchenwald, and new camps were set up, eventually, at the granite quarries of Flossenbuerg, Mauthausen, Gross-Rosen, and Natzweiler. Granite was the gold of this small Kolyma; one must imagine for oneself the horror of the forced labor of cutting and carrying heavy rocks. Since the new expansion had a clear economic rationale, camps were rebuilt and redesigned on larger scale, and the advanced structure of the Nazi concentration camps emerged at this stage. (I will immediately return to describe the architecture of the SS camp.)

Resources were available, but where would the inmates come from? This was a problem in 1937, and Himmler had to arrange, at first, for common criminals to be sent to the camps. Soon the inmates would be found: the outward expansion of the Reich, with its escalation of violence, brought new victims of political repression (the best kind of prisoner for forced labor). The original regime of terror imposed on Germany in spring 1933 was repeated in Austria in the spring of 1938, and then, in the fall of the same year, in the newly acquired Czech territories; then some ten thousand Jews were arrested as part of the Kristallnacht pogrom of November 9, 1938. By the beginning of the war, there were already 25,000 prisoners in the SS system. With the war itself, their numbers grew much further. First came internment proper: enemy civilians, residing in Germany, sent to concentration camps.[152] Further, previously arrested enemies of the regime were now rearrested as a measure of precaution.[153] Across Europe, Resistance fighters were sometimes sent to German concentration camps (instead of being shot on the spot); so were prominent citizens of conquered lands, arrested on the standard preventive basis.[154]

Of course, outside the SS system, Germany also had many prisoner-of-war camps. Some were genuine camps, built on the World War I model: this is where western prisoners of war were kept. Others were the death traps for Soviet prisoners, mentioned earlier. Gradually many Soviet prisoners of war trickled from their camps into the SS concentration camps, especially under the pressure of labor shortage (it did not make sense just to let them die in their barbed wire pens without being exploited).[155] By the beginning of 1942 there were thus already about 100,000 prisoners in the camps, and the infrastructure of the system was already greatly expanded. Many new camps were set up, growing in size. Auschwitz was an extreme case. This new camp—lying on an important rail junction in the part of Poland annexed to the Reich—was planned on a massive scale, with the capacity for accommodating 200,000 inmates. (This building program was never completely achieved, but even so, the Auschwitz complex did hold, at its peak, more than 100,000 inmates simultaneously: many more, of course, passed there.)[156]

We see, once again, how availability affects the growing uses of barbed wire. The Final Solution called for arresting and killing a very large number of people in a relatively short time. The SS could make a credible claim to be able to do this. Why? Because the SS had available to it the infrastructure and experience—accumulated for the different purposes of terror and forced labor. One function led to another: barbed wire had already become a standard tool for terror and forced labor, and mass killing looked sufficiently similar in character to allow an extension of the same tool.

I now move on to discuss the death camps. The system is in some senses not unlike previous ones discussed in the book. Once again, centers of barbed wire served to control space on a massive scale as, across Europe, a system was created with the death camps in its center. The main feature of this practice was a total asymmetry between the powerful and the powerless, so that many parallels emerge with human control over animals. To put this crudely, but precisely: the Jews in Europe were controlled with the same efficiency earlier reserved for such animals as the cows in the American West.

There were two aspects to this practice: life and death. Both were extraordinary. I will describe them briefly, in order.

Life inside the death camps was constrained by extreme spatial limitations, marked, as we have seen already, by a camp system that was relatively rich in resources. The basic model was obtained in Buchenwald in 1937 and essentially repeated in the death camps themselves. The camp would be surrounded by electrically charged barbed wire (the redundancy of electric charge *and* barbs is very typical of the Nazi regime, of violence multiplied by itself). Guardhouses were built every 250 feet—much denser than the Gulag, then, with its 200 yards between one guardhouse and the next. Floodlights illuminated the entire compound by night. The main feature we notice is a relative abundance of resources. As a consequence, it is not surprising to find that the compound was divided *internally* by further lines of barbed wire. The SS camp was like a Mondrian picture, a rectangle divided and subdivided into smaller rectangles of varying sizes, always defined by heavy barbed wire.[157] Space was heavily curtailed and defined, always through barbed wire: this was no Vorkuta, with its barbed wire shortage.

And this must be stressed: for the inmates of the SS camps, barbed wire was not a trivial detail. It was the unique defining feature of their landscape. Sofsky uses the following quotation from a survivor as motto for his description of camp space: "We're separated from each other by barbed wire. The Germans evidently have a very special affection for barbed wire." This is a correct observation; the same was noticed already in World War I trenches and prisoner-of-war camps, in both of which the Germans were superior in the use of barbed wire. "Wherever you go, barbed wire. But you gotta give credit where credit's due: the quality's good, stainless steel. Densely covered with long barbs." This is "vicious" barbed wire: "Barbed wire horizontally, barbed wire vertically."[158] It should be added that the fences were particularly tall (in Auschwitz, for instance, thirteen feet high):[159] horizons were literally limited so that even the sky would be dominated by an ever-present barbed wire.

As explained in the quotation from Sofsky, barbed wire fences were, routinely, thickly arranged as a thick lattice pattern; they were then arranged together—as noted earlier—to form larger structures of camps within camps. Belzec, the first specially designated death camp, was gradually built from February 1942 onward: a near-square structure of 265 by 275 yards of which, eventually, two small rectangles were carved out to form special areas for accommodation and extermination, all surrounded by barbed wire (see map 8).[160] Sobibor, a death camp constructed in March and April 1942, was a more complex structure (see map 9).[161] Of a rough rectangular shape defined by three layers of barbed wire, it was then internally divided into four camps, two of which were surrounded by their own barbed wire perimeter. Inside these minicamps, certain barracks were set apart by having their own barbed wire to surround them—a camp within a camp within a camp. A further barbed wire construction, winding its way between all those camps and minicamps, was a "tube," namely, two lines of barbed wire enclosing a narrow road, leading from the train station to the gas chambers.[162] (I will discuss this structure in greater detail when describing the process of death in the camps.) This Sobibor architecture was the model followed, almost exactly, in the next specially designated death camp, Treblinka (see map 10):[163] so now a standard was formed. It must be stressed that the entire Sobibor rectangle was no more than 400 by 600 yards in size; in the death camps, space was extraordinarily constricted, the horizons of life limited to the few yards between one barbed wire layer and another.

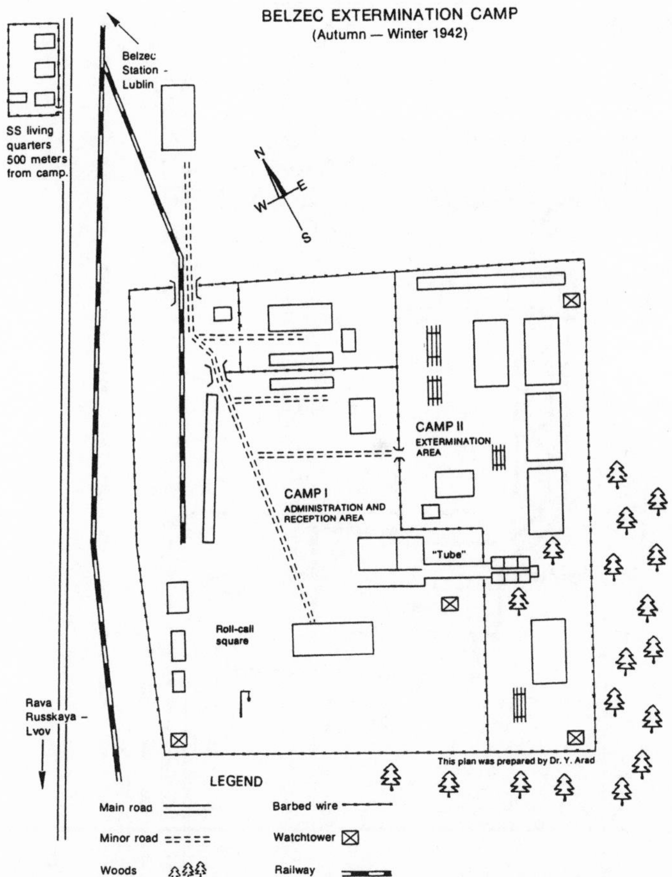

MAP 8 *Belzec Camp, fall–winter 1942. Reproduced from Arad 1987, 437. Reprinted with permission, Indiana University Press.*

Auschwitz itself was not a specially designated death camp, being simply the largest SS camp that was gradually transformed to participate in Jewish genocide. The camp was therefore of massive size, with 440 acres enclosed within barbed wire. Yet the same constriction of space held. The main living space at the subcamp of Birkenau was divided (by a simple grid pattern of six by two) into twelve smaller subcamps; added to that were many specially designed areas and barracks defined by their own perimeters, for

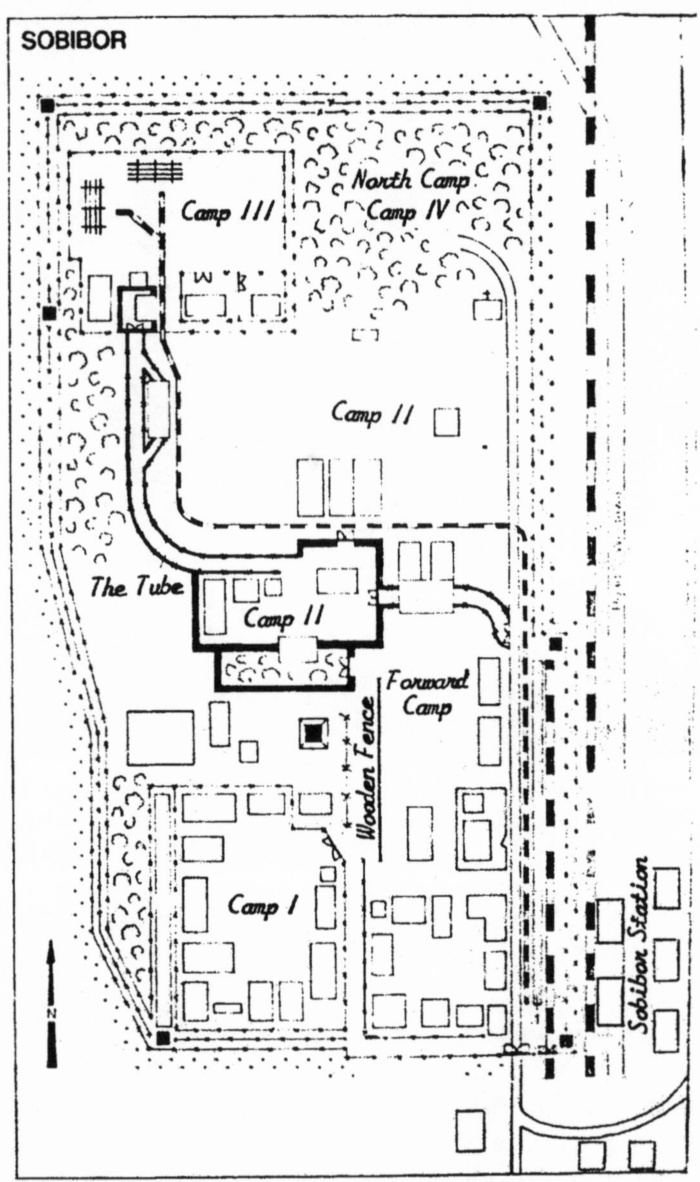

MAP 9 *Sobibor Camp.*
Reproduced from Arad 1987, 35. Reprinted with permission, Indiana University Press.

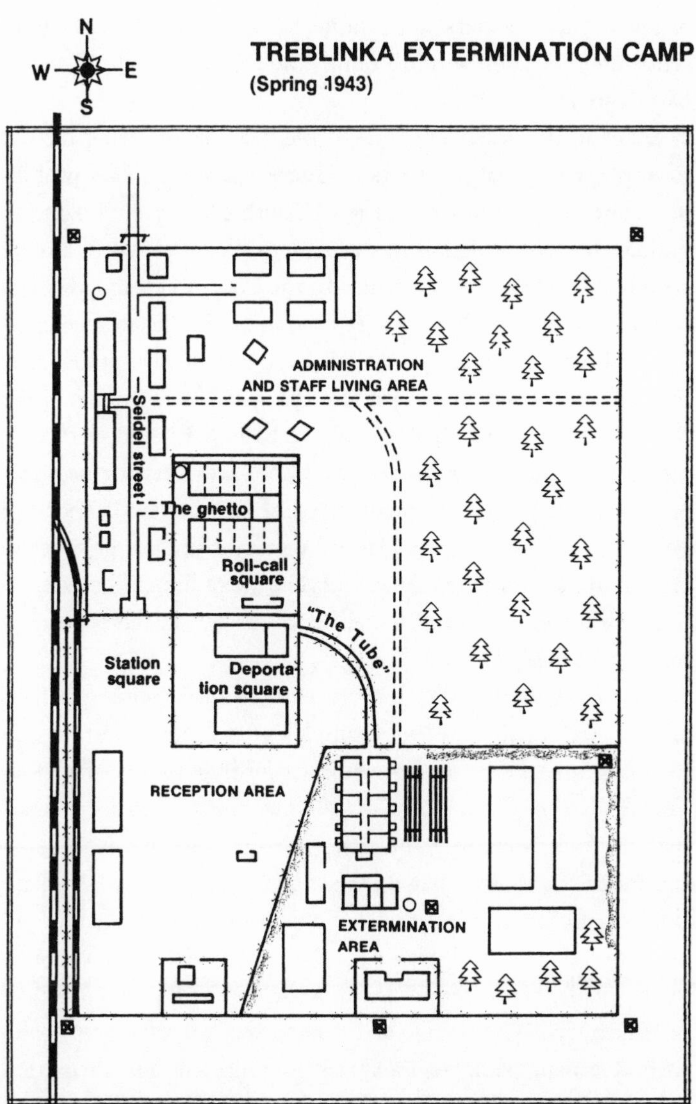

MAP 10 *Treblinka Camp, spring 1943.*
Reproduced from Arad 1987, 39. Reprinted with permission, Indiana University Press.

instance, the prisoners' quarantine to which sick inmates were sent—another camp within a camp (and another "medical" use of barbed wire).[164]

Many of the practices of life in the death camps went further to emphasize spatial constriction. There was the standard prohibited zone next to the external fence. With space overall being so limited, however, this too was enormously constricted to a mere strip of a few feet near the fence. In the early SS camps, this was still marked by a low barbed wire barrier, but in the advanced system, the prohibited zone was left as a completely symbolically defined area. It should be seen that the spatial constriction of the prohibited zone, and its eventual symbolic definition, served to *intensify* its presence. Prisoners could not avoid getting near this zone—and so lived in constant dread of crossing the barrier and being shot. (It was a game played by guards: order a prisoner to cross into the prohibited zone, and then shoot him.) The external fence emanated an area of lethality, obscurely and therefore even more terrifyingly defined.[165]

The space left for life itself was extraordinarily circumscribed as well. We recall the many examples of prisoners' barracks, in previous internment camps, built according to the model of military barracks. The same was followed in the main enlargement of Auschwitz, with the difference that—to save expenses—the model used was that of German *military stables.* Military stables were always designed for quick, cheap construction (an army would often find itself with the need to house many horses in the field); hence they were appropriate for the new building in Auschwitz. Their original capacity was for fifty-two horses each. German planners took this to represent the theoretical capacity for 550 men, and then—simply to accommodate more prisoners—the capacity was revised upward to 744. In practice there were often a thousand prisoners or more inside a single barracks. (I will discuss the ratio of human to animal space when discussing the cattle cars leading to the concentration camps.) Prisoners were packed closely together on their bunks.[166] This is the logical conclusion of the project of concentrating the Jews: less and less space was allowed to be used by Jews until the point, as Primo Levi explains, that “to have a bed companion of tall stature is a misfortune and means losing hours of sleep.”[167] It was impossible to move anywhere without hitting another body. The only personal spatial presence left to the prisoners—as long as they lived—was that of their own flesh.

Even this flesh, however, was no longer their own. Especially in Auschwitz, Jewish prisoners were now bodily marked. This practice had antecedents in the symbolic marking of clothing. Thus, for instance, from their very beginning, the SS camps articulated a complicated symbolic system of cloth strips sewn to the uniform. This heraldic system signaled various types of prisoners: a red triangle for a political prisoner, pink for homosexual, yellow for Jewish (which could then be combined to form Stars of David with two triangles: red on yellow for Jewish *and* political, pink on yellow for Jewish *and* homosexual, etc.).[168] Added to this, prisoners' numbers would be sewn to their clothes. (The same was done in the Gulag.)[169] The inmates of Auschwitz—not, however, those who were immediately sent to die—were under a similar symbolic regime, now attached not only to the clothes but to flesh itself. This was done by a kind of needled stamp. A combination of characters (standing for the prisoner's type) and numbers (representing the prisoner's serial number) were combined on the stamp; the stamp was then impressed into the prisoner's flesh. In early days, this wound was inflicted on the chest; later, the left arm was preferred. A dye was then rubbed into the wound, and a permanent sign resulted.[170] This branding—strictly speaking, tattooing—had a practical function in that it imposed yet another obstacle on any planned escape, yet another tool for tracing the fugitive. It was for this reason that slaves and animals had always been branded (as, for instance, we have seen in the American South). But it also served symbolically to sever the prisoner from a sense of control over his or her own body.

Escape was hardly an option anyway. The basic reason for this is simple: escapes from camps demand time and energy—which the prisoners did not have. British prisoners of war during World

War II were still playing the World War I game of digging tunnels, being caught, sometimes even succeeding;[171] but the inmates of the death camps spent their days in unending labor, trying as best they could to sleep the few hours they were allowed to. This labor illustrates, more than anything else, the total asymmetry of power between masters and prisoners. Even in the Gulag, labor was extracted not only by violence but also by incentives. There were different food rations, depending on the different fulfillment of work quotas (this was a continuation of Soviet practices outside the Gulag):[172] one worked, in the main, because of the carrot, not the stick. It is rare indeed to have human labor extracted by sheer violence, even in slave societies. But this was precisely the practice at Auschwitz. Primo Levi describes this with great elegance. Levi and his coworker struggle to carry a wooden sleeper weighing 175 pounds, and he notes on the experience: "I bite deeply into my lips; we know well that to gain a small, extraneous pain serves as a stimulant to mobilize our last reserves of energy. The Kapos also know it: some of them beat us from pure bestiality and violence, but others beat us when we are under a load almost lovingly, accompanying the blows with exhortations, as cart-drivers do with willing horses."[173] Of course, a horse (unlike the Auschwitz inmate) may get a piece of sugar, say, in return for his labor, but the comparison is illuminating. There is nothing in the world that could rationally convince a starved, doomed man that it is in his best interest to carry a weight of 175 pounds. Reason fails as a way of extracting labor, and violence must take its place. Thus the divide between human and animal labor disappears: labor is no longer based on any kind of exchange, or on verbal promises and threats. It is instead extracted, by force, from the victim—the way it is extracted from animals.

An even more extreme example of this asymmetry of power was yet another form of violent control: the medical experiment. Now, when we say that, for example, the Nazis used inmates as human guinea pigs, the operation appears simpler than it really is. We take it for granted that a certain animal is naturally used for experiments, and all the Nazis needed to do was to break a certain moral barrier and cross from the guinea pig to the human. However, even the guinea pig is not naturally a subject of experiments. The point I am making is historical, not ethical: to create the laboratory animal, a certain structure of power needs to be put into place. To begin with, the animal must be prepared to reach a "background" biological condition against which the experiment will test it; then everything about it must be monitored, and it can be allowed no action that might interfere with the experiment itself. Without these preconditions, we cannot have the intensive, precise control that a scientific experiment requires. In Auschwitz, we see considerable resources (relatively speaking) expanded on the biological preparation of subjects for experiments. A small selection of inmates—of whom the largest contingent was that of twins—were reasonably fed, before experimentation (for this reason, a relatively large number of victims of experimentation survived). Detailed documentation, such as blood tests and x rays, were taken daily. Then the experiments took place: for instance, inmates would have color agents injected into their eyeballs. (Dr. Mengele, the chief physician at Auschwitz, had a special interest in eye color. It should be said that experiments were mostly designed to develop methods of sterilization and were even more ghastly.)[174] The newly available experimental subjects were seen as a valuable asset. Hilberg recounts an example: "Dr. Dohmen of the Army Medical service wanted to do research on jaundice; so far, he had only injected healthy animals with virus from jaundiced humans, but now he wanted to reverse the process and inject humans with virus from diseased animals."[175] On the whole, while affording an extreme example of the extreme power assumed by Nazis over their inmates, medical experiments did not have a significant presence in the camps. Experiments are inherently expensive, and the camps, while much richer in resources than the Gulag, were still trying to operate on the cheap: it was wartime, after all.

Paradoxically, the camps were such effective tools of control *by* being cheap. We have seen the savings on space—with the result that the inmates were reduced to possess nearly nothing beyond their own flesh. Of course, the camps saved on food itself; the official ration in Auschwitz consisted of 350 grams of bread per day, a bowl of ersatz coffee for breakfast, and a bowl of turnip and potato soup for lunch. (This theoretical ration was not achieved in fact.)[176] Starvation, as usual, served in the biological reduction of the inmates into mere organic receptacles: naturally enough, everything in the inmates' life now revolved around the basic need for food. But perhaps the one concern to rival that of food was that of excrement. Here was one of the major pieces of savings in the planning of the camp. The twelve subcamps of Auschwitz-Birkenau each had twelve barracks housing prisoners, which stood for about ten thousand people in a subcamp; these were served by a single latrine.[177] "We stood in line to get into this tiny building, knee-deep in human excrement. As we all suffered from dysentery, we could rarely wait until our turn came, and soiled our ragged clothes, which never came off our bodies, thus adding to the horror of our existence by the terrible smell which surrounded us like a cloud. The latrine consisted of a deep ditch with planks thrown across it in certain intervals. We squatted on these planks like birds perched on a telegraph wire, so close together that we could not help soiling one another."[178] Terrence des Pres, in his study *The Survivor*, suggests that this "excremental assault"—as he calls it—was deliberately planned to reduce the prisoners further into mere biological objects. Whether planned or not, the biological consequences are indeed obvious. The standard dangers of concentration—starvation, overcrowding, and filth—were all brought to an unprecedented extreme. Dysentery was almost normal, and typhus epidemics frequently broke out. As mentioned earlier, there were areas of the camp that were fenced apart to become "hospitals" (in effect, in these quarantines the inmates were simply left to die). In this new type of camp, however, control over disease could be even simpler: sick inmates, or entire infected barracks, would often be killed—sent to the gas chambers.[179] (This reminds us of the standard response to outbreaks of epidemics among domesticated animals: the culling of the herd, that is, the killing of the infected and those suspected of infection.)

These gas chambers, in fact, were the main feature of the death camps. Just as the entire geography of Jewish Europe now revolved around the death camps, so each death camp revolved around its gas chamber, and it was death that defined life itself. I will now move on to describe this death.

As killing institutions, the geographic reach of the death camps (in particular that of Auschwitz) was remarkable. The death camps killed people coming from the entire continent—all the way from Greece to Norway, from France to the Soviet Union. This was based on a geography of concentration and transportation spread across the continent.

In Poland, we recall, the Jews were concentrated in ghettos and marked by the Star of David, from early on in the occupation. Adapting to local political conditions (in many places, Nazi control was exerted through local regimes), these policies were extended, for the Final Solution, all over Nazi-dominated Europe.

The victims were already concentrated within a defined perimeter—say, a Polish ghetto. When their turn came, the victims would be ordered to congregate at a specified location—typically, some open place left in the ghetto area. Depending on their response to the order, it could be supplemented by searches made through the ghetto and the forcible evictions of victims from houses, all until the quota for transportation was fulfilled. (Of course, when the plan was for the final clearing of a locality, searches would be very thorough.) If the train was already prepared, the victims would be marched to it immediately; otherwise they could be locked up pending further action, in some disused building—the usual practice for improvised incarceration. Thus, for instance, Lublin: "Small units of Trawniki men [Ukrainian volunteers], under the command of Germans, woke up the sleeping inhabitants with shouting and ordered them to leave their apartments without delay and to congregate in the street. . . . [They] were lined up in marching columns and led under escort to the synagogue. There they had to remain until dawn, when they were taken on foot to the Umschlagplatz [transfer station] near the slaughterhouse, where they embarked for Belzec."[180]

As we recall, ghettos were sited (in line with previous practices of concentration) next to railroad stations. Trains transported Jews *into* the ghettos; now they transported them *out* of the ghetto, to a death camp. Such trains would usually be made up of one or two passenger cars, for the guards, and several dozen cattle cars for the victims. This practice should be explained. There were plenty of precedents for transporting humans in cattle cars: we have seen this in the transport of the "kulaks" to the Gulag; and to quote a less sinister example, Allied soldiers on the western front often commented on the inscription on their railcars, "40 hommes ou 8 cheveaux," that is, forty men or eight horses.[181] (By the same ratio, the Auschwitz barracks, whose design was originally planned for fifty-two horses, should have held 260 people.) A cattle car is better suited for mass transportation than the passenger car is. It is cheaper to maintain, being, in fact, no more than a box on wheels. This immediately suggests a further advantage of the cattle car for transporting prisoners: the cattle do not require windows, and so the box is easy to contain. In practice, the apertures in the cars serving for Jewish transports were usually covered with barbed wire.[182] The two technologies, of the train and barbed wire, always went hand in hand: now finally they were amalgamated. In line with the general savings on space in such concentration camps, the cars were crammed, far beyond the "forty men" recommendation of World War I. Typically a car would hold a hundred people or more, so that the train as a whole could carry several thousand—the usual batch for such a transport. The entire train became a kind of mobile concentration camp, and the standard features of the death camps were all forced immediately on the victims: "We were packed into a closed cattle train. Inside the freight cars it was so dense that it was impossible to move. . . . The air inside the car was poisoned by the smell of bodies and excrement. Nobody thought about food, only about water and air."[183] The special feature of this stage of the journey, indeed, was the immense thirst. Most Polish Jews were killed during the summer of 1942, but even in winter, the heat was unbearable: when closely packed, human bodies create much heat (I will return to consider this biological effect hereafter). The trips were long, as logjams were often created (killing took time, and so the trains of those still living had to wait for their turn). Now, even when shipping cows—where more care is taken for the welfare of the shipped beings—there is usually some death in transit. A publication of the U.S Department of Agriculture from 1931, for instance, warned that "the death rate in affected shipments usually ranges from 1 to 3 per cent, but in some instances it may be as high as 10 or 15 per cent. Conservative estimates place the average yearly toll of shipping fever and kindred ailments at fully a million dollars."[184] In the cattle cars leading to the death camps, mortality was often even higher—and likewise was perceived by planners as a *flaw* in the process.

This, too, calls for an explanation. Surprisingly, death inside the train cars was not a result desired by the Nazis. While the goal was of course to kill all the victims, it was preferable to have them die later: corpses inside the cars complicated the problem of disposal, as they now had to be carried a few hundred yards to the crematorium or to the mass grave. This all took time and slave labor, which the Nazis were trying to economize. In practical terms, what the Nazis wanted was that the victims walk, on their own feet, as near as possible to the area where their corpses could be disposed of. I mention this not for the cheap irony but for the important lesson we learn about the Nazi practice: it all fits together, as soon as we consider it *from the corpse backward.* The fundamental feature of the death camps is that humans were perceived as future corpses, and so planning was dictated by the problem of disposing of such corpses.

But I am pushing ahead. Let us return to the victims in the mobile concentration camp of the cattle cars. They started out (in the typical Polish case) from the train depot right next to the ghetto; now they had reached another train depot, at the entrance to the death camp itself. The memoirs repeat the same description as the doors open to a frightening barrage of impressions: "Outside we heard all kinds of noises, stench, language, commands we didn't understand. It was in German but we didn't know what it meant. Dogs barked. The doors flung open . . ."[185] (The presence of dogs is familiar from the Gulag, and they were ubiquitous in the SS camps, as well.) Now the prisoners would be ordered—herded by dogs, beaten, shot at—to form in order. In Auschwitz, they would now face selection, that is, a moment of explicit reduction into mere receptacles of organic matter. Doctors (such as Mengele, the experimenter mentioned earlier) would inspect the prisoners qua organisms and decide whether they were fit for exploitation through either forced labor or medical experimentation. Those found fit—typically, a small minority —would be sent to the right, tattooed, and made to become part of the life described earlier. The rest would be sent to the left. This was the operation in Auschwitz. In the death camps proper —such as Belzec, Sobibor, and Treblinka—victims were (with few exceptions) sent through "the tube." This, as mentioned already, was a narrow passage between two high barbed wire fences, winding for as long as a few hundred yards through the camp and opening into one of the smaller camp areas.[186] Appropriately, barbed wire served to mark the final road the victims took. They were not alone there; along the route, the static violence of barbed wire was accompanied by active violence, pushing the victims ahead: "On both sides of the fence, stood Germans with dogs. . . . The Germans beat the people with whips and iron bars so they would run and push to get into the 'showers' quickly. The women's screams could be heard far off in other sections of the camp. The Germans urged the running victims on with yells of 'faster, faster, the water's getting cold, and others have to use the showers, too.'"[187]

At this point, we must detach ourselves once again from the perspective of the victims and return, finally, to consider the killers' perspective. How did the gas chambers come about?

The answer is complicated: the gas chambers were in constant evolution. In this book, we have seen many examples of the gradual adaptation of technology, based on little explicit planning. Certain tools are available and are therefore used to deal with a new problem, eventually giving rise to the standardization of new practices. The same formula holds for the history of the gas chambers themselves.

To begin with, Germany already had an experience of mass murder based on gas, the so-called euthanasia of the mentally ill in Germany itself in 1940 and 1941. Some seventy thousand people were killed in this operation. It targeted extremely vulnerable individuals who were already under the control of the asylums supposed to guard them. The killing of the mentally ill was now to be extended against the Jews.[188]

The agent used for killing the mentally ill was carbon monoxide. This gas can be easily obtained from the exhaust of, say, car engines, and in the "euthanasia" program, with its relatively small numbers of victims (typically twenty to thirty in each killing), the provision of gas was not a limiting factor. This changed as gas was used in the much more extensive campaign against the Jews. In Treblinka—the main site of killing in 1942 itself—the carbon monoxide engines were unreliable, so that killing was not continuous, leading to the logjams and the blocked trains, as mentioned earlier. Treblinka represents an early stage in the development: lethal, indeed (some 750,000 Jews were killed there), but unsatisfactory in terms of Nazi planning.[189]

We should now consider another route of development in the history of the gas chambers. As already explained, the fundamental concern in the camps was not the problem of killing—that is, dealing with living beings—but rather the problem of dealing with corpses. We have by now seen many concentration camps, in this chapter, and we see that any concentration camp—even without it being a death camp—would have a large number of corpses. In the SS concentration camps, in particular, discipline was enforced by torture and executions, and conditions overall were especially harsh—all resulting in high mortality. This poses a problem of biological control, as already mentioned in chapter 1. There we considered the situation of slaughterers in Chicago once they had killed a cow. Now that—as cow—it was brought under complete control, a new battle for biological control would start, against it *as dead body*. One had to fight against the bacteria and insects that claimed the corpse. The Chicago solution was refrigeration—obviously, an expensive solution, made possible only because this corpse would later on be sold and thus finance its own processing.

A cheaper way must be found for disposing of human corpses. In times of peace, burial can be taken care of properly, and the number of fresh graves is not large. When death occurs on a mass scale, however, and under what is otherwise the economic strain of war, disposal of corpses becomes a serious problem. One often resorts, still, to the solution of burial—however inadequate—in some improvised mass grave. This, indeed, was the solution taken by the Nazis in their mobile killings of Jews in the occupied area of the Soviet Union (to begin with, this was also the practice in some concentration camps, such as Treblinka).[190] Another alternative would be cremation: the burning of the corpses inside specially designed ovens. While more expensive than simple burial, cremation offers the only real answer to the biological hazard posed by the massive piling of corpses. Camps such as Auschwitz were therefore equipped, from their very inception, with crematoriums: that is, they had buildings designed for the ovens to burn corpses.[191]

A significant part of the prisoners' labor in all SS camps had to do with corpses: carrying them to the crematorium and burning them there. This labor could be made more productive (i.e., prisoners' labor could be better exploited) if killing and cremating were made contiguous. Already by late 1941—when Auschwitz was not yet a death camp—the logical conclusion was reached when prisoners were executed *inside* the crematoriums themselves. That is, prisoners chosen for execution would be made to enter the crematorium; they were shot there; then other prisoners would put the corpses to burn in the ovens.[192]

While Auschwitz was experimenting with its crematoriums, it was also experimenting with its methods for fumigating against lice. The standard agent—Zyklon B—had been used by the German army since 1917, and its operation was by now routine. An empty room would be sealed and Zyklon B released inside it by operators wearing gas masks; twenty-four hours later, the operators would return (once again, gas masks were required) and open the room. It would be aired for twenty hours. Zyklon B was an effective agent, securing the extermination of all insects, but we can see that its operation was time consuming. More to the point, it consumed *space*: for almost two days, a room would be inaccessible. In the Nazi concentration camps, space was very carefully saved, and so ways were investigated to speed up the operation of Zyklon B. In July 1941 German engineers found a way forward: in a heated room (with a temperature of thirty degrees Celsius or higher), Zyklon B evaporated more effectively and killed insects within one hour instead of twenty-four. As for the following period required for airing the room, this obviously could be shortened by providing the room with artificial ventilation. Thus a heated, ventilated room could serve for delousing clothes, all within seventy-five minutes. Soon special gas chambers were built for the purpose.[193]

When killing humans on a mass scale, speed is important: they should be quickly killed, and their corpses quickly disposed of, all allowing the continuous operation on a mass scale. Thus Zyklon B—taking a long period to kill, and then to be aired away—did not suggest itself originally as an agent to be used against humans. Now the equation was altered: in an appropriately heated room, Zyklon B would be a quick killer, and with appropriate ventilation, the corpses could be quickly approached and brought to the crematorium. Experiments were made in Auschwitz in September 1941, in which Soviet prisoners of war were killed with the new Zyklon B chamber method, which proved itself appropriate to the Nazi specifications.[194]

We are about to see now the most developed form of killing and disposal of corpses, as obtained in Auschwitz, and we are in a position to answer the most important question for this section. Why did the Nazi genocide use the apparatus of the concentration camps? In other words, why not keep to the method of mobile killing? Part of the answer to that has been mentioned already: simply as existing institutions, the SS camps sought ways of expansion, and they were thus eager to contribute to the killing of the Jews. This is the simple, institutional explanation for the phenomenon of the death camp, and we can see it as part of the more general trend, seen throughout the book, of seeking applications for an available technology. There is another explanation, which clarifies the advantage of the death camps as tools of genocide. The camps, by concentrating death, allowed a concentration of corpses, as well, and therefore allowed a better control over the biological hazard posed by mass killing. Since the killing of the Jews was planned from the corpse backward, concentration was logical. Thus the tools for concentrating living beings—barbed wire and railroads—were taken as the basic architecture and, at their terminus, were provided by gas chambers. In the death camps, barbed wire and gas chambers were a functional whole.

Let us finally consider this functional whole in operation. From 1943 onward, the Final Solution came to be based primarily in Auschwitz. After much experimentation, the system was reduced to its most basic constituents, put in clear order. These constituents were the use of Zyklon B, operated by heat, and the combination of killing and cremating inside a single operation.

We may return to follow the victims on their way to what they believe to be their reception, through showers, into a concentration camp. The building in front of them has several stages, of which they are as yet unaware. The first stage is a "dressing room," where they are ordered to undress. Then they are allowed inside the "showers" themselves. These have a convincing appearance and are in a relatively large room, of some fifty to two hundred square yards. The prisoners are pushed inside in the typical crowding of the camps, with perhaps one thousand people in a batch. Then the doors back to the "dressing room" are locked. It is thought that at this stage many victims understood that they were about to be murdered. Zyklon B is now thrown into the room from special openings (usually in the roof). As we recall, when humans are closely crowded together, they emit considerable heat. The bodies of the victims, in short, were made to contribute the energy required for their own death. Triggered by the heat, the Zyklon B would quickly evaporate and kill all the victims.

The ventilation system was now operated, and another door opened, now in the direction opposite that of the "dressing room." The building—we can now explain—has three stages: following (1) an undressing area, and (2) a killing area, comes (3) the crematorium itself, integrated inside the same structure as the gas chamber. Jews—forced to perform this particularly terrible labor—are now brought in to clean the "showers" (in preparation for the next batch), cut the victims' hair, extract any gold teeth, and then place the bodies in the ovens.[195] We can see how all the elements of the system are brought together: the victims undress themselves; their own flesh—the only thing they are left with—brings about the operation of the Zyklon B; this flesh, now dead, is quickly transferred to the ovens.

The most remarkable thing about the operation is its biological nature: the victims are reduced to biological organisms and are considered, throughout, as organisms. To repeat: the main feature of the Auschwitz crematoriums is that they were conceived in view of the biological problem of disposing of corpses. It sounds crude to say that Auschwitz was unique, among other things, in being an environmentally driven form of genocide. But while crude, this is not as absurd as it may sound: the Nazis, from the beginning, conceived of their anti-Jewish policy as a form of public hygiene operation. Nazism was a biologically driven ideology: its most extreme appearance, the Holocaust, had therefore to be driven by biological considerations. This might be a fundamental reason why the treatment of Jews by the Nazis was, indeed, so reminiscent of the treatment of slaughtered animals.

We have now seen the history of barbed wire, from invention to culmination, and I will stop now to remark on the significance of the instrument.

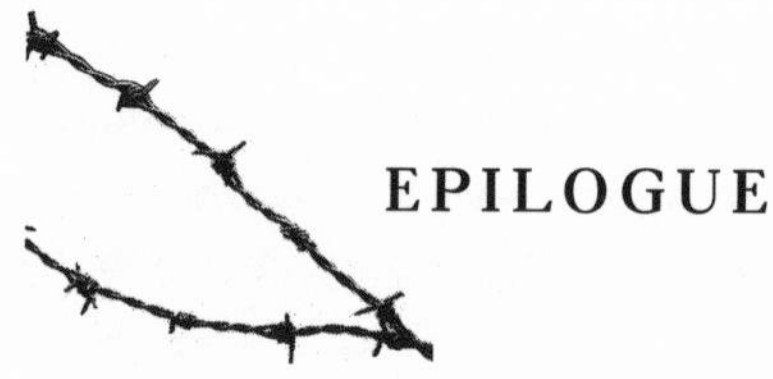

EPILOGUE

The history I have followed led in many directions, but in the end, the argument of the book is simple. I find I can sum it up in five theses.

1. The first thesis is straightforward: history is embodied. We sometimes think as if history is made of names, dates, and ideas that interact in an abstract space of relations and influences. But history is not at all abstract: it is a matter of flesh-and-blood individuals interacting in material space. History is not like chess; it is more like wrestling. Of course, this point is hardly new, and already Marx has taught us that before people do anything else, they must first eat, drink, and clothe themselves. In this book, I have stressed that even before people do those things, they must move, and they must occupy space. Thus history is not just about sociology or economics. History takes place as flesh moves inside space; it is thus, among other things, about the biology of flesh—as well as about the topology of space.

2. The second thesis is less widely accepted than the first, though I believe it follows directly from it. If history is about flesh-and-blood individuals interacting in material space, it also follows that history is not confined to humanity alone. Once again, history is not like chess, where you can take the thirty-two pieces on the board and ignore all the rest. We often think that we can take humans apart from their world, but everything counts, on the board, if only because it is *on the same board*—inside the same space. Or perhaps another simile would be more precise. We tend to concentrate on humans because we consider humans as *actors* in history—they have desires, they move about, and thus they shape reality. But all living beings have desires and move

about, and so they shape reality as well; and in another way, the same is true even of material reality itself. Thus there are no extras, and they are all actors—humans, animals, and their shared terrain. And because all these actors occupy the same stage, they cannot fail to interact; no species is an island. Thus history is embodied—and not only inside human bodies but in the bodies of all species.

These first two principles can be taken as a summary of the general approach of environmental history. In this book, I have made three further specific claims.

3. One of the main features of history is the prevention of motion. Biologically, animals just move around: history arrives when they are confined to a place. We usually start our histories with the tilling of fields, the domestication of animals, and the rise of towns—all emanating from the same principle: space is no longer open. Some parts are marked out from others, and certain humans and animals are confined *out* of a field, *inside* a pen, *away* from a city. We have seen, through this book, how the prevention of motion is tied to landownership and exploitation, to military history, and to forms of political control. The prevention of motion has to have this kind of wide application because it is elementary: to be affected by it, all you need to do is to be able to move. So it directly brings together all the actors of history. In a formula, this is history: humans change the terrain to prevent the motion of animals as well as other humans. And much of what matters in history is this: different periods are defined by different equations between humans, terrain, and animals, so that different forms of prevention of motion are made possible.

4. In particular, one can point to a modern equation between the actors. With industrial production—particularly of iron—humans could lay out, quickly and cheaply, effective barriers extending along large spaces. The prevention of motion could be dictated from a single center, on a mass scale. This was a new development. In the premodern world, control reached to points and to the lines connecting them; there simply was not enough prevention of motion to go around to cover an entire plane and

bring it all under control. In the modern world, this changed, and the topology was inverted: control reached everywhere, and only isolated points were left for motion, that is, *not* controlled from a center. The historical significance of barbed wire is that it served as an agent in this topological inversion.

5. To have our motion prevented is unpleasant, at the basic biological level. We want to move around, and to be denied that is in itself painful. Even more directly, prevention of motion is usually painful for a simple reason: usually, the way to prevent us from doing what we wish is to cause us pain. There is thus a direct relationship between the prevention of motion and violence. The reason barbed wire was so effective was that it could exert pain, on a mass scale, quickly and cheaply; and it was used to achieve control over a mass scale. It thus led, naturally, to violence and pain on a mass scale. This was the main feature of the period from 1874 to 1954.

Of course, in 1874, people did not think the next eighty years would be based on pain and violence. But we can easily explain the mistake of the optimists: they did not think in terms of environmental history. They thought of humans as essentially different from everything else. Marx, whom we can take as an example, thought of history as a process of growing human control over nature (which was of course correct), and he also thought that as this control became total, humans would no longer need to exploit one another: modernity would usher in the kingdom of freedom. The promise of Marxism—the essence of the promise of modernism—was to enslave nature so as to free humanity. But what if humanity itself is part of nature? Modernity, indeed, brought everything under control—the world with all its species—and humans, naturally, shared the same fate. In this particular case, at least, it turned out like this: a species that enslaves another forges its own chains.

Is this a simple cause-and-effect story—the enslavement of animals leading to the enslavement of humans? This book has unfolded, generally speaking, chronologically, from the invention of barbed wire in the American West, through its military applications in colonial wars and in World War I, leading to its well-known uses in the Gulag and Auschwitz. It would be too simplistic to argue that in this sequence, each link in the chain caused the following. After all, the Nazis would have persecuted the Jews with or without barbed wire. But there are some important causal links.

Barbed wire would probably have been invented with or without Henry Rose's experiments with his breachy cow. But the invention's early agricultural history *was* significant for its later development. A bit of barbed wire is, literally, no more than a thorn, a meaningless piece of iron. It is the fact that miles upon miles of such pieces of iron can be arranged in lines that turns this into a new tool of special significance for control. But how to get to have those thousands of miles? Arguably, these would never have been formed without American agriculture.

The same materials and the same ingenuity that led to the invention of barbed wire in 1874 had been there, no more than a decade earlier, when the American Civil War spawned all kinds of military inventions (the machine gun, the ironclad ship, the submarine). The need for something like barbed wire was also there—in the war itself, and in its prisoner-of-war camps. And yet barbed wire was not used. How could it be? This is what we have learned in this book: for barbed wire to be used in war or political control, it first had to be cheap and widely available. And the profitable use of barbed wire, even when relatively expansive, came from agriculture—with the need to exploit huge spaces quickly. This took place in America during the 1870s. Barbed wire entered human history—effectively, in the Boer War—only after its price had been pushed down through two decades of agricultural development. In retrospect, barbed wire could be seen to be an effective tool for military and political purposes. But it is likely that without the direct economic incentive of agriculture, barbed wire could never have passed the enormous gap separating a little bit of barbed wire (which, historically speaking, is nothing) from lots of barbed wire (which, historically speaking, is so much). To precede the uses of barbed wire in war and human repression, barbed wire had to undergo what may be conceived as its period of capital formation—when, quite literally, piles of barbed wire were put into stock. Only then could the later applications arrive.

In this limited sense, we can say that barbed wire did in fact arise from American agricultural history and, possibly, would not have been invented otherwise, so that, without the American West, the persecution of the Jews would possibly have taken a different form. Strange as this may sound, then, it may be that without the barbed wire ranches imprisoning Texan cows, there might have been no Auschwitz, either. I wish to make myself clear, so I rephrase: I do not make the preposterous suggestion that, without the ranches, there might have been no Holocaust. I'm just saying that without the ranches, there might have been no Auschwitz. The Holocaust was the product of a huge historical process involving European and German ideologies and the failure of modern German society, which was all independent from the history of barbed wire as such. And yet the form of the Holocaust—the death camps—was certainly a product of the technological and environmental history surveyed in this book. Without barbed wire, camps would have been too expensive to build in the first place and so would not have formed the obvious technique they came to be by the mid-twentieth century. Regimes would have relied on other tools of control. And so the Nazi persecution of the Jews would have taken different forms, as well. For instance, it might have taken the form of large-scale pogroms—which was what contemporary Jews mostly feared. The specific novelty of the Holocaust—the death camps—represented a specific technical development, starting in 1874; there is nothing implausible in suggesting that without this technical development, there would have been no death camps, either. And while merely a matter of form, this is by no means a trivial consideration—for is Auschwitz not the most powerful symbol of the catastrophes of the twentieth century?

This counterfactual exercise, however, assumes a world in which barbed wire would not have been invented in agriculture and yet would have been required in war and politics. This is a fundamentally false premise. Barbed wire was invented for a reason: because an entire panoply of technological advances led in a single direction, and the possibility arose—and with it, the desire—to control space not merely as a sequence of isolated points but in a total way extending across a plane. One therefore required—in agriculture, in war, and in politics—a cheap tool of control over space, quickly deployed on a mass scale. Considered from this perspective, the order of events is almost immaterial. In retrospect, we can see why agriculture—with its economic incentive—would be where the invention itself could most naturally take place. But the need was the same everywhere, and this is why the same tool was everywhere used. This idea, rather than cause and effect, structures the argument of my book. I do not suggest that the enslavement of cows in the American West *caused* World War I, the Gulag, or the Holocaust. The main theme, rather, is the similarity and continuity between these events. They all involved, on a mass scale, control over space, which is tantamount to the prevention of motion, which is tantamount to violence.

There is an inherent mistake in a statement such as "the Nazis did to the Jews what is normally done to animals." This makes us think in terms of a false picture. On the one hand are the European Jews, who, in the normal run of things, would go about their life—perhaps take the tram to work, board ships, ride in passenger trains. On the other hand there are certain animals—for example, cows—who, in the normal run of things, live enclosed inside barbed wire and are then concentrated to be killed. Then came the Final Solution, with Jews treated as cows normally are. But this is false: in the normal run of things, cows seek food through an open space of great grasslands; they graze, bear offspring, form herds, move on. They try as best they can to avoid predators and, when successful, die in old age. This is the natural life of the cow, and the ranch—its opposite—is every bit as artificial as the death camp. The Nazis, then, did not follow on some primordial treatment of animals; both what they did to Jews, and what ranchers did to cows, was in a sense *contemporary*:

an expression of the same order of historical control. Primo Levi has asked, about the inmate of Auschwitz, "if this is a man?"; one can equally ask, about the ranch inmate, "if this is a cow?" and the question, in both cases, is difficult to answer. In both cases, what we have is not a natural animal but the product of a special historical process—the same in both. Modernity made possible a total asymmetry between the powerful and the powerless. With this asymmetry of power, everything about an organism's life could be controlled, and as a result, a new kind of living being was created. Both cows and humans suffered the same modern equation of iron over flesh, and so both were transformed into what may be considered an altogether new species: the victim of extreme control. This victim—animal or human—is the hero of the twentieth century.

Barbed wire has by now lost the centrality to history that it enjoyed from 1874 to 1954. Why is that? An obvious suggestion is that we have moved from the prevention of motion to its facilitation, that ours is an age of globalization. Of course, we are now used to the boosterism or criticism of globalization. People have been equally enthusiastic or dismayed about the same phenomenon ever since the sixteenth century, and in a wider view still, the world has accumulated lines of connection throughout its history. Of course, different ages do have qualitatively different levels of connection. But it is simply an illusion to think of our own age as constituting a major transition in this respect; probably, the major transition took place in the middle of the nineteenth century. Much of the recent illusion has to do with the journalistic celebration of the Internet as a revolution. The Internet is an interesting historical phenomenon: it is also, essentially, a user-friendly interface of the telephone, which in turn is essentially a user-friendly interface of the telegraph. Although this growing user-friendliness is certainly of great importance, we should keep a sense of what has actually been achieved. The crucial function of the Internet in terms of world history—that it allows the global synchronization of commerce and politics—is *precisely* the achievement of the telegraph. When we say that in terms of world history, we live in the age of the Internet, we really mean—which is true—that we live in the age of the telegraph. This must be stressed: ours is a world that, in many ways, is contemporary with the entire period from the mid-nineteenth century onward. Massive ocean and continental transportation, government control that reaches everywhere, global economic and political interdependence—this has been the shape of the world for the last 150 years.

With this realization, we can offer a more sober assessment of global connection. Let us concentrate on the railroad, probably the single most important technology of connection in world history. This vividly brings out the relationship between connection and disconnection: the first, I argue, is reciprocally related to the second. The same lines serve both, and it is simply that connection is easier to perceive. Everyone thought of the railroads as great connectors, not as disconnectors. But they did disconnect. The railroad network was put into place, and soon barbed wire protected the railroads, and the network became a vehicle for the parceling of space into cells limited by barbed wire. The same lines of connection acted as lines of disconnection. This can be generalized as a geometrical law of which we have seen many examples in the book, which I will now set out formally: *Every connection has an equal disconnection orthogonal to it.*

A railroad, say, connects New York and Chicago, in a line connecting East to West; and soon a line of barbed wire is erected, disconnecting North from South. History, of course, is not geometry, and the law cannot be applied with the same mathematical necessity in some other cases, but it is widely applicable. The car and the telephone connected families to their distant relatives and friends and ultimately disconnected them from their neighbors; television, arguably, then went on to disconnect members of the family from each other. This is not a value judgment—the telephone is better than some neighborhoods, and the television is better than some families. But the principle is worth bearing in mind. After all, we have just one body to occupy space with and to connect with: if we move here, we do not move there; if we listen or look here, we do not listen or look there. It is as simple as that, and so it is impossible to change the net connectivity of the world. What has happened with the rise of the technologies of connection is not a rise in *net* connectivity but a change in the *nature* of connectivity. There is the same amount of connection between people as there ever was, but now more and more of it is channeled through artificial networks. These can then become sources of profit as well as of control, and this is the fundamental reason for their construction in the first place. We live not in a world where connection has grown but merely in a world where it has grown as an economic and political asset. Once again, I do not mean this as a criticism of our world: what is important for my argument here is that it would be false to ascribe the diminishing role of barbed wire to the rise of a new age of connectivity. For one thing, this age has been going on for the last century and a half; for another, it has always been simultaneously an age not only of connection but also of disconnection.

Still, it might be suggested now that the relative roles of connection and disconnection have changed: as the technologies of connection become greater sources of profit, there is less importance to disconnection itself. There is less need to prevent motion, then, and the world has become less violent. And this is certainly, to a certain extent, true. The second half of the twentieth century never did produce quite the equal of Auschwitz. Even more important, violence seems to have been historically marginalized. There were in fact tremendous outbursts of violence in the second half of the twentieth century. In China during the 1950s and 1960s, Stalinism—itself a mad, imitative modernization—was even more madly imitated by Maoism. This led to history's greatest human catastrophe, as measured in the absolute number of victims—many tens of millions dead of government-induced famine and repression. Then the Cambodian imitation of Maoism from 1975 to 1979, while much smaller in absolute terms, was—relative to the size of the population as a whole—worse even than Maoism. We can mention much more: in Rwanda, as late as 1996, more people were killed every day, on average, than at Auschwitz—using no more than machetes and clubs. All the while, violence had been sliding down the technological scale, just as it was sliding away from the centers of world history. Violence no longer mattered as much. The events we have followed in this book—colonialism, the two world wars, the Soviet experiment, the Holocaust—were also the major events of the period: the events that determined everything else. But Rwanda or Cambodia, and even, arguably, Maoism, were no more than sideshows.

In short, violence has not been reduced; it has been more concentrated on the margins and has thus become less visible to the people of the center. In other words, we have returned to the pre-1914 world. I suspect that this is how the late twentieth century will be remembered: not as a period of a break with the past but as exactly the opposite: a closing of the circle that began at the beginning of the century. The beginning of the century was a period of transition—the period of the coming of modernity. The technological revolution of the second half of the nineteenth century led to a crisis of transition. The new technologies allowed total control and concentrated it in a few centers of power. The world did not know quite what to do with this: fear of the potential of the railroad gave rise to World War I; dreams of the potential of modern control gave rise to the Soviet experiment; the transition to a single world center in America gave rise to the Great Depression; all of this gave rise to World War II. By this time, the center had learned its lesson. Europe was re-formed as a single entity, world finance was rearranged with an American center, the Cold War was managed to avoid eruption and finally folded. There was no longer a need for violence because effective control had already been established. The world had finally become a single system, which was, apparently, stable. So we can definitely see the role of barbed wire: it was a tool of transition, when world domination from a center had to be established through violence. It is not the case that barbed wire diminished in importance because history changed its course: instead, it *succeeded,* and for this reason was no longer needed.

If barbed wire retreated from the center stage of human history because of the lesser role of violence there, barbed wire has also largely retreated from animal history because, in that history, violence and control grew considerably. The subtle control of barbed wire was no longer sufficiently effective. Barbed wire, used to prevent the motion of animals, presupposes considerable animal movement: they can, at the very least, go as far as the fence. Such is no longer the case in the contemporary animal industry. Operating on a much larger scale than in the past, the industry needs to accommodate many more animals in a space that—with the growing number of humans and with ever-cheaper transportation—becomes more valuable. The result is that animals are not so much fenced as caged. The space allowed individual animals inside the contemporary structures of the animal industry extends, generally speaking, to their flesh and nothing more—replicating the bunks of Auschwitz. Cows tied to their milking machines; calves fixed inside dungeons of absolute nonmobility; chickens packed together in immense wire cages—we see that against such animals, barbed wire has become redundant. The comparison to the bunks of Auschwitz is meaningful: contemporary animals, even while alive, are being squeezed out of space. In this case, this squeezing is motivated not by politics but by economics: space is an element of cost and therefore must be reduced.

Here we can clearly see the correlation between center and margins. The growing violence against animals has been directly correlated with the peace at the human centers. Animals are mass-produced because of the growth of consumption in a prosperous economy, in turn the result of the long period of peace. Having killed and tortured each other enough, as it were, the people of the center now take a break as they concentrate on killing and torturing animals. Our view of that process is of course a question of ethics, not of history, and so, at this point, I bring my book to an end.

NOTES

INTRODUCTION, *pp. xi–xiv*

1. There is a long tradition of writing on the history of barbed wire from the perspective of the history of the American West. This history—a mixture of patriotic history and guide to the barbed wire collector—reaches its culmination in McCallum 1965. In such histories, the use of barbed wire for human repression is never mentioned. Histories of human repression, on the other hand, never mention animal history as such and, when discussing the history of barbed wire, would not even register its beginning in the American West. Two recent books—Razac 2000 and Krell 2002—do mention that origin of barbed wire. The first, however, mentions it in the context of the fate of Native Americans, while the second (an excellent study of the iconography of barbed wire) is essentially focused on the human cultural perceptions of the artifact. Thus, surprisingly, this book (following on my article [Netz 2000]) is indeed the first work to recognize the history of barbed wire as crossing species—from the animal to the human.

1. EXPANSION, *pp. 1–55*

1. The term "Great Plains" refers to the area of today's United States between the Mississippi River and the Rocky Mountains. There is much continuity between the plains and their surroundings. The lack of simple boundaries may, indeed, be seen as the main theme of the area's history. It is a largely flat space, short on distinguishing features, allowing unhindered movement for thousands of miles: a challenge to the would-be preventer of motion.

2. Du Pratz 1763, 200.

3. Keats 1973; Houck 1901; "Sylvestris" 1803.

4. I follow—as we all do—Braudel 1979.

5. McPherson 1988, 486.

6. Utley 1984.

7. Both terms, "bison" and "cow," call for some explanation. "Bison" is simple: this is the term biologists (and most contemporary historians) prefer when speaking about the species *Bison bison*, frequently referred to also as buffalo. My rationale for the term "cow" is more complex. Of course, it is only cows that can be forced to produce milk or, indeed, further cows, for human consumption. Hence, in the agricultural setting, male calves tend to be killed younger, creating a gender disparity in the population as a whole. Cows are therefore historically much more common than steers. (Steers are castrated bulls;

uncastrated bulls are of course rare in the agricultural setting.) Further, the word "cattle" can easily suggest a commodity rather than a living being. I therefore prefer to speak of "cows" when referring to both cows and bulls, avoiding the term "cattle" altogether. A further complication is that the female of the bison is also called a cow; it should be clear that I use "cow" only for the common cow, *Bos taurus*.

8. Crosby 1986.

9. Clutton-Brock 1992, 38.

10. Isenberg 2000, 23–30; Webb 1931, 226.

11. Frison 1991, chap. 3.

12. Isenberg 2000, chaps. 3–4.

13. White 1994, 248.

14. Isenberg 2000, 130.

15. Isenberg 2000, 16–20.

16. Arnold and Hale 1940, vii, 17, 92. See also Boorstin 1973, 19–26.

17. Rosa 1982, 1996, esp. 130–33.

18. White 1994, 263–70.

19. See, e.g., Neeson 1993. I will return to consider this development in greater detail in the next chapter. The partition of the open field in Europe was—as we will see—also a major event in military history, changing the nature of the European battlefield.

20. Cronon 1983, 119–20.

21. Webb 1931, 287–88.

22. Basalla 1988, 52.

23. Cronon 1991, chap. 4.

24. McCallum and McCallum 1965, 29–31.

25. Raichle 1979. It should be noted, however, that the period as a whole was one of a gradual erosion of corporal punishment as applied to humans.

26. Crosby 1986, 184.

27. McCallum and McCallum 1965, 48.

28. Industrial Museum: American Steel and Wire Company 1929. Photographs of Exhibits (1926?), book no. 2. Under the category "Specimen of Barbed Wire."

29. Basalla 1988, 49–55.

30. A useful perspective into the nineteenth-century embrace of wire is the enthusiastic yet sober account in J. B. Smith 1891, esp. chaps. 1 and 5.

31. Butts and Johnson 1856, 1.

32. Webb 1931, 297.

33. James 1966, 9–13.

34. McFadden 1978.

35. Industrial Museum: American Steel and Wire Company. Photographs of Exhibits (1926?), book no. 2. Under the categories "Specimen of Barbed Wire" and "First Barbed Wire Circular."

36. Washburn and Moen 1881, 16.

37. Cronon 1991, chap. 4.

38. Cronon 1991, 68.

39. This is the claim of Washburn and Moen (1881, 27), of course a biased source and at any rate no more than an estimate. But assuming that the pound-length ratio is not too far from the truth—after all, this ratio was the basis on which customers bought wire—fifty thousand miles of barbed wire fences translate into somewhat more than 100 million pounds of barbed wire. Webb (1931, 309) estimates that total production

up to 1880, inclusive, was about 174 million pounds, while the more conservative McFadden (1978, 465) puts the figure at 127 million pounds, substantiating the manufacturers' claim.

40. Baker MSS 596: DcC 847, Baker Library, Cambridge, Mass.

41. The same type of leaflet, issued by Washburn and Moen in 1883—three years after the one quoted in the text—contained exactly the same comparison, but with the wire prices reduced by about 20 percent (still way above actual market prices).

42. J. B. Smith 1891, 314–15.

43. White 1994, 260.

44. See Gressley 1966 for an analysis of the role of investors in cattle. Of 93 American investors sampled there, more than half resided in either New York or Boston (71); according to Nimmo 1885, some 20 million acres of land were purchased in the West for European owners before 1885 (45). With a handful of exceptions, all those owners were from Great Britain. For the perception of bonanza, see Gressley 1966, chap. 2.

45. Nimmo 1885, 21.

46. Nimmo 1885, 42–44.

47. Brown 1994, 401.

48. Nimmo 1885, 177.

49. McCallum and McCallum 1965, chap. 10.

50. R. Richardson 1978.

51. R. Richardson 1978. Although this goes beyond the chronological bounds here, it is appropriate to mention the remarkable way by which the screwworm would finally be eradicated from the plains. Insects are much more tenacious than mammals are, and their extermination calls for some ingenuity. The extermination of the screwworm would, in fact, call forth true scientific genius. This method, invented by the biologists Raymond C. Bushland and Edward F. Knipling, was employed in the 1960s on the plains, and the species, with rare exceptions, has never since been seen there. It works like this. Vast numbers of screwworm males are reared; using irradiation during the appropriate time in their growth, they are rendered sterile; then they are released. Now the flies do the work for you. The males seek out the females far better than any humans ever could do. They mate, and each sterile mating event renders a female infertile for a cycle. The bona fide males, as it were, are put out of business through a dumping form of competition. It is obvious that with sufficient cycles, and sufficiently large numbers of sterile males released, the species will disappear. In fact, hundreds of millions of sterile flies were released each week for over a decade. (A complication of the project should be added: since the extermination was not global but confined to the United States, it had to be defended perpetually on the Mexican border.) There is something truly dizzying about this image of humans mass-producing flies whose contribution is their own destruction. The entire

operation was in fact a harbinger of modern genetic control over populations, and so the plains cow, the trigger for an early kind of modernity based on control through iron, served also as the trigger for the contemporary kind of modernity based on the more subtle controls of biotechnology (Knipling 1960).

52. Washburn and Moen 1881, 21–33.

53. Vermont General Assembly 1880, 1.

54. James 1966, 30–31.

55. James 1966, 137.

56. Printed by J. W. Gates and Co., 1882, in Baker MSS 596: DcE 1558.

57. Printed by Washburn and Moen, 1883, in Baker MSS 596: DcE 1558.

58. McCallum and McCallum 1965, 135–39.

59. See, e.g., Frink, Jackson, and Spring 1956, 117; White 1994, 267.

60. Nimmo 1885, 22.

61. Jordan 1993.

62. Baker MSS 596: DcC 759.

63. Baker MSS 596: DcC 648.

64. See, e.g., Scobie 1964, esp. 44–45.

65. Sbarra 1955, 102.

66. Baker MSS 596: DcC 840.

67. Baker MSS 596: DcC 844.

68. Baker MSS 596: DcC 844.

69. Baker MSS 596: DcC 844.

70. J. B. Smith 1891, 93.

71. J. B. Smith 1891, 133–34.

72. Crosby 1986, 187.

73. McMichael 1984, 216–19, 274–77.

74. Quoted in T. J. Keegan 1987, 228.

75. For agricultural transformation in South Africa in the late nineteenth century, see T. J. Keegan 1987.

76. Statistics based on Baker MSS 596: DcC 877, a document produced in the 1930s for historical purposes, by the auditor department of American Steel and Wire Co.

77. Tariff Commission, Comparative Statistics of Imports by Countries, 1931–1935, V.8 Group 6 (W.P.A. Statistical Project 65-31-2075), 237.

78. I should mention that in the years following World War II, steel and iron products lost much of their dynamism in the American economy, and other countries (for instance, Japan) came to the fore. In 1985 the world could see the amazing sight of an American tariff raised against the dumping of barbed wire from Argentina. By then America was a net importer, importing about 170,000 tons for a paltry 5,000 tons export (U.S. International Trade Commission 1985, 104, 124). Even so, the importance of America for the consumption of barbed wire remains robust.

79. Including, significantly, a new awareness of animal pain; see Turner 1980.

80. Rinderpest is a viral disease leading to high fever and a failure of several tissues, including the membranes of the mouth. The animal stops eating and dies quickly, with

marked internal pain. Even today, no treatment is known (from the 1920s onward, though, vaccines were developed, and the disease may perhaps be eradicated in the twenty-first century).

81. Swabe 1999, 99–104.

82. Indeed, it is worth noting in passing that the entire idea of contagion as the basic model of disease transmission was shaped by the experience of controlling the motion of cows. The Pasteur turn in medicine started out, following the devastation of 1865, as French science was trying to prevent new economic disasters caused by animal disease.

83. *American Veterinary Review* 1881, 321.

84. See, e.g., Schlosser 2000.

85. Soon the idea of the refrigerating railroad car would be extended to the refrigerating oceangoing ship, connecting the Old World with the New (Strickton 1965, 235).

86. Cronon 1991, chap. 5.

87. Levenstein 1988, introduction.

88. Hooker 1981, 113.

89. This is the name by which the company was famous; at its foundation, it was called the American Steel and Wire Company of New Jersey, and it changed names several times afterward.

90. McFadden 1978, esp. 483–85.

91. FTC 1916, 233.

92. FTC 1916, 211.

93. FTC 1916, 236.

94. The dossier of documents relating to the Roberts Wire Company of Pittsburgh, Pennsylvania, kept in the American Steel and Wire Company Archives (Baker MSS: 596 DcB 1119), includes, among other things, the telegraph code issued by the company in 1888. This is a list of single-word equivalents for long expressions, designed to save on telegraph expenses. Instead of the phrase "delivered at Mobile, Ala.," for instance, the Roberts salesman would telegraph the single word "defensive," and so forth. The attached map simply lists all the "delivered at . . ." locations specified in this telegraph code.

The indication this code offers of barbed wire distribution is, of course, very rough. This is only one company, and no quantitative values are shown here at all. However, it is clear that Roberts was an important producer (with total sales in 1889 of more than $2 million, the company's barbed wire sales were probably in the range of a few tens of thousands of tons, i.e., perhaps one-fifth of American consumption: possibly, indeed, the largest producers). Furthermore, the areas of distribution accord with what is otherwise known of distribution at that time, especially the predominant position of Texas. The West itself is clearly underrepresented (possibly better served by producers closer to Chicago), but on the whole, the map makes sense for 1888, when barbed wire was a feature of agriculture anywhere in the United States. It should be borne in mind, after all, that telegraph codes are designed to anticipate the possible, not to state the actual: the points of delivery sketched here are the centers of distribution, near which, experience shows, barbed wire is most likely to be in demand.

95. Immediately following the resolution of the legal battles for the barbed wire patent, in January–February 1881, Washburn and Moen reached a series of arrangements with the various producers of barbed wire, defining the weight of barbed wire they were henceforth allowed to produce (and the payment they would owe Washburn and Moen). These are summarized for the United States in Baker MSS 596: DcC 827, and in original form for Canada in Baker MSS 596: DcC 839.

The amounts stated are not precise indications of actual production, either before or after the signing of the agreements. Overoptimistic companies might ask for quotas larger than they actually produced, or companies might in practice break the limit set upon them (indeed, some small firms continued to operate outside licenses, and the Washburn and Moen archives are replete with efforts to fight such infringements). Overall, however, the resulting map representing the relative volumes is very plausible, showing a marked concentration in the greater Chicago area (especially toward the Illinois-Iowa prairie area, where barbed wire originated) and, to a lesser extent, in the steel-manufacturing areas toward Lake Erie. The total production limit set for 1881 would be 55,600 tons (in the United States), which compares interestingly with the actual production (estimated) for that year, 60,000 tons.

The main lacuna of this document is the production by Washburn and Moen themselves, in Worcester, Massachusetts (the amounts stated for that city refer not to Washburn and Moen but to a local rival): holding the patent rights, the firm would need to sign no license. It is clear that Washburn and Moen were great producers of barbed wire, but their estimated production for 1891 (when production overall was more than double that of 1881) was a mere 25,000 tons (Baker MSS 596: DcC 618), less than one-fifth of overall production for that year. It is likely that the addition of Washburn and Moen to the map would result in Massachusetts appearing as a third central area of production, equal in importance to the other two, but not eclipsing any of them.

The map represents each 250 tons by one square millimeter. When more than one company operates in the same town, the amount represented is the aggregate for the town (Joliet, Illinois, for instance, today a Chicago suburb, had seven barbed wire producers in 1881).

96. Cronon 1991, chap. 6.

97. Hurt 1981, 51.

98. For the Dust Bowl, see Worster 1979; Hurt 1981.

2. CONFRONTATION, *pp. 56–127*

1. Woods 1992.

2. For inventories of warfare, see L. Richardson 1960; Hoover Institution 1971.

3. J. Keegan 1998, 10–18. Keynes was the architect of British financial survival during the war, and his famous tract, *The Economic Consequences of the Peace* (Keynes 1919), remains the best short description of the European system before the war—and its failure thereafter.

4. Davenport 1987, 470.

5. For the background to the Boer War, see, e.g., Davenport 1987, 83–87, 187–91.

6. Davenport 1987, 211–12.

7. Davenport 1987, 212–16.

8. The following technical discussion is based on War Office, General Staff 1906, 4:568–76.

9. Lee 1985, 159.

10. Pakenham 1979, 569.

11. Calculated from Davenport 1987, 253; Pakenham 1979, 588.

12. Pakenham 1979, 570.

13. Pakenham 1979, 607.

14. For the Spanish colonial experience in Morocco, see Alvarez 2001. (See there, p. 37, and Woolman 1968, 100–101, for the general features of the *blocao* system.)

15. For the Arab Revolt and responses to it, see Naor 1987.

16. See Gvati 1981, 299; Naor 1987, 35–46.

17. For a survey of practices surrounding the domesticated horse, see Clutton-Brock 1992.

18. See Ellis 1978, 8–9, for the following discussion of the horse in warfare.

19. The conquest of the Inca empire is especially remarkable; see Hemming 1970, 111–13, for the role of the horse.

20. Porch 2000, 100.

21. Waldron 1990.

22. In what follows, I am indebted to White 1962, a masterpiece that is often criticized for its detail but stands for its overall interpretation.

23. See Clutton-Brock 1992, 73–77, and references there.

24. Von Schmidt 1881, iii.

25. Von Schmidt 1881, 74.

26. Von Schmidt 1881, 10.

27. Von Schmidt 1881, 74.

28. Von Schmidt 1881, 31–36.

29. Von Schmidt 1881, 35.

30. Chandler 1966, 2:51.

31. It should be said that agricultural development did not follow a single line. British enclosure was not directly imitated in Europe, where local peasant landowning remained central. This too, however, came to be based more and more on the individual fenced plot, so that the European countryside, if anything, was more parceled than the British one (in Britain, capitalist landowners would benefit more from the economies of scale, with somewhat larger fields as a consequence). The literature on this question is large, and there is considerable regional variety. See, e.g., Grantham and Leonard 1989, pt. 3; Hopcroft 1999.

32. Mingay 1977, 273–74.

33. Howard 1961, 118–19, 156–57.

34. Ellis 1978, 147.

35. "Pour la lance" 1902, 16; translation mine.

36. Rimington 1912, 53–55.

37. Rimington 1912, 51.

38. Dundonald 1926, 181.

39. Loir 1911, 121.

40. Dallas 2000, 17.

41. Von Poseck 1923, 228.

42. Moore 1931, 11.

43. DiNardo 1991, 5.

44. DiNardo 1991, 40.

45. Mahan 1862, 44–48. The French terminology—Mahan himself was American—is typical of military writing of the period.

46. Brackenbury 1888, 53.

47. Brackenbury 1888, 56.

48. Brialmont 1879, 324–25; translation mine.

49. Wheeler 1893, 173.

50. Wheeler 1898, 89.

51. Baden-Powell 1903, 193.

52. Baden-Powell 1903, 193.

53. Baden-Powell 1903, 194.

54. Baden-Powell 1903, 193.

55. See Walder 1973, 102–4.

56. War Office, General Staff 1906, 1:636.

57. U.S. War Department 1907, 79.

58. U.S. War Department 1906, 113.

59. Soloviev 1906, 29.

60. The best overall technical description of trench construction is War Office, General Staff 1906, 2:633–38.

61. Sedgwick 1908, 140.

62. War Office, General Staff 1906, 1:641.

63. War Office, General Staff 1906, 2:269.

64. War Office, General Staff 1906, 2:301.

65. War Office, General Staff 1906, 1:233.

66. War Office, General Staff 1906, 2:39.

67. Walder 1973, 272.

68. For the classic discussion, see Ellis 1975.

69. War Office, General Staff 1906, 2:233–34. There were five Japanese armies, each comprising two or three divisions.

70. Porch 2000, 187.

71. For readable overviews of the general course of the war, see Martin 1967; Walder 1973.

72. J. Keegan 1998, chap. 3.

73. War Office, General Staff 1917–1918, 32.

74. Ellis 1976, 25.

75. McCallum and McCallum 1965, 224.

76. Industrial Museum: American Steel and Wire Company. Photographs of Exhibits (1926?), book no. 2. Under the category "Military Barb Wire."

77. Ellis 1975, 24.

78. Ellis 1975, 116.

79. Gilbert 1994, 541.

80. J. Keegan 1976, 258.

81. J. Keegan 1976, 334.

82. Ellis 1976, chap. 13.

83. Stone 1975, 197.

84. Remarque 1929, 84–86.

85. Quoted from Gilbert 1994, 441. Compare also "The Old

Barbed Wire," a British popular war song quoted by Krell (2002): "If you want to find the old battalion, / I know where they are, I know where they are . . . / They're hanging on the old barbed wire" (57).

86. J. Keegan 1998, 278–86.

87. Prentiss 1937, 637.

88. Hammond 1999, 16.

89. Haber 1986, 33–34.

90. Haber 1986, 56.

91. Swinton 1932, 32.

92. Harris 1995, chap. 1.

93. Williams 1987, chaps. 1–2.

94. Naumann 1977, 8–9.

95. Naumann 1977, 9–10.

96. Williams 1987, chap. 3.

97. Quoted from Harris 1995, 52–53.

98. Figes 1996, chap. 7, sec. 2.

99. Figes 1996, chap. 6, sec. 3.

100. Stone 1975, chap. 13.

3. CONTAINMENT, *pp. 128–227*

1. See, e.g., J. Smith 1994, chap. 1; Foner 1972, esp. chaps. 6 and 9.

2. Musicant 1998, 69–70.

3. Quoted in Foner 1972, 113.

4. J. Smith 1994, 22.

5. Foner 1972, 115.

6. J. Smith 1994, chap. 2.

7. Linn 2000, 303.

8. Linn 2000, esp. 214–15.

9. See Fairbank 1992, 189–91. Tikhvinsky 1983, 103–5—a Soviet account—is useful for its interest in details of peasant insurrections.

10. Wilson 1902, 498–99.

11. Pakenham 1979, 466–67.

12. Pakenham 1979, 608.

13. Spies 1977, 144–51; Pakenham 1979, 522.

14. See Davenport 1987, 216. There is a large literature on the subject, which still is, quite justifiably, controversial in South Africa. The most thorough studies remain Spies 1977 and Otto 1954.

15. Spies 1977, 363–64.

16. Parliamentary Report 1901a, 23.

17. Davenport 1987, 217.

18. Spies 1977, 148.

19. See Van Rensburg 1980, 46–47.

20. Parliamentary Report 1901b, 13–14.

21. Parliamentary Report 1901b, 268.

22. Parliamentary Report 1901b, 300.

23. Quoted in Raath 1999, 51.

24. Parliamentary Report 1901b, 304.

25. Parliamentary Report 1901a, 299.

26. Parliamentary Report 1902, 8; see also 14.

27. Parliamentary Report 1901b, 15–17.

28. Parliamentary Report 1902b, 91.

29. Spies 1977, 296.

30. Parliamentary Report 1902a, 8–9.

31. Marvel 1994, 38.

32. Marvel 1994, 238.

33. Lawrence and Glover 1964.

34. Hesseltine 1930, 114.

35. Vance 2000, 72.

36. Vance 2000, 299, 103.

37. Solzhenitsyn 1989, 441.

38. Moynihan 1978, chap. 1.

39. Jackson 1989, 38.

40. Dennett 1919, 48.

41. The literature on escape is enormous: see, e.g., Moynihan 1978, chap. 3; Dennett 1919, chap. 8.

42. See Jackson 1989, 31.

43. Vance 2000, 322.

44. Jackson 1989, 39–40.

45. Jackson 1989, 41–42.

46. Bird 1986, 48–49.

47. Bird 1986, 169.

48. Bird 1986, 134, 141, 159.

49. Bird 1986, 153.

50. Bird 1986, 155.

51. Jackson 1989, chap. 4.

52. Fischer 1989.

53. Kordan and Melnycky 1991. Map 6 is based on p. 9 there.

54. Fischer 1989, 199–201; Splivalo 1982, chap. 13.

55. Lafitte 1988.

56. Weglyn 1976, 37–38.

57. The literature on the Japanese internment is huge; Weglyn 1976 is a useful entry point to this literature.

58. Malsagoff 1926, 45.

59. Malsagoff 1926, 44.

60. Werth 1999, 114, 118.

61. Leggett 1981, 178–80.

62. Malsagoff 1926, 55–56.

63. Cederholm 1929, 298.

64. Malsagoff 1926, 77–80. Map 7 is based on p. 80.

65. Werth 1999, 138.

66. Solzhenitsyn 1974, 70; see pt. 3, chap. 2, for the "Solovki" in general.

67. Werth 1999, 137.

68. See Figes 1996, chap. 3.

69. Conquest 1986, 87.

70. See Figes 1996, 775–80.

71. Conquest 1986, 182.

72. Fitzpatrick 1994, 137.

73. Brooks 2000, 36–37, 80.

74. Werth 1999, 152–53.

75. Ivanova 2000, 73–76.

76. Zurichenko 1950, 12–13.

77. Archive, Obshchestvo Memorial–Moscow, f. 2, op. 1, d. 96, l. 36. Translations from Obshchestvo Memorial archive are mine.

78. Pavel Negretov, quoted in Ivanova 2000, 80.

79. A peasant quoted in Conquest 1986, 229.

80. Fitzpatrick 1994, 66.

81. Hosking 1992, 166.

82. Quoted in Conquest 1986, 159.

83. Archive, Obshchestvo Memorial–Moscow, f. 2, op. 1, d. 91, lines 16–17.

84. Conquest 1986, 179.

85. Conquest 1986, 180.

86. From the Web site of AntiqueTractors.com, http://www.antiquetractors.com (accessed June 2001).

87. Conquest 1986, 181.

88. Conquest 1986, 253.

89. Conquest 1986, 301.

90. Archive, Obshchestvo Memorial–Moscow, f. 2, op. 2, d. 4, l. 6.

91. Hosking 1992, 166, 356–60.

92. See Pryor 1992, 37.

93. Fitzpatrick 1994, 138.

94. Fitzpatrick 1994, 90–96.

95. Conquest 1986, 327–28.

96. Mandelshtam 1970.

97. Solzhenitsyn 1974, 34–36.

98. Rossi 1989, s.v. "zona, 2.1 bol'shaya zona."

99. Werth 1999, 238.

100. Archive, Obshchestvo Memorial—Moscow, f. 2, op. 1, d. 112, l. 126.

101. Rossi 1989, s.v. "zona."

102. Rossi 1989, s.vv. "Barak," "vyshka 2.1 storozhevaya vyshka," "zapretka," "zona."

103. Solzhenitsyn 1975, 534.

104. Conquest 1978, 102–3.

105. Clutton-Brock 1999, chap. 4.

106. Ivanova 2000, 108.

107. Werth 1999, 238.

108. Solzhenitsyn 1975, 80–102.

109. Ivanova 2000, 78.

110. Solzhenitsyn 1975, 101.

111. Conquest 1990, 332; Ivanova 2000, 105.

112. Kizny 1997, 49–55.

113. Ivanova 2000, 105.

114. School of Slavonic and East European Studies in the University of London 1934, 22–23.

115. Conquest 1978, chap. 9.

116. Conquest 1978, 162.

117. Conquest 1978, 214–15.

118. Conquest 1978, 152–62.

119. See Conquest 1990, chap. 9.

120. Solzhenitsyn 1974, pt. 1, chap. 6.

121. Werth 1999, 218–19.

122. Werth 1999, 236–38.

123. Werth 1999, 249.

124. Werth 1999, 256.

125. See Hitler 1939, chap. 11.

126. Hamilton 1982.

127. Broszat 1968, 401.

128. Berben 1975, 2.

129. Sofsky 1997, 56.

130. Broszat 1968, 410.

131. Broszat 1968, 407–8.

132. Broszat 1968, 444–45.

133. Friedländer 1997, 139, 122–23.

134. Hilberg 1961, 106.

135. Friedländer 1997, 285.

136. Friedländer 1997, 143.

137. See Hilberg 1961, 127.

138. Noakes and Pridham 1988, 1052.

139. Gilbert 1985, 116.

140. See Shavit 1995, 37–50.

141. Hilberg 1961, 152.

142. Hilberg 1961, 172.

143. Hilberg 1961, 169.

144. On disease in the Warsaw Ghetto, see Roland 1992, esp. chaps. 7–8.

145. Hilberg 1961, 173–74.

146. See Dwork and Van Pelt 1996, 119–20.

147. See Hitler 1939, 294.

148. Jansen 1997.

149. Noakes and Pridham 1988, 1090.

150. Dwork and Van Pelt 1996, 261–62.

151. See Hilberg 1961, sec. 7.

152. Kogon 1950, 180–83.

153. Broszat 1968, 464–71.

154. Broszat 1968, 471–72.

155. Broszat 1968, 472.

156. Broszat 1968, 473–75.

157. Kogon 1950, 51–52, Sofsky 1997, chap. 4.

158. Sofsky 1997, 47, quoted from Herzberg, on Bergen-Belsen.

159. Gutman and Berenbaum 1994, 14.

160. Based on Arad 1987, 437.

161. Based on Arad 1987, 35.

162. Arad 1987, 23–43.

163. Based on Arad 1987, 39.

164. Dwork and Van Pelt 1996, 263–64, and chap. 8.

165. Sofsky 1997, 56–57.

166. Dwork and Van Pelt 1996, 263–67.

167. Levi 1960, 65.

168. Berben 1975, 227.

169. Solzhenitsyn 1978, 58–59.

170. See Pawelczynska 1979, 92.

171. See Vance 2000.

172. Rossi 1989, s.vv. "norma," "raportichka."

173. Levi 1960, 67.

174. Gutman and Berenbaum 1994, chap. 13.

175. Hilberg 1961, 601–2.

176. Gutman and Berenbaum 1994, 24.

177. Dwork and Van Pelt 1996, 264–66.

178. Gisella Perl, quoted in Des Pres 1976, 54.

179. Gutman and Berenbaum 1994, 328.

180. From a trial against SS men held in Wiesbaden, quoted in Arad 1987, 57.

181. See Farwell 1999, 94.

182. See Hilberg 1981, 17, 188; Arad 1987, 65, 81; Gilbert 1985, 408.

183. Arad 1987, 63.

184. Miller 1931, 2. As pointed out by Tsovel (2004), this is already the result of a long process whereby the shipping of animals is adapted to modern transportation, at the first stage with truly horrific rates of mortality (and so loss for the owners). The transportation of Jews to the camps was comparable not so much to the contemporary transportation of animals but to that of the mid-nineteenth century, when death in transit of some 15 percent of the animals was commonplace.

185. Quoted in Dwork and Van Pelt 1996, 340.

186. Arad 1987, 68–89.

187. Abraham Goldfarb, quoted in Arad 1987, 86.

188. Dwork and Van Pelt 1996, 124–26; Arad 1987, 9–11.

189. Arad 1987, 87.

190. Arad 1987, 167.

191. Dwork and Van Pelt 1996, 176–77.

192. Dwork and Van Pelt 1996, 178–79.

193. Dwork and Van Pelt 1996, 219–21.

194. Dwork and Van Pelt 1996, 292–93.

195. See Gutman and Berenbaum 1994, chap. 7.

REFERENCES

Alvarez, J. E. 2001. *The Betrothed of Death: The Spanish Foreign Legion during the Rif Rebellion, 1920–1927*. London.

Anglesey, the Marquess of. 1986. *The History of the British Cavalry, 1899 to 1913*. Vol. 4 of *The History of the British Cavalry, 1816 to 1919*. London.

Arad, Y. 1987. *Belzec, Sobibor, Treblinka: The Operation Reinhard Death Camps*. Bloomington.

Arnold, O., and J. P. Hale. 1940. *Hot Irons: Heraldry of the Range*. New York.

Azan, P. 1918. *The Warfare of Today*. Boston.

Baden-Powell, B. F. S. 1903. *War in Practice*. London.

Basalla, G. 1988. *The Evolution of Technology*. Cambridge.

Berben, P. 1975. *Dachau, 1933–1945: The Official History*. London.

Bird, J. C. 1986. *Control of Enemy Alien Civilians in Great Britain, 1914–1918*. New York.

Boorstin, D. J. 1973. *The Americans: The Democratic Experience*. New York.

Brackenbury, C. B. 1888. *Field Works: Their Technical Construction and Tactical Application*. London.

Braudel, F. 1979. *Civilization and Capitalism, 15th–18th Century*. New York.

Brialmont, A. 1879. *La Fortification du Champ de Bataille*. Bruxelles.

Brooks, J. 2000. *Thank You, Comrade Stalin! Soviet Public Culture from Revolution to Cold War*. Princeton.

Broszat, M. 1968. "The Concentration Camps, 1933–1945." In *Anatomy of the SS State*, ed. H. Krausnick, H. Buchheim, M. Broszat, and H.-A. Jacobsen. New York.

Brown, R. M. 1994. "Violence." In *The Oxford History of the American West*, ed. C. A. Milner II, C. A. O'Connor, and M. A. Sandweiss. Oxford.

Bunyan, J. 1967. *The Origin of Forced Labor in the Soviet State, 1917–1921: Documents and Materials*. Baltimore.

Cederholm, B. 1929. *In the Clutches of the Tcheka*. Boston.

Cesarani, D., and T. Kushner, eds. 1993. *The Internment of Aliens in Twentieth Century Britain*. London.

Chandler, D. G., ed. 1966. *A Guide to the Battlefields of Europe*. 2 vols. Philadelphia.

Clifton, R. T. 1970. *Barbs, Prongs, Points, Prickers, and Stickers: A Complete and Illustrated Catalogue of Antique Barbed Wire.* Norman, Okla.

Clutton-Brock, J. 1992. *Horse Power: A History of the Horse and the Donkey in Human Societies.* Cambridge, Mass.

———. 1999. *A Natural History of Domesticated Animals.* Cambridge.

Cohen, P. A. 1997. *History in Three Keys: The Boxers as Event, Experience, and Myth.* New York.

Conquest, R. 1978. *Kolyma: The Arctic Death Camps.* New York.

———. 1986. *The Harvest of Sorrow: Soviet Collectivization and the Terror-Famine.* Oxford.

———. 1990. *The Great Terror: A Re-assessment.* London.

Cook, T. 1999. *No Place to Run: The Canadian Corps and Gas Warfare in the First World War.* Vancouver.

Cronon, W. 1983. *Changes in the Land: Indians, Colonists, and the Ecology of New England.* New York.

———. 1991. *Nature's Metropolis: Chicago and the Great West.* New York.

Crosby, A. W. 1986. *Ecological Imperialism: The Biological Expansion of Europe, 900–1900.* Cambridge.

Dallas, G. 2000. *1918: War and Peace.* London.

Davenport, T. R. H. 1987. *South Africa: A Modern History.* Toronto.

Davies, R. W. 1995. "Forced Labour under Stalin: The Archive Revelations." *New Left Review* 214.

Dennett, C. P. 1919. *Prisoners of the Great War.* New York.

Des Pres, T. 1976. *The Survivor: An Anatomy of Life in the Death Camps.* Oxford.

Diamond, J. 1997. *Guns, Germs, and Steel: The Fates of Human Societies.* New York.

DiNardo, R. L. 1991. *Mechanized Juggernaut or Military Anachronism? Horses and the German Army of World War II.* New York.

Dundonald, Twelfth Earl. 1926. *My Army Life.* London.

Du Pratz, M. le Page. 1763. *The History of Louisiana, or of the Western Parts of Virginia and Carolina: Containing a Description of the Countries That Lye on Both Sides of the River Missisipi: With an Account of the Settlements, Inhabitants, Soil, Climate, and Products.* London.

Dwork, D., and R. J. Van Pelt. 1996. *Auschwitz: 1270 to the Present.* New York.

Ellis, J. 1975. *The Social History of the Machine Gun.* Baltimore.

———. 1976. *Eye Deep in Hell.* London.

———. 1978. *Cavalry: The History of Mounted Warfare.* New York.

Fairbank, J. K. 1992. *China: A New History.* Cambridge, Mass.

Farwell, B. 1999. *Over There: The United States in the Great War, 1917–1918.* New York.

Federal Trade Commission. 1996. *Report on Cooperation in American Export Trade.* Washington, D.C.

Fiebeger, G. J. 1909. *A Text-Book on Field Fortification.* New York.

Figes, O. 1996. *A People's Tragedy: The Russian Revolution, 1891–1924.* London.

Fischer, G. 1989. *Enemy Aliens: Internment and the Homefront Experience in Australia, 1914–1920.* Queensland.

Fitzpatrick, S. 1994. *Stalin's Peasants.* Oxford.

Foner, P. S. 1972. *The Spanish-Cuban-American War and the Birth of American Imperialism, 1895–1902.* New York.

Foucault, M. 1977. *Discipline and Punish.* New York.

Friedländer, S. 1997. *The Years of Persecution, 1933–1939.* Vol. 1 of *Nazi Germany and the Jews.* New York.

Frink, M., W. T. Jackson, and A. W. Spring. 1956. *When Grass Was King: Contributions to the Western Range Cattle Industry Study.* Boulder, Colo.

Frison, G. C. 1991. *Prehistoric Hunters of the High Plains.* San Diego.

FTC. *See* Federal Trade Commission.

Gilbert, M. 1985. *The Holocaust: A History of the Jews of Europe during the Second World War.* New York.

———. 1994. *First World War.* London.

Grantham, G., and C. S. Leonard. 1989. *Agrarian Organization in the Century of Industrialization: Europe, Russia, and North America.* London.

Gressley, G. M. 1966. *Bankers and Cattlemen.* New York.

Gutman, Y., and M. Berenbaum, eds. 1994. *Anatomy of the Auschwitz Death Camp.* Bloomington.

Gvati, C. 1981. *A Century of Settlement.* Tel Aviv.

Haber, L. F. 1986. *The Poisonous Cloud: Chemical Warfare in the First World War.* Oxford.

Hamilton, R. F. 1982. *Who Voted for Hitler?* Princeton.

Hammond, J. W., Jr. 1999. *Poison Gas: The Myths versus Reality.* London.

Harris, J. P. 1995. *Men, Ideas, and Tanks: British Military Thought and Armoured Forces, 1903–1939.* Manchester.

Hemming, J. 1970. *The Conquest of the Incas.* San Diego.

Hesseltine, W. B. 1930. *Civil War Prisons: A Study in War Psychology.* Columbus, Ohio.

Hilberg, R. 1961. *The Destruction of the European Jews.* Chicago.

———. 1981. *Sonderzüge nach Auschwitz.* Frankfurt.

Hitler, A. 1939. *Mein Kampf.* Trans. D. C. Watt. London.

Hooker, R. J. 1981. *Food and Drink in America: A History.* New York.

Hopcroft, R. L., ed. 1999. *Regions, Institutions, and Agrarian Change in European History.* Ann Arbor.

Hosking, G. 1992. *The First Socialist Society: A History of the Soviet Union from Within*. Cambridge, Mass.

Houck, L. 1901. *The Boundaries of the Louisiana Purchase: A Historical Study*. St. Louis.

Howard, M. 1961. *The Franco-Prussian War*. London.

Hurt, R. D. 1981. *The Dust Bowl: An Agricultural and Social History*. Chicago.

Iliffe, J. 1979. *A Modern History of Tanganyika*. Cambridge.

Industrial Museum: American Steel and Wire Company. Photographs of exhibits. 1929. Worcester, Mass.

Isaac, Benjamin. 1990. *The Limits of Empire: The Roman Army in the East*. Oxford.

Isenberg, A. C. 2000. *The Destruction of the Bison: An Environmental History, 1750–1920*. Cambridge.

Ivanova, G. M. 2000. *Labor Camp Socialism: The Gulag in the Soviet Totalitarian System*. London.

Jackson, R. 1989. *The Prisoners, 1914–1918*. London.

James E. Butts Jr. & Co. 1856. *A Treatise on Wire Fencing . . . Dedicated to Agriculturalists*. Boston.

James, J. S. 1966. *Early United States Barbed Wire Patents*. Maywood, Calif.

Jansen, H. 1997. *Der Madagaskar-Plan*. Munich.

Jordan, T. G. 1993. *North American Cattle-Ranching Frontiers: Origins, Diffusion, and Differentiation*. Albuquerque.

Kaminski, A. J. 1982. *Konzentrationslager 1896 bis heute: Eine Analyse*. Stuttgart.

Keats, J. 1973. *Eminent Domain: The Louisiana Purchase and the Making of America*. New York.

Keegan, J. 1976. *The Face of Battle*. London.

———. 1998. *The First World War*. New York.

Keegan, T. J. 1987. *Rural Transformations in Industrializing South Africa*. London.

Keynes, J. M. 1919. *The Economic Consequences of the Peace*. London.

Kizny, T. 1997. *Czas Imperium/The Time of the Empire*. Warsaw.

Knipling, E. F. 1960. "Use of Insects for Their Own Destruction." *Journal of Economic Entomology* 53 (3): 415–20.

Kogon, E. 1950. *The Theory and Practice of Hell*. New York.

Kordan, B. S., and P. Melnycky, eds. 1991. *In the Shadow of the Rockies: Diary of the Castle Mountain Internment Camp, 1915–1917*. Edmonton.

Krell, A. 2002. *The Devil's Rope: A Cultural History of Barbed Wire*. London.

Lafitte, F. 1988. *The Internment of Aliens*. London.

Lawrence, F. L., and R. W. Glover. 1964. *Camp Ford, C.S.A.: The Story of Union Prisoners in Texas*. Austin.

Lee, E. 1985. *To the Bitter End: A Photographic History of the Boer War, 1899–1902*. London.

Leggett, G. 1981. *The Cheka: Lenin's Political Police*. Oxford.

Levenstein, H. A. 1988. *Revolution at the Table: The Transformation of the American Diet*. New York.

Levi, P. 1960. *Survival in Auschwitz*. Trans. S. Woolf. New York.

Linn, B. M. 1989. *The U.S. Army and Counterinsurgency in the Philippine War, 1899–1902*. Chapel Hill, N.C.

———. 2000. *The Philippine War, 1899–1902*. Lawrence, Kans.

Loir, M. E. 1911. *Cavalerie*. Paris.

Mahan, D. E. 1862. *A Treatise on Field Fortification*. New York.

Malsagoff, S. A. 1926. *An Island Hell: A Soviet Prison in the Far North*. London.

Mandelshtam, N. 1970. *Hope against Hope*. Trans. Max Hayward. New York.

Martin, C. 1967. *The Russo-Japanese War*. London.

Marvel, W. 1994. *Andersonville: The Last Depot*. Chapel Hill.

McCallum, H. D., and F. T McCallum. 1965. *The Wire That Fenced the West*. Norman, Okla.

McFadden, J. M. 1978. "Monopoly in Barbed Wire: The Formation of the American Steel and Wire Company." *Business History Review* 52 (4): 465–89.

McMichael, P. 1984. *Settlers and the Agrarian Question: Capitalism in Colonial Australia*. Cambridge.

McPherson, J. M. 1988. *Battle Cry of Freedom: The Civil War Era*. New York.

Meinig, D. W. 1998. *Transcontinental America, 1850–1915*. Vol. 3. of *The Shaping of America*. New Haven.

Miller, A. W. 1931. *Maintaining the Health of Livestock in Transit*. U.S. Department of Agriculture Leaflet 38. Washington, D.C.

Milner, C. A., II, et al. 1994. *The Oxford History of the American West*. Oxford.

Mingay, G. E., ed. 1977. *The Agricultural Revolution: Changes in Agriculture, 1650–1880*. London.

Moore, J. 1931. *Our Servant the Horse*. London.

Moynihan, M. 1978. *Black Bread and Barbed Wire: Prisoners in the First World War*. London.

Musicant, I. 1998. *Empire by Default: The Spanish-American War and the Dawn of the American Century*. New York.

Naor, M. 1987. *Yemey Homa Umigdal* [Days of Wall and Watchtower]. Jerusalem.

Naumann, W. L. 1977. *The Story of Caterpillar Tractor Co.* New York.

Neeson, J. M. 1993. *Commoners: Common Right, Enclosure, and Social Change in England, 1700–1820*. Cambridge.

Netz, R. 2000. "Barbed Wire." *London Review of Books* 22 (14): 30–35.

Nimmo, J., Jr. 1885. *Report in Regard to the Range and Ranch Cattle Business of the United States.* Washington, D.C.

Noakes, J., and G. Pridham, eds. 1988. *Foreign Policy, War, and Racial Extermination.* Vol. 2 of *Nazism: A History in Documents and Eyewitness Accounts, 1919–1945*. New York.

Otto, J. C. 1954. *Die Konsentrasie-Kampe.* Johannesburg.

Pakenham, T. 1979. *The Boer War*. New York.

———. 1991. *The Scramble for Africa, 1876–1912*. New York.

Parliamentary Report. 1901a. *Reports Etc. on the Working of the Refugee Camps in the Transvaal, Etc.* Vol. 1. Parliamentary Report Cd. 819. London.

Parliamentary Report. 1901b. *Reports Etc. on the Working of the Refugee Camps in the Transvaal, Etc.* Vol. 2. Parliamentary Report Cd. 853. London.

Parliamentary Report. 1902a. *Report on the Concentration Camps in South Africa, by the Committee of Ladies, Etc*. Parliamentary Report Cd. 893. London.

Parliamentary Report. 1902b. *Further Papers Relating to the Working of the Refugee Camps in South Africa, Etc*. Parliamentary Report Cd. 934. London.

Patterson, R. 1985. *Historical Atlas of the Outlaw West*. Boulder, Colo.

Pawelczynska, A. 1979. *Values and Violence in Auschwitz: A Sociological Analysis*. Berkeley, Calif.

Poggi, C. 1997. "Dreams of Metallized Flesh: Futurism and the Masculine Body." *Modernism/Modernity* 4:19–43.

Porch, D. 2000. *Wars of Empire*. London.

"Pour la lance." 1902. *Revue de Cavalerie* 35:14–22.

Prentiss, A. M. 1937. *Chemicals in War*. New York.

Pryor, F. L. 1992. *The Red and the Green: The Rise and Fall of Collectivized Agriculture in Marxist Regimes*. Princeton.

Raath, A. W. G. 1999. *The British Concentration Camps of the Anglo-Boer War, 1899–1902: Reports on the Camps*. Bloemfontein.

Raichle, D. R. 1979. "The Abolition of Corporal Punishment in New Jersey Schools." In *Corporal Punishment in American Education*, ed. I. A. Hyman and J. H. Wise. Philadelphia.

Rakestraw, D. A. 1995. *For Honor or Destiny: The Anglo-American Crisis over the Oregon Territory*. New York.
Razac, O. 2000. *Histoire politique de barbelé: La prairie, la tranchée, le camp*. Paris.
Remarque, E. M. 1929. *All Quiet on the Western Front*. Trans. A. W. Wheen. Boston.
Richardson, L. F. 1960. *Statistics of Deadly Quarrels*. Pittsburgh.
Richardson, R. H. 1978. *The Screwworm Problem: Evolution of Resistance to Biological Control*. Austin.
Rimington, M. F. 1912. *Our Cavalry*. London.
Roland, C. G. 1992. *Courage under Siege: Starvation, Disease, and Death in the Warsaw Ghetto*. Oxford.
Rosa, J. G. 1982. *The West of Wild Bill Hickok*. Norman, Okla.
———. 1996. *Wild Bill Hickok: The Man and His Myth*. Lawrence, Kans.
Rossi, J. 1989. *The Gulag Handbook*. New York.
Royal Flying Corps. 1917. *German Prisoners in Great Britain*. London.
Sbarra, N. H. 1955. *Historia del Alambrado en la Argentina*. Buenos Aires.
Schlosser, E. 2000. *Fast Food Nation*. Boston.
School of Slavonic and East European Studies in the University of London. 1934. *The Gold Industry and the Gold Reserves of the Soviet Union*. London.
Scobie, J. R. 1964. *Argentina: A City and a Nation*. New York.
Sedgwick, F. R. 1908. *The Russo-Japanese War on Land*. London.
Selby, J. 1978. *The Eagle and the Serpent: The Spanish and American Invasions of Mexico, 1519 and 1846*. London.
Service, R. 1998. *A History of Twentieth-Century Russia*. Cambridge, Mass.
Shavit, Y. 1995. *Geto Varsha Be-Tmunot: Kibbutz Lochamey Ha-Getaot* [The Warsaw Ghetto in Pictures]. Kibbutz Lochamey Ha-Getaot.
Smith, J. 1994. *The Spanish-American War: Conflict in the Caribbean and the Pacific, 1895–1902*. London.
Smith, J. B. 1891. *A Treatise upon Wire, Its Manufacture and Uses, Embracing Comprehensive Descriptions of the Constructions and Applications of Wire Ropes*. London.
Sofsky, W. 1997. *The Order of Terror*. Princeton.
Soloviev, L. Z. 1906. *Actual Experiences in War*. Washington, D.C.
Solzhenitsyn, A. I. 1974. *The Gulag Archipelago, 1918–1956*. Vol. 1. New York.
———. 1975. *The Gulag Archipelago, 1918–1956*. Vol. 2. New York.
———. 1978. *The Gulag Archipelago, 1918–1956*. Vol. 3. New York.
———. 1989. *August 1914*. New York.

Spies, S. B. 1977. *Methods of Barbarism? Roberts and Kitchener and Civilians in the Boer Republics, January 1900–May 1902*. Cape Town.

Splivalo, A. 1982. *The Home Fires*. Fremantle, Western Australia.

Stewart, W. W. 1919. *Prices of Iron, Steel, and Their Products*. Washington, D.C.

Stone, N. 1975. *The Eastern Front, 1914–1917*. New York.

Strickton, A. 1965. "The Euro-American Ranching Complex." In *Man, Culture, and Animals*, ed. M. Harris and E. B. Ross. Washington, D.C.

Swabe, J. 1999. *Animals, Disease, and Human Society: Human-Animal Relations and the Rise of Veterinary Medicine*. London.

Swinton, E. D. 1903. *The Defence of Duffer's Drift*. London.

———. 1932. *Eyewitness*. London.

"Sylvestris." 1803. *Reflections on the Cession of Louisiana to the United States*. Washington, D.C.

Taylor, J. G. 1976. *Louisiana: A Bicentennial History*. New York.

Tikhvinsky, S. L., ed. 1983. *Modern History of China*. Trans. V. Schneierson. Moscow.

Tsovel, A. 2004. "Alienated Contact: Transformations in the Relation of Humans to Other Species from the Eighteenth to the Early Twentieth Centuries." In *Humans and Other Animals in Historical Perspective*, ed. B. Arbel. Jerusalem.

Turner, J. 1980. *Reckoning with the Beast: Animals, Pain, and Humanity in the Victorian Mind*. Baltimore.

U.S. International Trade Commission. 1985. *Trade Shifts in Selected Commodity Areas—Annual 1985*. U.S. International Trade Commission Publication no. 1864. Washington, D.C.

U.S. War Department. 1906. *Reports of Military Observers*. Vol. 3. Military Information Division, General Staff. Washington, D.C.

———. 1907. *Reports of Military Observers*. Vol. 5. Military Information Division, General Staff. Washington, D.C.

Utley, R. M. 1984. *The Indian Frontier of the American West, 1846–1890*. Albuquerque.

Vance, J. F., ed. 2000. *Encyclopedia of Prisoners of War and Internment*. Santa Barbara, Calif.

Van Rensburg, T. 1980. *Camp Diary of Henrietta E. C. Armstrong: Experiences of a Boer Nurse in the Irene Concentration Camp, 6 April–11 October 1901*. Pretoria.

Von Poseck, M. 1923. *The German Cavalry: 1914 in Belgium and France*. Berlin.

Von Schmidt, C. 1881. *Instructions for the Training, Employment, and Leading of Cavalry*. Trans. C. W. B. Bell. London.

Walder, D. 1973. *The Short Victorious War: The Russo-Japanese Conflict, 1904–5*. London.
Waldron, A. 1990. *The Great Wall of China: From History to Myth*. Cambridge.
War Office, General Staff. 1906. *The Russo-Japanese War: Reports from British Officers Attached to the Japanese Forces in the Field*. London.
———. 1917–1918. *British Trench Warfare, 1917–1918: A Reference Manual*. Published by the Imperial War Museum, London, 1997.
Washburn and Moen Manufacturing Co. 1881. *The Fence Question in the Southern States, Etc.* Pamphlets. Worcester, Mass.
Webb, W. P. 1931. *The Great Plains*. Boston.
Weglyn, M. 1976. *Years of Infamy: The Untold Story of America's Concentration Camps*. New York.
Werth, N. 1999. "A State against Its People: Violence, Repression, and Terror in the Soviet Union." In *The Black Book of Communism: Crimes, Terror, Repression*, ed. Stépahne Courtois et al. Cambridge, Mass.
Wheeler, J. B. 1893. *The Elements of Field Fortification for the Use of the Cadets of the United States Military Academy at West Point*. New York.
———. 1898. *The Santiago Campaign, 1898*. Boston.
White, Lynn, Jr. 1962. *Medieval Technology and Social Change*. Oxford.
White, R. 1994. "Animals and Enterprise." In *The Oxford History of the American West*, ed. C. A. Milner II, C. A. O'Connor, and M. A. Sandweiss. Oxford.
Williams, R. C. 1987. *Fordson, Farmall, and Poppin' Johnny: A History of the Farm Tractor and Its Impact on America*. Chicago.
Wilson, H. W. 1902. *After Pretoria: The Guerilla War*. London.
Woolman, D. S. 1968. *Rebels in the Rif: Abd El Krim and the Rif Rebellion*. Stanford, Calif.
Woods, F., ed. 1992. *Winston S. Churchill, War Correspondent, 1895–1900*. London.
Worster, D. 1979. *Dust Bowl: The Southern Plains in the 1930s*. Oxford.
Zurichenko, A. 1950. "How a Camp Was Built." *Challenge* 1 (2): 12–13.

INDEX

ABOUT THE AUTHOR

Reviel Netz is Professor of Classics at Stanford University. He has written numerous books and articles, focusing on philosophy and the history of mathematics and science. His books include *The Shaping of Deduction in Greek Mathematics: A Study in Cognitive History* (1999) and *Archimedes: Translation and Commentary* (2004). He received his B.A. and M.A. from Tel Aviv University and his Ph.D. from Cambridge University.

Library of Congress Cataloging-in-Publication Data
Netz, Reviel.
Barbed wire : an ecology of modernity / Reviel Netz.
p. cm.
Includes bibliographical references.
ISBN 0-8195-6719-1 (cloth : alk. paper)
1. Barbed wire—Political aspects. 2. Wire fencing—History. 3. Wire obstacles—History. 4. Concentration camps—History. I. Title.
TS271.N48 2004
909.8–dc22
2004041267